electronics

data

handbook

SECOND EDITION

electronics
data
handbook

SECOND EDITION

MARTIN CLIFFORD

TAB BOOKS

BLUE RIDGE SUMMIT, PA. 17214

This book is dedicated
to the memory of
Philip I. Pryzant

FIRST EDITION
8 PRINTINGS

SECOND EDITION
FIRST PRINTING—JULY 1972

Printed in the United States
of America

Hardbound Edition: International Standard Book No. 0-8306-2118-X

Paperbound Edition: International Standard Book No. 0-8306-1118-5

Library of Congress Card Number: 72-82250

Contents

CHAPTER   **PAGE**

INTRODUCTION   9

1   **DC CIRCUITS**   11
Resistors—Resistors in series—Resistors in parallel—Two
parallel resistors of equal value—Three parallel resistors of
equal value—Two parallel resistors having widely different
values—Resistors in parallel—Selecting a shunting resistor—
Conversions—Conductance—Ohm's law for conductance—
Resistors in series parallel—Tolerance—Preferred values of
resistors—Resistor color code—Resistance of wire—Resistance
per thousand feet at 68º F—Resistance of solid copper, single
wire-any length (at 68º F)—Single wire layer solenoid—Length
of wire used in single layer solenoid—Length of wire-resistance
method—Temperature—Coefficient of resistance—Positive
temperature coefficient of capacitors—Negative temperature
coefficient of capacitors—Temperature coefficient color code—
Ohm's law—Polarity of IR drops—Basic units—Loading—
Power—Total power dissipation—Total power—Work—
Efficiency—Power units—Power vs energy—Heating effect of
current—Horsepower—Phase—The shunt law—Line and
branch currents—Voltage divider (potentiometer)—
Proportional voltages and resistances—Voltages in series
aiding and opposing—Cells in series aiding—Cells in parallel—
Voltage reference points—Kirchoff's voltage law—Voltages in a
closed network—Kirchhoff's current law—Series-parallel
resistive circuit—Time constants in DC circuits—For a series R-
L circuit—For a series R-C circuit—One time constant—Two
time constants—Three time constants—The R-L circuit—Time
constants in AC circuits—Time constant of a coupling circuit

2   **AC CIRCUITS**   51
Period—Velocity of wave—Voltage and current
measurements—Average value—Instantaneous values—
Effective or RMS values of a sine wave of voltage or current—
Average and effective values—Relationships—Nonsinusoidal
waves—Wave shape symmetry—Rise time and fall time—

Capacitors—Conversions—Multiples and submultiples—
Exponents—Capacitors in parallel—Capacitors in series—For
two capacitors in series—For any number of capacitors in
series—Capacitors in series parallel—Change of a capacitor—
Energy stored in a capacitor—Working voltage of a capacitor—
Capacitive reactance—Capacitors as storage dividers—Ohm's
law for a capacitive circuit—Impedance of an R-C circuit—
Voltages in a series R-C circuit—Inductors (coils)—
Conversions—Single layer air-core coils—Inductance of air-
cover multi-layer coil—Inductors in series—Inductors in
parallel—Coefficient of coupling and mutual inductance—
Inductors in series aiding—Inductors in series opposing—
Inductors in parallel aiding—Inductors in parallel opposing—
Reactance of an inductor—Ohm's law for an inductive circuit—
Inductive voltage divider—Capacitive-inductive divider—
Resistive-inductive   voltage   divider—Resistive-capacitive-
inductive voltage divider—L-C voltage divider—R-C voltage
divider—Impedance in an R-L circuit—Voltages in a series R-L
circuit—Effective resistance—Q of a coil—Q of a capacitor—
Voltage transformer step up and step down—Current trans-
former, step up and step down—Impedance transformers—
Power transformer color code—IF transformer color code—
Audio and output transformer color code (single ended)—Audio
and output transformer color code (push-pull)—Phase angle—
Phase angle in resistive circuits—Phase angle in inductive
circuits—Phase angle in capacitive circuits—Phase angle of a
series R-L circuit—Phase angle of a series R-C circuit—
Impedance and phase angle of single resistor—Impedance and
phase angle of series resistors—Impedance and phase angle of
parallel resistors—Impedance and phase angle of series-
parallel resistors—Impedance and phase angle of single inductor—Impedance and phase angle of coils in series—
Impedance and phase angle of a single capacitor—Impedance
and phase angle of series capacitors—Impedance and phase
angle of parallel capacitors—Impedance and phase angle of
coils in parallel—Impedance and phase angle of a series L-C
circuit—Impedance and phase angle of a series R-L-C circuit—
Complex series circuit—Net reactance—Impedance and phase
angle of a parallel R-L circuit—Impedance and phase of a
parallel R-C circuit—Impedance and phase angle of a parallel
L-C circuit—Impedance and phase angle of a parallel R-L-C
circuit—Impedance and phase angle of series R-L shunted by
R—Impedance and phase angle of series R-L shunted by C—
Impedance and phase angle of R-C in parallel with R-L—
Reactance-resistance ratio—Admittance of a series circuit—
Susceptance—Conductance—Ohm's law for AC—Power in AC
circuits—Apparent power—Power factor—Power factor of
coils—Power factor of capacitors—Power—Current—Voltage—
Impedance—Resonance in a series circuit—Q of a series
resonant circuit—Decibels and nepers—Reference levels (0
db)—Volume units (VU)—High pass filter (constant K)—Low

pass filter (constant K)—Bandpass filter (constant K)—Band
elimination filter (constant K)—T type low-pass filter (constant
K)—π type low-pass filter—π type high-pass filter—m-derived
filters—Types of m-derived filters—L attenuator—L-pad—
Nonsinusoidal waves—Fundamental and harmonic relationships

3 **VACUUM TUBES AND VACUUM TUBE
CIRCUITS** 141
Tube currents and voltages—Amplification factor—AC plate
resistance—Plate efficiency—Mutual conductance—
Relationships of u, rp and gm—Merit coefficient (figure of
merit)—Voltage amplifiers—Cathode followers—Resistance-
coupled audio amplifiers (triodes) — Amplification at intermediate or medium frequencies (triode)—Amplification at
low frequencies (triodes)—Amplification at high frequencies
(triodes)—Resistance-coupled audio amplifiers (pentodes)—
Amplification at medium frequencies (pentodes)—
Amplification at low frequencies (pentodes)—Amplification at
high frequencies (pentodes)—Negative feedback—Power
amplifiers—Power sensitivity—Power output—Maximum
transfer of power to the load—Power in the plate load—
Undistorted power output—Single pentode audio power output

4 **SEMICONDUCTORS** 157
Direction of current flow—Electrode voltages—Electrode
currents—Current amplification—Resistance gain—Voltage
gain—Power gain—Basic circuits—Phase reversal—Base
current amplification factor—Alpha cutoff frequency—Interval
input and output resistances—Base resistance—Emitter
resistance—Collector resistance—Static leakage current—
Power dissipation—Current efficiency—Rise time—Fall time—
Storage time—Delay time

5 **TELEVISION** 173
Television waveforms—Television channels (VHF)—UHF
channels—Finding the channel number—Television channels
(UHF)—Aspect ratio—Scanning frequencies for monochrome
TV—Frequency response—Horizontal sweep frequency
(monochrome)—Composition of a single line—Horizontal
blanking pulse composition—Vertical blanking—Deflection
frequencies—Color subcarrier—Beat interference—Reversal of
picture and sound signals—Video IF

6 **ANTENNAS AND TRANSMISSION LINES** 183
Physical length of an antenna—Full wave antennas—Antenna
impedance—Radiation resistance—Radiated power—Power

CHAPTER   **PAGE**

gain—Wave angle—Transmission lines—Two wire open transmission line—Attenuation—Concentric transmission line—Resistance of coaxial transmission line—Resistance of open two-wire copper line—Standing wave ratio (SWR)—Characteristic impedance—Matching impedances—Table of antenna types—Parabolic reflector antennas—Cosecant squared reflector—Horn antennas—End-fed Hertz (zepp)—Center-fed Hertz (tuned doublet or center-fed zepp)—Fuchs antenna—Corner reflector—Marconi—Parasitic array—Rhombic antenna—Vertical J—Coaxial antenna (sleeve antenna)—Ground plane antenna—Crow foot antenna—Turnstile antenna—Skin antenna—Ilas antenna—Omni-range (vor)—Adcock antenna—Loop antennas—Stub mast—Half rhombic (inverted V or tilted wire)—Beverage antenna—Folded dipole—Velocity factor—Length of transmission line

7 **MEASUREMENTS**   **207**
How to determine the resistance of a d'Arsonval meter movement—Shunt resistance—Multiplier resistance—Meter sensitivity—Resistance measurements—Shunt ohmmeter for low resistance measurements—Bridges—Wheatstone bridge—Slide wire bridge—The scope

8 **TABLES AND DATA**   **217**
Conversion factors—Equivalents—Electronic abbreviations—Decimal equivalents of fractions of an inch—Wavelength and frequency bands—Math symbols—Math data—Greek alphabet—Comparison of electric and magnetic circuits—Powers of two—Fundamentals of Boolean algebra—Relations of rules of operation—Squares, lobes and roots—Powers and numbers—Trigonometric functions—Conversion of inches to millimeters—Conversion of millimeters to inches—Common logarithms of numbers—Binary numbers—Decimal to binary conversion rules—Binary to decimal conversion rules—Fusing currents of wires—Roman numerals—Numerical data—Common integrals—Linear measure—Square measure—Cubic measure—Liquid measure—Dry measure—Circular measure—Communications industrial

INDEX   **247**

Introduction

The amount of data faced by those who become involved in the study of electronics is simply staggering. Some of it, once purely the province of the electrical engineer, has become necessary even for those who have made electronics their avocation, their hobby.

Where is this data? Every book on electronics is filled with it. There is no scarcity of information. There is a definite problem, though, in being able to reach it with minimum effort and minimum time. The research, however, generally involves considerable reliance on memory, on the availability of a number of text books, and the ability to use the contents pages or indexes of these books to best advantage.

This brings us directly to the purpose of this book. Its function is to help minimize the research needed to find specific electronics information. No claim is made for completeness, but every effort has been made to include those formulas which are commonly used.

What is a formula? It is just an extremely convenient, shorthand way of writing information. There is nothing unusual or special about formulas, but because they often make use of mathematical symbols, the impression is sometimes raised that they represent the height of accuracy and that the answers they yield are beyond question or challenge. Nothing of the sort. Quite often a formula will represent nothing more than a reasonably good approximation. Similarly, calculating a formula to several decimal places is ridiculous, when slide rule accuracy would be all that is required.

The solution to a problem in electronics may involve the use of several formulas. The ability to solve such a problem will require judgment in the selection of the formulas and their use in the proper sequence. A knowledge of elementary algebra and trigonometry and some skill in handling algebraic functions will be of considerable help. Quite often the stumbling block in electronics is not electronics but the failure to realize that electronics relies on mathematics as a tool.

Every book requires that the author make certain assumptions—assumptions of prior knowledge on the part of his readers.

This book is no exception. This is not a book of electronic theory. Since a formula is usually the end product of theory, the only intent here is to provide formulas in an easily accessible manner. Where explanatory material is given in this text, its function is to clarify the use of a formula, or its derivation.

Many additional and useful formulas can be obtained through the use of transpositions and-or substitutions. Ohm's law is a notable example since, basically, we have just one formula. Practically speaking, though, we have three by transposing quantities from one side of the formula to the other. Substituting equal quantities from one formula into another also produces "new" formulas that may lend themselves very nicely to particular applications.

Mathematical computations laboriously performed with pencil and paper are subject to frequent error brought on by fatigue and an elusive decimal point. Data in this book were checked with the invaluable help of the Adler Model 1210 electronic calculator. We acknowledge with particular thanks the courtesy of Adler Business Machines, Inc. in supplying their Model 1210 electronic calculator for this purpose.

Our special thanks also to Automatic Electric Co. (division of General Telephone & Electronics) for permission to reproduce material supplied by them. The cover photo is by Harry Seawell—taken at IBM's Thomas J. Watson Research Center at Yorktown Heights, New York.

Martin Clifford

Chapter 1

DC Circuits

For the purpose of this book we are going to consider that there are only five basic components used in any electronic apparatus—whether a small receiver or a complex computer. These basic components are resistors, capacitors, inductors (or coils), tubes and transistors.* But these components lend themselves to a tremendous number of variations and combinations. The rules, the laws and the formulas of electronics help us understand the behavior of these components, taken together or separately, and to predict their behavior.

RESISTORS

Resistors enable us to control the flow of electric currents. With their help we can divide voltages. In combination with other components we use them to make electrical waves into shapes most suited for our needs. Resistors can be used individually, in series, in parallel, in series-parallel.

Resistors in Series. See Fig. 1-1.

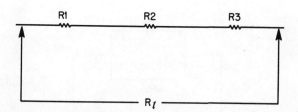

Fig. 1-1. When wiring resistors in series, the total resistance is not affected by the order in which the resistors are connected.

---

*A battery might be considered as still another component, but it is not regarded so here.

$$R_t = R1 + R2 + R3 \ldots \qquad (1\text{-}1)$$

R_t is the total resistance. **R1, R2** and **R3** are the individual resistors. The dots indicate that you can have any number of resistors. The resistors can be arranged in any order and their values can be added in any order. Before using the formula, make sure that the resistors are in the same units—ohms, kilohms, or megohms.

In this formula, and all the others that follow, the assumption is made that the resistance of the wires and the connections is negligible. This is generally true when R_t is large, approximately 10 ohms or more, and when the circuit current is small, possibly a few milliamperes or less. When **R** is small and currents are large and are measured in terms of amperes, the resistance of connecting wires or conductors and the resistance of joints becomes significant.

When resistors are wired in series, the total resistance, R_t, is always larger than the value of the largest resistor in the network. When resistors are wired in parallel, the total resistance is always smaller than the value of the smallest resistor in the network.

Two Resistors in Parallel. See Fig. 1-2.

$$R_t = \frac{R1 \times R2}{R1 + R2} \qquad (1\text{-}2)$$

This formula is useful only for two resistors in parallel. R_t is the total resistance. R1 and R2 are the individual resistors.

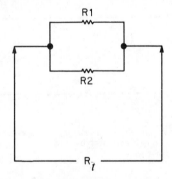

Fig. 1-2. For resistors in parallel, the total resistance is less than the value of either resistor.

12

Two Parallel Resistors of Equal Value

If two resistors of equal value are placed in parallel, the total resistance is one-half the value of either resistor. If **R1** and **R2** are the parallel connected resistors:

$$R_t = \frac{R1}{2} \text{ or } \frac{R2}{2}$$

Three Parallel Resistors of Equal Value

If three resistors of equal value are placed in parallel, the total resistance is one-third the value of any of the resistors. If **R1**, **R2** and **R3** are the parallel connected resistors:

$$R_t = \frac{R1}{3} \text{ or} \frac{R2}{3} \text{ or} \frac{R3}{3}$$

Two Parallel Resistors Having Widely Different Values

If two resistors are connected in parallel, and one of the resistors has a value that is 10 times, or more, greater than the other, it may be possible to consider the total resistance equal to the resistor having the smaller value. Example: A 10-ohm resistor is in parallel with a 100-ohm resistor. What is the total resistance?

$$R_t = \frac{R1 \times R2}{R1 + R2} = \frac{10 \times 100}{10 + 100} = \frac{1000}{110} = 9.1 \text{ ohms} \quad \text{approximately}$$

Depending on circuit requirements, an answer of 10 ohms might be considered satisfactory. In any event, in problems of this kind it is often helpful to be able to know the approximate answer as a check on the arithmetic.

Three Resistors in Parallel. See Fig. 1-3.

$$R_t = \frac{1}{\dfrac{1}{R1} + \dfrac{1}{R2} + \dfrac{1}{R3} \cdots} \tag{1-3}$$

R_t is the total resistance. This formula is suitable for adding as many resistors in parallel as you wish, as indicated by the dots. It can also be used for adding two resistors in parallel.

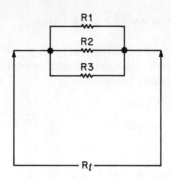

Fig. 1-3. Several formulas are available for calculating the total resistance of three or more resistors in parallel. The total resistance will always be less than the value of any resistor in the parallel combination.

An algebraic variation of the same formula is:

$$\frac{1}{R_t} = \frac{1}{R1} + \frac{1}{R2} + \frac{1}{R3} \cdots \qquad (1\text{-}4)$$

Any Number of Resistors in Parallel.

$$R_t = \frac{R1}{1 + R1/R2 + R1/R3 + R1/R4 \ldots} \qquad (1\text{-}5)$$

This formula can be extended to include any number of parallel resistors. It can also be combined with the formula for series resistors to supply the answer to a series-parallel combination. To make the work easier when using this formula, make R1 the largest resistor in the parallel combination. The reason for doing so is that you will be working with whole numbers. If R1 is one of the smaller value resistors the arithmetic will involve fractions. However, the formula is applicable no matter how the resistors are coded.

Tables 1-1 and 1-2 are charts which can be conveniently used to find the total resistance of two resistors in parallel. However, for values of resistors not shown in the charts, it will still be necessary to use a formula.

To use Table 1 and Table 2 for a two-resistor parallel network, identify one resistor as R1 and the other as R2. Locate the value of R2 in the left-hand column. Move horizontally to the right and stop in the appropriate R1 column. Example: A 15-ohm resistor is in parallel with a 68-ohm resistor. Locate 15 in the R2 column at the left. Move to the right to the 68 column. The equivalent resistance is 12.2 ohms.

Similarly, use the two tables to find the parallel resistors corresponding to a single value. Example: What two resistors are needed to produce an equivalent resistance of 4.58 ohms? Locate

Table 1-1. Total resistance, R, for two resistors, R1 and R2, in parallel, with resistance values from 1 to 100 ohms (kilohms, megohms).

R1	1	1.5	2.2	3.3	4.7	6.8	10	15	22	33	47	68
R2												
1	0.50	0.60	0.69	0.77	0.83	0.87	0.91	0.93	0.95	0.97	0.98	0.99
1.5	0.60	0.75	0.89	1.03	1.14	1.22	1.30	1.36	1.40	1.43	1.45	1.46
2.2	0.69	0.89	1.10	1.32	1.50	1.66	1.82	1.92	2.00	2.06	2.10	2.13
3.3	0.77	1.03	1.32	1.65	1.94	2.22	2.48	2.70	2.87	3.00	3.08	3.14
4.7	0.83	1.14	1.50	1.94	2.35	2.78	3.20	3.58	3.87	4.12	4.27	4.39
6.8	0.87	1.22	1.86	2.22	2.78	3.40	4.05	4.58	5.79	5.64	5.94	6.18
10	0.91	1.30	1.82	2.48	3.20	4.05	5.0	6.0	6.9	7.7	8.3	8.7
15	0.93	1.35	1.92	2.70	3.58	4.68	6.0	7.50	8.9	10.3	11.4	12.2
22	0.95	1.40	2.00	2.87	3.87	5.19	6.9	8.90	11.0	13.2	15.0	16.6
33	0.97	1.43	2.06	3.00	4.12	5.64	7.7	10.3	13.2	16.5	19.4	22.2
47	0.98	1.45	2.10	3.08	4.27	5.94	8.3	11.4	15.0	19.4	23.5	27.8
68	0.99	1.45	2.13	3.14	4.39	6.18	8.7	12.2	16.6	22.2	27.8	34.0

4.58 in the table. Move straight up and the value of R1 is given as 15 ohms. Move straight left and the value of R2 is 6.8 ohms. 6.8 ohms in parallel with 15 ohms is 4.58 ohms.

Find larger values by moving the decimal point to the right by one place. Example: To find the equivalent resistance of 330 ohms and 470 ohms, locate 33 in the R2 column in Table 1-2. Move the decimal point one place to the right and 33 becomes 330. Locate 47 ohms in the R1 row. Move the decimal point one place to the right and 47 becomes 470. Move horizontally to the right from 33 to the 47 column. The intersection of the two columns is at 19.4. Move the decimal point one place to the right to get 194 ohms. 330 ohms and 470 ohms in parallel equals 194 ohms.

Also use Tables 1-1 and 1-2 to find the equivalent of three resistors in parallel. Combine two of the resistors and get an equivalent value. Combine this equivalent value with the remaining resistor.

Table 1-2. Total resistance, R, for two resistors, R1 and R2 in parallel, with resistance values from 10 to 1,000 ohms (kilohms, megohms).

R1	10	15	22	33	47	68	100	150	220	330	470	680
R2												
10	5.0	6.0	6.9	7.7	8.3	8.7	9.1	9.3	9.5	9.7	9.8	9.9
15	6.0	7.5	8.9	10.3	11.4	12.2	13.0	13.6	14.0	14.3	14.5	14.6
22	6.9	8.9	11.0	13.2	15.0	16.6	18.2	19.2	20.0	20.6	21.0	21.3
33	7.7	10.3	13.2	16.5	19.4	22.2	24.8	27.0	28.7	30.0	30.8	31.4
47	8.3	11.4	15.0	19.4	23.5	27.8	32.0	35.8	38.7	41.2	42.7	43.9
68	8.7	12.2	16.6	22.2	27.8	34.0	40.5	46.8	51.9	56.4	59.4	61.8
100	9.1	13.0	18.2	24.8	32.0	40.5	50	60	69	77	83	87
150	9.3	13.6	19.2	27.0	25.8	46.8	60	75	89	103	114	122
220	9.5	14.0	20	28.7	38.7	51.9	69	89	110	132	150	166
330	9.7	14.3	20.6	30.0	41.2	56.4	77	103	132	165	194	222
470	9.8	14.5	21.0	30.8	42.7	59.4	83	114	150	194	235	278
680	9.9	14.6	21.3	31.4	43.9	61.8	87	122	166	222	278	340

SELECTING A SHUNTING RESISTOR

A common problem is having a resistor on hand whose value is too high for a particular application. The resistor can be shunted with another resistor so that the two resistors in parallel will have the required resistance value.

$$R1 = \frac{R_t \times R2}{R2 - R_t}$$

R1 and R2 are the two parallel resistors. R_t is the equivalent value. Example: What value resistor should be shunted across a 30-ohm resistor so that the equivalent value of the two parallel resistors will be 20 ohms?

$$R1 = \frac{R_t \times R2}{R2 - R_t} = \frac{20 \times 30}{30 - 20} = \frac{600}{10} = 60 \text{ ohms}$$

A 30-ohm resistor when shunted by a 60-ohm resistor will have an equivalent value of 20 ohms.

CONVERSIONS

The basic unit of resistance is the ohm. Multiples are the kilohm, or thousand ohms, and the megohm, or million ohms. To convert from one unit to another:

1 ohm = 10^{-3} kilohm = 0.001 kilohm = 1/1,000 kilohm
1 ohm = 10^{-6} megohm = 0.000001 megohm = 1/1,000,000 megohm
1 kilohm = 10^{3} ohms = 1,000 ohms
1 kilohm = 10^{-3} megohm = 0.001 megohm = 1/1,000 megohm
1 megohm = 10^{3} kilohms = 1,000 kilohms
1 megohm = 10^{6} ohms = 1,000,000 ohms

CONDUCTANCE

Conductance and resistance are related since they are the inverse of each other.

$$G = \frac{1}{R} \qquad (1\text{-}6)$$

and

$$R = \frac{1}{G} \qquad (1\text{-}7)$$

The basic unit of resistance is the ohm. The basic unit of conductance is the mho. The mho is simply the ohm spelled backward.

Resistors in Parallel (Conductance Method). See Fig. 1-4.

$$G_t = G1 + G2 + G3 \ldots \ldots \tag{1-8}$$

This formula regards the components shown in Fig. 1-4 as conductors. G_t is the total conductance in mhos. Conversion can be made to the more familiar resistance form by dividing each term into the number 1.

$$G_t = G1 + G2 + G3 = \frac{1}{R_t} = \frac{1}{R1} + \frac{1}{R2} + \frac{1}{R3} \tag{1-9}$$

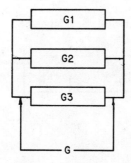

Fig. 1-4. The solution of a problem involving parallel resistors is often made easier by considering them as conductors.

Which leads us directly back to formula given in (1-4).

Ohm's Law For Conductance

Conductance and resistance are reciprocals. Since resistance problems, such as a number of resistors in parallel, often involves working with fractions, it can be helpful to shift from resistance to conductance and work with decimals. Ohm's law for conductance is similar to Ohm's law for resistance.

$$E = \frac{I}{G} \qquad (1\text{-}10)$$

$$R = \frac{1}{G} \qquad (1\text{-}12)$$

$$I = E \times G \qquad (1\text{-}11)$$

I is the current in amperes; **G** the conductance in mhos; **R** is the resistance in ohms.

For current through two resistors **R1** and **R2** in parallel:

$$I_{R1} = \frac{I_t \times G1}{G1 + G2}$$

I_{R1} is the current (in amps) through **R1**; I_t is the line or total current (in amps): **G1** is the conductance of **R1**; **G2** is the conductance of **R2**, both in mhos.

For the current through **R2**:

$$I_{R2} = \frac{I_t \times G2}{G1 + G2}$$

Resistors in Series-Parallel. See Fig. 1-5.

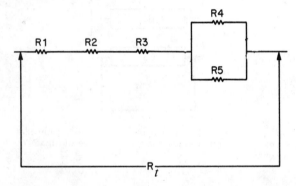

Fig. 1-5. Basically, finding the total resistance of a circuit of this type involves the use of two different formulas.

The formula for resistors in series can be combined with any of the formulas for resistors in parallel to supply the answer to problems involving resistors in series-parallel combinations.

$$R_t = R1 + R2 + R3 + \frac{R4 \times R5}{R4 + R5} \qquad (1\text{-}13)$$

Often, working with three or more resistors in parallel, calculation of the total resistance can be tedious. It may be desirable to round off resistance values to make the arithmetic easier, keeping in mind that the resistance, as indicated in the circuit, will not take the tolerance into consideration.

In any parallel combination, if there is a 10 to 1 ratio, or better, between resistor values, the total resistance will be only slightly lower than the value of the smallest resistor.

TOLERANCE

Electrical components have physical and electrical tolerances. Both are expressed in percent. To change percent to a decimal, divide percent by 100. To change a decimal to percent, multiply by 100.

There are three types of tolerances: the plus tolerance, the minus tolerance, and the plus-minus tolerance. Plus tolerances are indicated by a plus sign. Example: A wire has a diameter of .065 mil + 2 mils. This wire can have a diameter ranging between these limits: .065 mil and .065 + 2 = .067 mil. A minus tolerance is shown by a minus sign. Example: The chassis cutout for a transformer is 3"−.025". The cutout can have any dimension ranging from 3" to 3−.025" 3" to 2.975". A plus-minus tolerance uses a plus-minus sign: Example: A resistor has a value of 1,000 ohms, ± 20%. 20% = 20/100 = 0.2. 1,000 x 0.2 = 200 ohms. 1,000 + 200 ohms = 1,200 ohms. 1,000 - 200 ohms = 800 ohms. A 1,000-ohm ± 20 % resistor can have any value between 800 and 1,200 ohms.

PREFERRED VALUES OF RESISTORS

Values of resistors follow the recommendations of the Electronics Industries Association (EIA). Table 1-3 shows the values for molded composition resistors. All the values in this list are available in a tolerance of ± 5 %. The values shown in bold-face type are for resistors with a tolerance of ± 10 %.

Table 1-3. Preferred resistor values.

			Ohms					Megohms	
2.7	13	68	360	**1800**	9100	**47000**	0.24	1.1	5.1
3.0	**15**	75	390	2000	**10000**	51000	**0.27**	**1.2**	**5.6**
3.3	16	**82**	430	**2200**	11000	**56000**	0.30	1.3	6.2
3.6	**18**	91	**470**	2400	**12000**	62000	**0.33**	**1.5**	**6.8**
3.9	20	**100**	510	**2700**	13000	**68000**	0.36	1.6	7.5
4.3	**22**	110	**560**	3000	**15000**	75000	**0.39**	**1.8**	**8.2**
4.7	24	**120**	620	**3300**	16000	**82000**	0.43	2.0	9.1
5.1	**27**	130	680	3600	**18000**	91000	**0.47**	**2.2**	**10.0**
5.6	30	**150**	750	**3900**	20000	**100000**	0.51	2.4	11.0
6.2	**33**	160	**820**	4300	**22000**	110000	**0.56**	**2.7**	**12.0**
6.8	36	**180**	910	**4700**	24000	**120000**	0.62	3.0	13.0
7.5	**39**	200	**1000**	5100	**27000**	130000	**0.68**	**3.3**	**15.0**
8.2	43	**220**	1100	**5600**	30000	**150000**	0.75	3.6	16.0
9.1	**47**	240	**1200**	6200	**33000**	160000	**0.82**	**3.9**	**18.0**
10	51	**270**	1300	**6800**	36000	**180000**	0.91	4.3	20.0
11	**56**	300	**1500**	7500	**39000**	200000	**1.0**	**4.7**	**22.0**
12	62	**330**	1600	**8200**	43000	**220000**			

RESISTOR COLOR CODE

The color code for resistors (Fig. 1-6) is that established by the EIA.

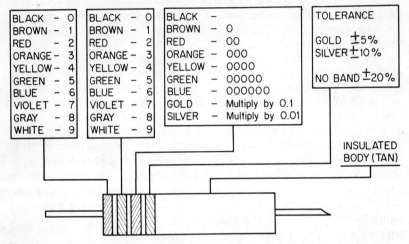

Fig. 1-6. The first three color bands supply the total resistance. The fourth color (if any) gives the tolerance. Example: A 5,600-ohm resistor would be green (first color—5), blue (second color—6) and red (third color—00).

RESISTANCE OF WIRE

The resistance of any solid, single conductor copper wire depends upon its length and cross-sectional area. Resistance increases with length, decreases as the cross-sectional area becomes greater. Expressed in a formula, we have:

$$R = \rho \, \frac{L}{A} \qquad (1\text{-}14)$$

R is the resistance in ohms, L is the length and A is the cross-sectional area. (See Fig. 1-7.) The length L is in feet and the area is in circular mils. 1 mil = 0.001 inch. The Greek letter ρ (rho) is the specific resistance or the resistivity of a metal—in this case, copper. The specific resistivity of copper is 10.4. The resistivity of most other metals is higher—aluminum is 17, brass is 45. Silver is 9.8, making it a better conductor than copper. To find the area of a

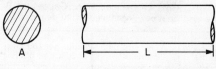

length x cross-sectional area

Fig. 1-7. The resistance of a conductor is based upon its length and cross-sectional area. Other factors, such as voltage and temperature, material of which the resistor is made, will also determine the resistance.

copper wire when the diameter is given in mils, square the diameter (multiply it by itself). A diameter of 5 mils is an area of 25 circular mils. This means that formula (1-14) can be written as:

$$R = \rho \, \frac{L}{d^2} \tag{1-15}$$

The resistance of copper wire varies with temperature. The resistivity of 10.4 for copper wire is at 20° Celsius. Table 1-4 lists the diameter in mils and the area in circular mils of copper wire from No. 0000 gauge to No. 40 gauge.

The formula for the resistance of copper wire does not take the effects of temperature into consideration. The resistance value, obtained by using the formula, is for wire in free space, not carrying current. The information given in Table 1-4 is for bare, annealed solid copper wire at 20 degrees Celsius, corresponding to 68 degrees Fahrenheit.

The diameter (d) of the wire table (Table 1-4) is the nominal diameter. There is a tolerance in the manufacturer of wires so there can be some variation from the diameter dimensions given in the table. Thus, No. 18 gauge wire, for example, has a nominal diameter of 40.303 mils. The minimum diameter is 39.9 mils and the maximum diameter is 40.7 mils. Since the resistance is a function of the diameter, wire having a minimum rather than nominal or maximum, will also have a greater resistance per unit length.

Table 1-4 shows that the smaller the gauge number, the thicker the wire. You will find it convenient to keep in mind that the area of wire approximately doubles for every three gauge numbers. Thus, No. 20 wire has double the area of No. 23. The significance here is that the current-carrying capacity is also doubled.

Every wire size becomes 12.3% greater in diameter as the wire guage number is decreased by 1. Thus, gauge 18 wire has a

21

AWG	Diameter, mils, d	Area, circular mils, d^2	Ohms per 1000 ft. at 20°C., or 68°F.	Pounds per 1000 ft.
0000	460.00	211,600	0.04901	640.5
000	409.64	167,805	0.06180	508.0
00	364.80	133,079	0.07793	402.8
0	324.86	105.534	0.09827	319.5
1	289.30	83,694	0.1239	253.3
2	257.63	66,373	0.1563	200.9
3	229.42	52,634	0.1970	159.3
4	204.31	41,743	0.2485	126.4
5	181.94	33,102	0.3133	100.2
6	162.02	26,250	0.3951	79.46
7	144.28	20,817	0.4982	63.02
8	129.49	16,768	0.6282	49.98
9	114.43	13,094	0.7921	39.63
10	101.89	10,382	0.9989	31.43
11	90.742	8,234.1	1.260	24.93
12	80.808	6,529.9	1.588	19.77
13	71.961	5,178.4	2.003	15.68
14	64.084	4,106.8	2.525	12.43
15	57.068	3,256.8	3.184	9.858
16	50.820	2,582.7	4.016	7.818
17	45.257	2,048.2	5.064	6.200
18	40.303	1,624.3	6.385	4.917
'19	35.890	1,288.1	8.051	3.899
20	31.961	1,021.5	10.15	3.092
21	28.462	810.10	12.80	2.452
22	25.347	642.47	16.14	1.945
23	22.571	509.45	20.36	1.542
24	20.100	404.01	25.67	1.223
25	17.900	320.41	32.37	0.9699
26	15.940	254.08	40.81	0.7692
27	14.195	201.50	51.47	0.6100
28	12.641	159.79	64.90	0.4837
29	11.257	126.72	81.83	0.3836
30	10.025	100.50	103.2	0.3042
31	8.928	79.71	130.1	0.2413
32	7.950	63.20	164.1	0.1913
33	7.080	50.13	206.9	0.1517
34	6.305	39.75	260.9	0.1203
35	5.615	31.53	329.0	0.0954
36	5.000	25.00	414.8	0.0757
37	4.453	19.83	523.1	0.0600
38	3.965	15.72	659.6	0.0476
39	3.531	12.47	831.8	0.0377
40	3.145	9.89	1049	0.0299

diameter of 40.30 mils. 40.30 x 12.3% = 40.30 x 0.123 = 4.95690. Add this result to the diameter of gauge 18 wire to find the diameter of gauge 17 wire. 40.30 + 4.95690 = 45.2569 = 45.26 mils.

A faster method is to use this formula:

wire gauge dia. (mils) x 1.123 = dia. next larger size.

Example: Gauge 22 wire has a diameter of 25.35 mils.

25.35 x 1.123 = 28.46805 mils = dia. of No. 21 wire

To find the next smaller diameter wire (wire having next larger gauge number)

$$\frac{\text{wire gauge dia. (mils)}}{1.123} = \text{dia. next smaller size}$$

RESISTANCE PER THOUSAND FEET AT 68°F

Table 1-4 shows that resistance increases as wire gauge number increases.

$$\frac{R \text{ in ohms per}}{1000 \text{ feet} \times 1.26} = \frac{R \text{ in ohms per 1000 feet of}}{\text{next higher gauge number}}$$

Example: R of No. 20 wire = 10.15 ohms per 1000 feet

$\quad$ 10.15 x 1.26 = 12.789 ohms for No. 21 gauge wire

Conversely, to find resistance, 1000 feet of next lower gauge number, divide by 1.26

RESISTANCE OF SOLID COPPER, SINGLE WIRE—ANY LENGTH (AT 68°F)

You can use Table 1-4 to find the resistance of any length of wire, even though the table specifies resistance in ohms per thousand feet. Divide the known length of wire by 1,000 and multiply by the resistance per thousand feet, taken from Table 1-4.

$$\frac{\text{length of wire}}{1000} \times \frac{\text{resistance per thousand feet} =}{\text{resistance of wire, any length}}$$

Thus, the resistance of 300 feet of No. 30 gauge wire is:

$$\frac{300}{1,000} \times 301.2 = 0.3 \times 103.2 = 30.96 \text{ ohms}$$

SINGLE WIRE LAYER SOLENOID

Before winding a coil, it may be necessary to determine how much space the coil will require. For a single layer solenoid:

Length of coil (in mils)=wire dia. in mils x number of turns.

First, determine what gauge of wire to use. Knowing the gauge, find the diameter in mils, d, from Table 1-4. Multiply this diameter by the number of turns to learn the length of the coil. To determine the length of the coil in inches:

$$\text{length of coil in inches} = \frac{\text{wire dia. in mils x no. of turns}}{1000}$$

Note: Since Table 1-4 is for bare wire, no allowance has been made for insulation. For enameled or Formvar coated wires the difference will be slight.

LENGTH OF WIRE USED IN SINGLE LAYER SOLENOID

The circumference of a single turn of a solenoid is $2\pi \times$ **R** or **d**. π is a constant and is equal to 3.14, approximately. The length of wire of a solenoid is:

length of wire, in inches = π x **d** x No. of turns

d is the diameter of the solenoid, in inches.

LENGTH OF WIRE—RESISTANCE METHOD

You can determine the length of a wire if you know its resistance and gauge number. Example: You have an unknown length of No. 18 wire whose resistance is 2½ ohms. What is the length of this wire in feet?

$$\text{length of wire} = \frac{1,000 \times \text{resistance of the wire}}{\text{resistance of 1,000 feet}}$$

The resistance of 1000 feet of No. 18 wire from Table 1-4 is 6.385 ohms.

$$\text{length of wire} = \frac{1,000 \times 2\frac{1}{2}}{6.385} = \frac{2,500}{6.385}$$

$$= 391 \text{ feet}$$

TEMPERATURE

In common practice, temperature is given in degrees Fahreheit or Celsius. (Other scales, more often found in laboratory rather than commercial or industrial use, include Kelvin, Reaumur and Rankine.)

To change degrees Celsius to degrees Fahrenheit:

$$F = (C \times 9/5) + 32 \qquad (1\text{-}16)$$

To change degrees Fahrenheit to degrees Celsius:

$$C = (F - 32) \times 5/9 \qquad (1\text{-}17)$$

F is in degrees Fahrenheit and C is in degrees Celsius. (Also see Table 1-5.)

Table 1-5. Celsius-Fahrenheit conversion.

Deg.C.	Deg.F.	Deg.C.	Deg.F.	Deg.C.	Deg.F.	Deg.C.	Deg.F.
−40	−40.0	80	176.0	210	410	310	590
−30	−22.0	90	194.0	220	428	320	608
−20	− 4.0	100	212.0	230	446	330	626
−10	14.0	110	230.0	240	464	340	644
0	32.0	120	248.0	250	482	350	662
10	50.0	130	266.0	260	500	360	680
20	68.0	140	284.0	270	518	370	698
30	86.0	150	302.0	280	536		
40	104.0	160	320.0	290	554		
50	122.0	170	338.0	300	572		
60	140.0	180	356.0				
70	158.0	190	374.0				
		200	392.0				

COEFFICIENT OF RESISTANCE

Resistors can change their value, the amount of change depending on how the resistors were made, the temperature rise or fall of the resistors, the ambient temperature, and the current through the resistors.

The term, coefficient of resistance, is used to describe a change in the value of resistance. A positive temperature coefficient means that the resistor will increase in value with an increase in temperature. A negative temperature coefficient means a decrease. Zero temperature coefficient means no change whether temperature goes up or down. Resistors can have either a positive or a negative temperature coefficient, depending on how the component is manufactured.

POSITIVE TEMPERATURE COEFFICIENT OF CAPACITORS

The temperature coefficient, T_c, of a capacitor is the value change of a capacitor for each 1° C increase in temperature. Like resistors, temperature coefficient is a function of capacitor construction. It is specified in terms of parts per million (PPM) per degree Celsius. Example: A 100 pf capacitor has a temperature coefficient of 300 PPM/deg. C. For a 1^c rise in temperature, the capacitance will increase 3×10^2 pf for each 10^6 pf.

$$\frac{capacitance}{10^6} \times T_c = capacitance\ increase/1^\circ C\ increase$$

The capacitance will increase by:

$$\frac{100}{10^6} \times 300 = \frac{10^2}{10^6} \times 3 \times 10^2$$
$$= \frac{3 \times 10^4}{10^6} = \frac{3}{10^2} = \frac{3}{100} = 0.03$$

The capacitance will increase by 0.03 pf for each 1° C increase in temperature.

With a positive temperature coefficient, the value of capacitance increases with a rise in temperature. Positive temperature coefficients are preceded by a plus (+) sign or may have no polarity sign.

NEGATIVE TEMPERATURE COEFFICIENT OF CAPACITORS

Negative temperature coefficients are also specified in PPM/1° C but are always preceded by a minus sign. Example: A .05 uf capacitor has a **Tc** of —600 PPM/deg. C.

$$\frac{.05}{10^6} \times (- 600) = \frac{5 \times 10^{-2}}{10^6} \times (- 600)$$
$$= 5 \times 10^{-8} \times (- 600)$$
$$= -3,000 \times 10^{-8}$$
$$= -3 \times 10^3 \times 10^{-8} = -3 \times 10^{-5}$$

The minus sign indicates a decrease in capacitance. This capacitor will decrease by 3×10^{-5} μf or 0.00003 μf for each 1° C rise in temperature. If the temperature rises 10° C, the capacitance will decrease by 10 x 0.00003 μf = 0.0003 μf. Since the original value is 0.05 μf, the actual capacitance for a 10°C rise will be:

$$.05 - [10 \ (0.00003)] = .05 - .0003 = 0.0497 \ \mu f$$

TEMPERATURE COEFFICIENT COLOR CODE

Tc is indicated on ceramic capacitors by this color code:

Color	Tc in PPM/deg. C
Black	0
Brown	-33
Red	-75
Orange	-150
Yellow	-220
Green	-330
Blue	-470
Violet	-750
Gray	+30
White	+500

OHM'S LAW

More widely used than any other formula in electronics (see Fig. 1-8), Ohm's law is simply:

$$E = I \times R \tag{1-18}$$

E is the voltage (in volts), I is the current in amperes, and R is the resistance in ohms. By dividing both sides of this formula by R, we get:

$$I = \frac{E}{R} \tag{1-19}$$

Or, by dividing both sides by I, we get:

$$R = \frac{E}{I} \tag{1-20}$$

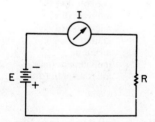

Fig. 1-8. Simple circuit showing three factors involved—voltage, current and resistance. When any two of these are known, the third and unknown value can be found by using Ohm's law.

By common practice, the unknown value (the value we are looking for) is placed on the left-hand side of the equation. These three forms of Ohm's law can be used to find any one value (such as voltage) when the other two values (current and resistance) are known.

POLARITY OF IR DROPS

If the direction of flow of current (Fig. 1-9) through a resistor is known, an arrow indicating that direction can be marked with plus (+) and minus (−) signs to show the polarity of the voltage drop. The head end of the arrow is plus, the tail end is minus.

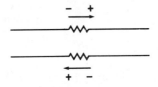

Fig. 1-9. Arrows indicate direction of electron current flow, and polarity of the voltage drop.

BASIC UNITS

The basic units used in Ohm's law are the volt, the ampere, and the ohm. Multiples and submultiples of these units are often convenient.

In Terms of Numbers

Unit	Symbol	Multiple	Value
volt	E	kilovolt (kv)	1,000 volts
volt	E	millivolt (mv)	1/1,000 volt
volt	E	microvolt (μv)	1/1,000,000 volt
ohm	R	kilohm	1,000 ohms
ohm	R	megohm	1,000,000 ohms
ampere	I	milliampere (ma)	1/1,000 ampere
ampere	I	microampere (μa)	1/1,000,000 ampere

The numbers used in problems involving Ohm's law are often very large whole numbers or large decimals. When this happens it is more convenient to use exponents. The relationships between the ohm, volt, and ampere in both numerical and exponential form is:

1 volt	$= 10^3$ millivolts	$= 10^6$ microvolts
1 millivolt	$= 10^{-3}$ volt	$= 10^3$ microvolts
1 microvolt	$= 10^{-6}$ volt	$= 10^{-3}$ millivolt
1 ohm	$= 10^{-3}$ kilohm	$= 10^{-6}$ megohm
1 kilohm	$= 10^3$ ohms	$= 10^{-3}$ megohm
1 megohm	$= 10^6$ ohms	$= 10^3$ kilohms
1 ampere	$= 10^3$ milliamperes	$= 10^6$ microamperes
1 milliampere	$= 10^{-3}$ ampere	$= 10^3$ microamperes
1 microampere	$= 10^{-6}$ ampere	$= 10^{-3}$ milliamperes

The two triangles shown in Fig. 1-10 are memory aids for remembering Ohm's law. Cover the unknown value with a finger tip and the triangle automatically reveals the correct formula to use. If you want to find the current in a circuit (just as an example) cover the letter **I** or the word "amps" and the formula is revealed as either **E** divided by **R** or volts divided by ohms.

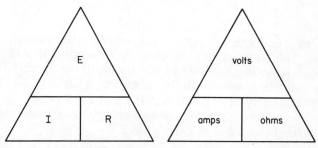

Fig. 1-10. These are memory aids for remembering Ohm's Law. Ohm's Law is one of the most widely used formulas in electronics.

LOADING

Any component that draws current from a voltage source is a load. A "heavy" load is one that requires more current than a "light" load. The terms are relative. A heavy load in one circuit might be regarded as a light load in another. The maximum load is that presented by a short circuit across a voltage source. The minimum load is zero load—an open circuit across a voltage source. However, an open-circuit condition does not guarantee zero current, since leakage current can exist due to dust, dirt, unusually high EMF's, defective components, stray varying magnetic fields, poor wire or component spacing, humidity, etc.

POWER

The power in a DC circuit involves values of voltage, current and resistance. In the basic power formula (Fig. 1-11):

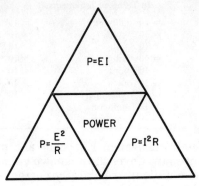

Fig. 1-11. These are the three basic power laws. The power laws can be combined with Ohm's Law to yield other useful formulas.

$$P = E \times I \qquad (1\text{-}21)$$

power (P) is in watts, voltage (E) is in volts and the current (I) is in amperes. This formula, like the Ohm's law formula, is of the $A = B \times C$ type. Knowing any two of the three values in this formula always yields the answer to the unknown. $A = B \times C$; $B = A/C$ and $C = A/B$. Similarly, $P = E \times I$; $E = P/I$ and $I = P/E$.

We can easily derive other power formulas from the basic power formula and use of Ohm's law.

$$P = E \times I \qquad \text{But } E = I \times R$$

substituting $I \times R$ for E in the power formula we have:

$$P = I \times R \times I \qquad \text{Note that } I \times I = I^2 \qquad (1\text{-}22)$$

$$\text{Thus, } P = I^2R \text{ or } I^2 \times R$$

This formula is still of the $A = B \times C$ type and so any two known values can be made to reveal the unknown quantity.

We can make another substitution in our power formula.

$$P = E \times I \qquad \text{But } I = E/R$$

substituting E/R for I in the power formula we have:

$$P = E \times E/R \qquad E \times E = E^2 \qquad (1\text{-}23)$$

$$P = E^2/R$$

30

Since **E**, **I**, and **R** are always used in some form of the power laws and in Ohm's law as well, a little algebraic manipulation leads to some new formulas:

$$E = I \times R \text{ and } P = E \times I \text{ or } I = \frac{P}{E}$$

then

$$E = \frac{P \times R}{E}$$

Multiplying both sides by **E** we have:

$$E^2 = P \times R \text{ or } E = \sqrt{P \times R} \tag{1-24}$$

Other formulas can be obtained more directly:

$$P = I^2 R \qquad I^2 = \frac{P}{R} \qquad I = \sqrt{\frac{P}{R}} \tag{1-25}$$

Similarly:

$$E = \frac{P}{I} \tag{1-26}$$

$$R = \frac{P}{I^2} \tag{1-27}$$

$$R = \frac{E^2}{P} \tag{1-28}$$

TOTAL POWER DISSIPATION

The total power dissipated by resistive loads (Fig. 1-12) whether in a series, parallel, or series-parallel circuit, is the sum of the individual powers. In Fig. 1-12, **R1** utilizes power **P1**; **R2** has power **P2**; and **R3** has power **P3**.

$$P_t = P1 + P2 + P3 \tag{1-29}$$

P_t is the total power in watts. **P1**, **P2**, and **P3** are also in watts.

The formulas used in Ohm's law and in problems involving power can be conveniently summarized and are shown in Table 1-6.

Table 1-6. Summary of power and Ohm's Law formulas for DC.

Watts	Amperes	Ohms	Volts
$P =$	$I =$	$R =$	$E =$
E^2/R	E/R	E/I	IR
I^2R	P/E	E^2/P	P/I
EI	$\sqrt{P/R}$	P/I^2	$\sqrt{PR}$

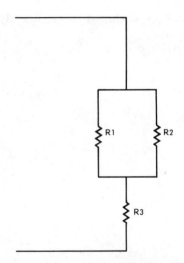

Fig. 1-12. The total power is the arithmetic sum of the individual powers utilized by each component.

WORK

Power used per unit of time is called work. That is, work $= P \times t$. The basic unit is the watt-hour.

When large amounts of power are involved, power used per unit of time is expressed in kilowatt–hours.

$$\text{kilowatt–hours} = \frac{P \times t}{1,000} \qquad (1\text{-}30)$$

P is the power in watts; t is the time in hours.

EFFICIENCY

Note that power always involves either voltage or current, but voltage or current **alone** do not represent an expenditure of energy. A battery is a voltage source but there is no utilization of the electrical energy stored in the battery until the battery is connected to a circuit component, such as a resistor.

Electronic circuits receive power from a battery (or a power supply), and use this power (called input power) to perform some function. The power may be modified or changed in some way and then, called output power, may be delievered to a load. The load may be a resistor, some other component, or another circuit.

Since part of the power will be used in the circuit itself, the output power will always be less than the input. The ratio of these two powers is called the efficiency:

$$\eta = P_o/P_i \qquad\qquad (1\text{-}31)$$

η is the efficiency, P_0 is output power, while P_i is input power. Since P_0 is always less than P_i, the answer must always be decimal—that is, less than one. To obtain efficiency in terms of percentage rather than a decimal, multiply the answer by 100.

$$\eta \times P_i = P_o$$

and

$$P_i = \frac{P_o}{\eta}$$

POWER UNITS

The basic unit of power is the watt. As in the case of Ohm's law large whole numbers or decimals may be involved, making the use of exponents desirable. The power formulas given are valid only for linear resistors—that is, resistors which obey Ohm's law.

		In Terms of Numbers	
Unit	Symbol	Multiple	Value
watt	P	microwatt	1/1,000,000 watt
watt	P	milliwatt	1/1,000 watt
watt	P	megawatt	1,000,000 watts
		In Terms of Exponents	
1 watt		$= 10^3$ milliwatts	$= 10^6$ microwatts
1 milliwatt		$= 10^{-3}$ watt	$= 10^3$ microwatts
1 microwatt		$= 10^{-6}$ watt	$= 10^{-3}$ milliwatt

POWER vs ENERGY

Energy is the ability to do work. The rate at which that work is done is called power. The unit of energy or work is the joule. The unit of power is the joule/second or watt. In electronics, electrical power is usually measured in watts. Electrical energy can be stored, but not in resistors. Electrical energy put into a resistor is given off by that resistor as heat.

HEATING EFFECT OF A CURRENT

A current produces heat when it passes through a resistor. The heat generated is proportional to the square of the current, in amperes, multiplied by the value of **R**, in ohms.

$$H = I^2 \times R \qquad\qquad (1\text{-}32)$$

H is in joules per second. Since joules per second = watts, the formula becomes:

$$P = I^2 \times R$$

P is the power in watts, I the current in amperes and **R** the resistance, in ohms.

If the heat produced is in terms of calories per second, the formula is:

$$H = 0.239 I^2 \times R$$

H is the heat in calories/sec.

HORSEPOWER

Horsepower (HP) is a unit of measurement used for motors and generators. Electrical power input to a motor is in watts or kilowatts; output in HP. Output of a generator is in watts or kilowatts; input in HP.

$$1\,HP = 746\,watts = 550\,ft\ lbs/sec.$$

and in terms of kilowatts

$$HP = \frac{\text{kilowatts} \times 1{,}000}{746}$$

These formulas can be transposed in terms of power in watts or kilowatts.

$$1\,\text{watt} = 1/746\,HP = 0.00134\ HP$$

$$KW = \frac{HP \times 746}{1{,}000} \tag{1-33}$$

PHASE

The DC voltage across a resistor and the DC current through it are always in step or in phase. If the voltage increases, the current will also increase, assuming the value of resistance remains constant. Under the same conditions, a decrease in voltage always results in a decrease in current.

THE SHUNT LAW

When a voltage is applied to resistors connected in parallel, the same voltage appears across each of the resistors. Since the voltage E is equal to $I \times R$, we can make the same statement in the shape of a formula:

$$I1 \times R1 = I2 \times R2 \tag{1-34}$$

If we get the current terms on one side of this equation and the resistance terms on the other side, we will have:

$$\frac{I1}{I2} = \frac{R2}{R1}$$

This new arrangement shows us that the ratio of the currents (see Fig. 1-13) is inversely proportional to the ratio of the resistances. This is just another way of saying that the larger the resistance, the smaller the current flowing through it. A formula, such as that above, is just another application of Ohm's law.

Formulas of this kind are of the $A \times B = C \times D$ type. They can be rearranged to supply four additional formulas. In each instance, though, there must be only one unknown—that is, you must have values for three of the four items in the formula. Using $I1 \times R1 = I2 \times R2$, we have:

in terms of current

$$I1 = \frac{I2 \times R2}{R1} \tag{1-35}$$

$$I2 = \frac{I1 \times R1}{R2} \tag{1-36}$$

in terms of resistance

$$R1 = \frac{I2 \times R2}{I1} \tag{1-37}$$

$$R2 = \frac{I1 \times R1}{I2} \tag{1-38}$$

LINE AND BRANCH CURRENTS

Current from a power source is line current. In a series network, line current is the same throughout the circuit. In the two-resistor parallel branch circuit of Fig. 1-13, the line current branches into two currents, $I1$ and $I2$. The sum of the branch currents equals the line current.

$$I_{line} = I1 + I2 \tag{1-39}$$

Transposing:

$$I1 = I_{line} - I2$$

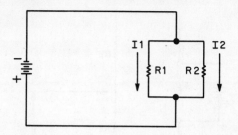

Fig. 1-13. While the currents flowing through R1 and R2 might not be equal, the voltages across each resistor are identical. Actually, there is only one voltage across the parallel units, but it is convenient to regard it as two equal voltages.

and:

$$I2 = I_{line} - I1$$

For three parallel branches:

$$I_{line} = I1 + I2 + I3$$

VOLTAGE DIVIDER (Potentiometer)

A fixed voltage, such as that supplied by a battery or power supply, is often not suitable for a particular circuit or component. Resistors can be used as voltage dividers to obtain any value of voltage less than that of the source. See Fig. 1-14. The smaller voltage, e, is equal to the source voltage multiplied by the ratio of the resistances:

$$e = E \times \frac{R1}{R1 + R2} \qquad (1\text{-}40)$$

As R2 is made smaller, the output voltage e becomes larger, reaching the value of E as a limit. The input voltage E remains constant. Since the resistors, R1 and R2 are in series, the same current flows through them.

Suppose a load of near-infinite resistance is placed across R1. But if the load does not draw current, then the formula can be used as is to find the value of e. If If the load does draw current, and its resistance is known, then R1 and the load may be considered as a pair of parallel resistors. Calculate the equivalent value of this parallel pair, substitute this value for R1, and the formula can then be used to determine the amount of e.

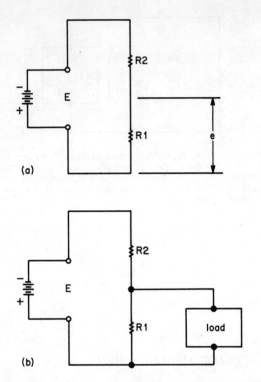

Fig. 1-14. It is often convenient to be able to calculate the voltage across a single resistor of a network.

PROPORTIONAL VOLTAGES AND RESISTANCES

In a series resistive network, the **IR** drops are proportional to the values of **R** and the total voltage, **E** (Fig. 1-15).

$$\frac{IR1}{E} = \frac{R1}{R_t}$$

IR1 is the voltage across R1; E is the applied EMF; R_t is the total resistance. $R_t = R1 + R2 + R3$.
Similarly:

$$\frac{IR2}{E} = \frac{R2}{R_t} \qquad \text{and} \qquad \frac{IR3}{E} = \frac{R3}{R_t}$$

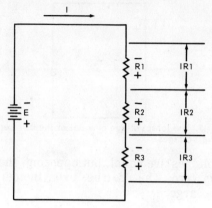

Fig. 1-15. IR drops in a series resistive network.

VOLTAGES IN SERIES AIDING AND OPPOSING

Voltage drops in series aiding are additive (see Fig. 1-16). The total voltage is equal to the sum of the individual voltages;

$$E_t = E1 + E2 + E3 \ldots \ldots$$ (1-41)'

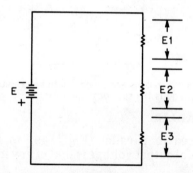

Fig. 1-16. The voltage across each resistor can be added to obtain the total voltage. See Fig. 1-15 for the polarities of the voltage drops.

Voltages can be connected in series opposing. The total voltage (see Fig. 1-17) is equal to the larger voltage minus that of the smaller one.

$$E_t = E2 - E1$$

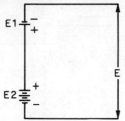

Fig. 1-17. The total voltage is equal to the difference of the two voltages.

If the two voltages are equal, but opposing, the total effective output voltage is zero. This is true, even though the individual voltages may be large.

CELLS IN SERIES AIDING

The total voltage of cells in sereis aiding, Fig. 1-18, is the sum of the individual cell voltages. The maximum available current is the current capability of the weakest cell in the series group.

$$E_t = E1 + E2 + E3 \ldots$$

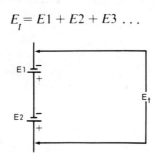

Fig. 1-18. When cells are connected in series aiding, the total voltage is the sum of the individual cell voltages.

CELLS IN PARALLEL

Cells are wired in parallel (Fig. 1-19) to increase current capability. The total output voltage is that of any individual cell.

VOLTAGE REFERENCE POINTS

Ground, a common bus, or a neutral wire are commonly used as voltage reference points, but any voltage point can also act as a reference., In Fig. 1-20 (circuit A), point A is 12 volts negative with respect to point B. Point B is 12 volts positive with respect to point A. In drawing (B), point A is 6 volts negative with respect to ground. Point B is 6 volts positive with respect to ground. The voltage from A to B is 12 volts. In drawing (C), both points, A and B, are 6 volts positive with respect to ground. The voltage between points A and B

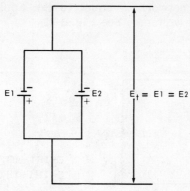

Fig. 1-19. When cells of identical voltages are wired in parallel, the total voltage is that of any individual cell.

is zero. In drawing (D) points A and B are both 6 volts negative with respect to ground. The voltage between points A and B is zero.

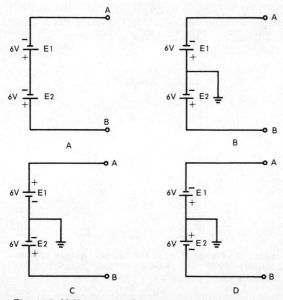

Fig. 1-20. Voltages are always measured between two points, one of which may serve as a reference. Ground or a common bus is often used as such a reference.

KIRCHHOFF'S VOLTAGE LAW

The algebraic sum of the voltages around a closed circuit or network is zero. More simply stated, the sum of the voltages in a closed circuit or network is equal to the applied EMF (electromotive force or voltage). See Fig. 1-21.

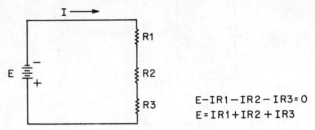

$$E - IR1 - IR2 - IR3 = 0$$
$$E = IR1 + IR2 + IR3$$

Fig. 1-21. If the voltage drops across each resistor are added, their sum will be equal to the voltage of the battery. If this sum is subtracted from the battery voltage, the result will be zero.

Consider Fig. 1-22. The sum of the voltage drops across the resistors is equal to that of the battery. Note the voltage polarities of the resistors and the battery. They oppose each other, but since the voltages are equal, the algebraic sum is zero.

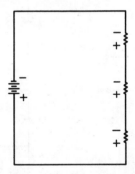

Fig. 1-22. The polarity of the battery voltage and the polarity of the voltage drops across the resistors are opposite.

More practically, in electronics we consider the sum of the voltage drops equal to the source voltage (Fig. 1-23). That is:

$$E_{\text{battery}} = I1R1 + I1R2 + I1R3 \qquad (1\text{-}42)$$

Since this is a series circuit, the same current (I1) flows through each of the resistors.

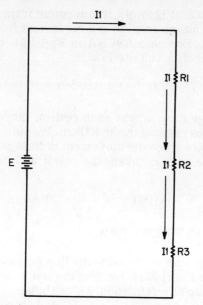

Fig. 1-23. In a series circuit, the same current flows through each component.

VOLTAGES IN A CLOSED NETWORK

The direction of current flow external to a voltage source is from minus to plus. Fig. 1-24 shows such a closed network. The

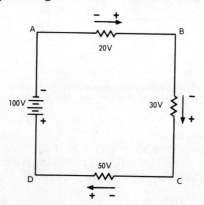

Fig. 1-24. The algebraic sum of the voltages in a closed network is equal to zero.

network path can be either clockwise or counterclockwise. The closed path in Fig. 1-24 is from A to B to C to D to A. Any starting point may be selected.

In a closed path (Fig. 1-24), if movement from minus to plus is considered as a voltage drop, then a movement from plus to minus is a voltage gain. For path ABCDA in Fig. 1-24, the voltages, according to Kirchhoff's voltage law is:

$$(-20) + (-30) + (-50) + 100 = 0$$

There is a voltage drop across each resistor since current travels from minus to plus in going through them. We gain 100 volts in going through the battery since the movement is from plus to minus. If a counterclockwise path is taken, the result will be the same. For path ADCBA:

$$(-100) + 50 + 30 + 20 = 0$$

KIRCHHOFF'S CURRENT LAW

The algebraic sum of the currents flowing toward a junction is equal to zero. See Fig. 1-25. If we take the conditions existing in this circuit and set it up as an equation, we will have:

$$I1 - I2 - I3 = 0$$

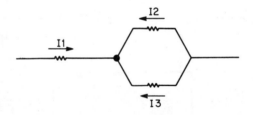

Fig. 1-25. The heavy dot represents the junction toward which the currents are flowing. The algebraic sum of these currents is zero.

While the conditions shown in Fig. 1-25 may be algebraically possible, it isn't a practical circuit condition. We can change Fig. 1-25 so that it looks like Fig. 1-26. We now have:

$$I1 = I2 + I3$$

If we put this into words it simply means that we have as much current flowing away from the junction (or meeting point of the three conductors) as we have flowing toward it. Obviously. If this

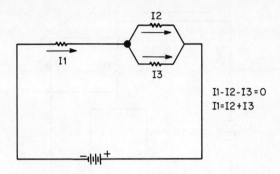

$$I1-I2-I3=0$$
$$I1=I2+I3$$

Fig. 1-26. The sum of the currents moving away from a junction is equal to the current flowing toward it.

were not the case, we would have an accumulation of current at the junction. What about the minus signs in front of $I2$ and $I3$? These indicate direction of current flow. If we use a plus sign to show current flowing from left to right, then a minus sign serves nicely to represent current moving from right to left. The transposition of $I2$ and $I3$ from the left side to the right side is an elementary algebraic operation.

SERIES-PARALLEL RESISTIVE CIRCUIT

In a series-parallel network the total voltage equals the sum of the IR drops across the series and parallel components. In Fig. 1-27, the total voltage E equals $E1 + E2$. $E1$ is the IR drop across $R1$. $E2$ is the drop across $R2$ and $R3$.

$$E_{total} = I \times R1 + I \times \left| \frac{R2 \times R3}{R2 + R3} \right. \qquad (1\text{-}43)$$

TIME CONSTANTS IN DC CIRCUITS

Combinations of resistors and capacitors, or resistors and coils (known as R-C or R-L circuits) can be used to control the time for a voltage or current to reach its peak value (see Fig. 1-28). The time, in seconds, required for the current or the voltage to reach 63.2 percent of its final value, is known as the time constant of the circuit.

45

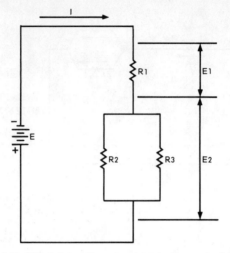

Fig. 1-27. The total voltage is equal to the sum of the drops across the series and parallel components.

For a Series R-L Circuit:

$$t = \frac{L}{R} \tag{1-44}$$

L is the total inductance in the circuit, in henrys; R is the total resistance, in ohms. The time constant, t, is the time required for the current to attain 63.2 percent of its ultimate peak amount.

For a Series R-C Circuit:

$$t = R \times C \tag{1-45}$$

R and t are the same as described for the series R-L circuit. C is the total capacitance in the circuit, in farads.

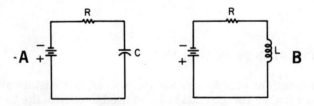

Fig. 1-28. The charge and discharge of a capacitor through a resistor is not something that takes place instantaneously. Similarly, in a circuit involving a coil and a resistor, it takes a definite amount of time for a current to reach its maximum value.

If, instead of charging through a resistor, a fully-charged capacitor is allowed to discharge through a resistor, the formula for the time constant in an **R-C** circuit would still apply. In this case, though, a time constant would be the time it takes for the capacitor to lose 63.2 percent of its full charge, or, to drop to 36.8 percent of its initial charge.

Generally, a capacitor is considered to be fully charged or fully discharged, after five time constants.

ONE TIME CONSTANT

In a series **R-C** circuit, at the end of one time constant, the effective voltage producing current flow is the source voltage minus 63 % of the source voltage. Thus, if an **R-C** circuit is connected across a 100-volt DC source, the net effective voltage at the end of one time constant is:

Source voltage—63% source voltage = net effective voltage
100 volts—(0.63 x 100) = 100-63 = 37 volts

The battery in this circuit (Fig. 1-28A) acts as though its voltage is only 37 volts. The time at which this takes place depends on the value of resistance and capacitance, and can be calculated from the formula: t=R x C.

TWO TIME CONSTANTS

At the end of one time constant, the source voltage has decreased to an effective value that is 63 % of its original value, or, the source is 0.37 x **E**, where **E** is the original value of the source voltage.

At the end of two time constants, the effect of the source voltage decreases another 63%. But since the net effective source voltage has dropped to 37% at the end of one time constant, its value at the end of two time constants is:

$$63\% \times 37\% = 0.63 \times 0.37 = 0.23 = 23\%$$

At the end of the first time constant, the effective source voltage decreased 63 %. At the end of the second time constant the effective source voltage decreased an additional 23%. The total decrease at the end of two time constants is 63% + 23% = 86%. If the voltage source is 100 volts, at the end of two time constants, the source voltage is effectively only 100—(0.86 x 100)=100—86 = 14 volts.

THREE TIME CONSTANTS

With the passage of another time constant, the effective source voltage decreases by another 63%. But at the end of two time constants the effective source voltage is 14% of its original value. Hence, 63% x 14% = 0.63 x 0.14 = 0.09 = 9%. The total percentage drop at the end of three time constants is:

$$63\% + 23\% + 9\% = 95\%$$

Thus, at the end of three time constants, the net effective voltage is:

source voltage — (.95 x source voltage)

If the original source voltage was 100 volts:

$$100 — (0.95 \text{ x } 100) = 100 — 95 = 5 \text{ volts}$$

At the end of four time constants, using the same arithmetic, the effective source voltage is 2 volts, and at the end of five time constants it is 1 volt.

THE R-L CIRCUIT

The behavior of the **R-L** circuit (Fig. 1-28B) is equally interesting. At the moment the circuit is closed, the current in the circuit is minimum, the voltage drop across the resistor is also minimum, while the induced voltage across the coil, L, is maximum.

As time moves forward (in fractions of a second), the voltage drop across the resistor increases, while the induced voltage goes down, both exponentially. Kirchhoff's voltage law is applicable at any instant since the voltage across the resistor and that across the coil must be equal to the applied EMF.

At the end of five time constants, or more, the induced voltage is zero, the voltage drop across the resistor is equal to the battery voltage, the current is maximum, the magnetic field around the coil is maximum, but is not changing. This clearly illustrates that the induced EMF across the coil is due to the **rate** of change of the current and not its amount.

The energy delivered to the resistor, because of the current flow, is dissipated by the resistor as heat. The energy delivered to the coil is stored in its magnetic field.

If, through some switching arrangement, the battery is disconnected and the coil is shunted across resistor **R**, the current flow curve will be exponential downward—that is, the current will be decreasing. Both the current and the voltage across the resistor will drop to 36.8 percent of their maximum amounts in **L/R** seconds.

TIME CONSTANTS IN AC CIRCUITS

The methods for calculating the time constant of a series **R-C** or series **R-L** DC circuit is also applicable to series **R-C** or series **R-L** AC circuits. However, in an AC circuit, time constants must be considered with respect to the time duration of a single complete cycle of the AC waveform. For a sine wave of the type supplied by an ordinary power outlet, the frequency is 60 Hz. A single cycle of this wave would require a time completion of 1/60 second, or 0.0166 second. $0.0166 \times 10^6 = 16,600$ microseconds. Any time constant that is 1/10 of this value (or less) is regarded as a "short" time constant. Any time constant that is more than 1/10th of 16,600 microseconds (in this example) is regarded as "long." Thus, in an AC circuit, a long or short time constant not only depends on the values of **R**, **C** or **L**, but also on the frequency of the AC waveform.

TIME CONSTANT OF A COUPLING CIRCUIT

A coupling circuit of the **R-C** type (Fig. 1-29) should have a long time constant compared to the lowest frequency supplied by the source voltage. **C** in Fig. 1-29 has a value of 0.1 uf and **R** is 0.5 megohm.

$$T = R \times C = (5 \times 10^5)\,(0.1 \times 10^{-6}) = 0.5 \times 10^{-1} = 0.05 \text{ second}$$

$$0.05 \times 10^6 = 50,000 \text{ microseconds}$$

$$f = 1\text{kHz} = 1000 \text{ Hz} \quad t = 1/1000 = 0.001 \text{ second}$$

$$0.001 \times 10^6 = 1,000 \text{ microseconds}$$

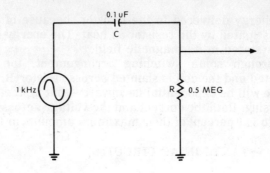

Fig. 1-29. R-C type coupling circuit.

The ratio of the time constant to the lowest frequency of the source is 50,000/1,000 = 50 to 1. The time constant in this circuit would be regarded as long since it is more than 10 times the time duration of a single complete wave of the source.

Chapter 2

AC Circuits

One of the characteristics of a direct current (as the name implies) is its motion in one direction. Although this current is often of constant strength, it can also vary, depending on voltage changes in the circuit. But whether constant or changing (or pulsing) it is still unidirectional. A characteristic of a direct voltage is that it does not change its polarity. This is true, even if the voltage is a fluctuating one.

An alternating current is bidirectional. It will flow first in one direction, and then reverse and move in the other. An alternating voltage is one whose polarity changes.

WAVELENGTH AND FREQUENCY

The wave shown in Fig. 2-1 is a sine wave of current or voltage. This is a periodic type of wave, meaning that the current (or

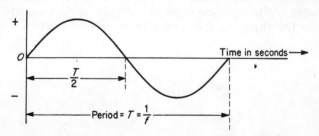

Fig. 2-1. This sine wave can represent either voltage or current.

voltage) changes its direction of flow at regular time intervals, and that the voltage assumes equal alternate positive and negative values. The length of a wave (or the wavelength) is the distance from the beginning of a single wave to its end. The wavelength is also the distance between successive positive peaks or successive negative peaks. The symbol for wavelength is the Greek letter lambda (λ).

The sine wave in Fig. 2-1 is a complete cycle and consists of two alternations—a positive alternation and a negative alternation. The frequency of a wave is the number of cycles completed per second. Cycles per second is abbreviated as cps. Cycles per second are now referred to as Hertz, abbreviated as Hz. Thus:

$$1 \text{ Hertz} = 1 \text{ Hz} = \text{cycles per second} = 1 \text{cps.}$$

A kiloHertz is 1,000 cps and a megaHertz is 1,000,000 cps.

The frequency of a periodic wave is also the number of wavelengths per unit of time—generally taken as one second. As the number of waves per second increases, the length of the wave decreases. We can express this as an inverse relationship:

$$f = \frac{1}{\lambda} \text{ or } \lambda = \frac{1}{f}. \qquad (2\text{-}1)$$

All that this means is that frequency and wavelength act as opposites. When one increases, the other decreases. And vice versa.

The wavelength (λ) of a radio wave, measured in meters from the beginning of one cycle to the end of that same cycle, is equal to its velocity in free space, 300,000,000 meters per second, divided by its frequency, f, in Hz.

$$\lambda = \frac{300,000,000}{f} = \frac{3 \times 10^8}{f}$$

In free space radio waves and light waves travel at the same speed—186,000 miles/second or 300,000,000 meters/second. Other formulas for changing frequency to wavelength are:

$$\lambda \text{ (in meters)} = \frac{3 \times 10^5}{f \text{ (in kiloHertz)}} \qquad (2\text{-}2)$$

$$\lambda \text{ (in centimeters)} = \frac{3 \times 10^4}{f \text{ (in megaHertz)}} \qquad (2\text{-}3)$$

To find the wavelength in feet when the frequency is in megaHertz convert the speed of radio waves from miles per second to feet per second. There are 5,280 feet in one mile. Hence:

$$\frac{186,000 \times 5280}{1,000,000} = \frac{186 \times 10^3 \times 528 \times 10^1}{10^6}$$

$$= \frac{186 \times 528 \times 10^4}{10^6} = 186 \times 528 \times 10^{-2}$$

$$= 186 \times 5.28 = 984 \text{ feet per microsecond}$$

Hence to find the wavelength in feet when the frequency in megaHertz is known:

$$\lambda \text{ (in feet)} = \frac{984}{f \text{ (in megaHertz)}}$$

To change wavelength to frequency:

$$f \text{ (in kiloHertz)} = \frac{3 \times 10^5}{\lambda \text{ (in meters)}}$$

$$f \text{ (in megaHertz)} = \frac{3 \times 10^4}{\lambda \text{ (in centimeters)}}$$

$$f \text{ (in megaHertz)} = \frac{984}{\lambda \text{ (in feet)}}$$

PERIOD

Frequency may also be regarded as the time duration of a number of waves. A wave having a frequency of 30 Hertz has 30 complete waves in one second. The time duration of a single cycle, or period, would be 1/30 second. In terms of a formula, the period would be:

$$T = \frac{1}{f} \qquad (2\text{-}4)$$

In this formula, **T** is in seconds and **f** is in Hertz.

VELOCITY OF A WAVE

The distance covered by a wave in a certain amount of time is known as its velocity. That is:

$$\text{Velocity} = \frac{\text{Distance}}{\text{Time}}$$

We can write this much more conveniently in a formula, as:

$$V = \frac{D}{T}$$

Defining the period as the time it takes a wave to travel a distance equal to its wavelength (λ), we can then make a substitution in the above formula and get:

$$V = \frac{\lambda}{T}$$

But we also know that **T** = 1/**f**. Making another substitution, we have:

$$V = \frac{\lambda}{1/f}$$

or

$$V = f \times \lambda \qquad (2\text{-}5)$$

VOLTAGE AND CURRENT MEASUREMENTS

The problem in measuring alternating voltages and currents stems from the fact that such voltages and currents are constantly changing. Because of this a reference point is needed. The reference is the peak or maximum value of the wave. In a pure sine wave, either the positive peak or the negative peak can be used, since both have the same amplitude. The polarity of the voltage (that is, whether the voltage is positive or negative) may be disregarded.

A single cycle of a sine wave (regardless of frequency) lasts for 360 degrees. During a single cycle we get two peaks, one positive and one negative—that is, we get one peak each 180 degrees. But while peak voltage measurements are often useful, they are not truly representative of a sine wave.

The peak value of a wave is an instantaneous value occurring at the 90° point and at the 270° point. Peak values are important since they represent the maximum potential that may be impressed across an electronic component. The peak-to-peak value is the EMF measured from the positive peak to the negative peak. Since a sine wave is symmetrical, the amplitude of the positive peak equals the amplitude of the negative peak.

AVERAGE VALUE

We have a drawing of a sine wave in Fig. 2-2. In the positive part of the wave we have a number of dashed lines drawn vertically. If we measure the heights of each of these lines (known as ordinates) and average them, our average value will be about 60%

54

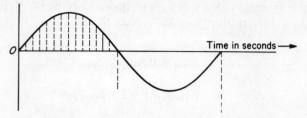

Fig. 2-2. Method used for obtaining the average voltage or current.

of the peak or maximum value. Using more lines to provide a more accurate sampling would show the average value to be 63.7% of the peak. We can write this as a formula:

$$E_{average} = 0.637 \times E_{peak} \qquad (2\text{-}6)$$

Note that Fig. 2-2 does not show actual values of voltage, nor is this required. Our peak is 100% or 1.

Since the formula is an $A = B \times C$ type, we can divide both sides of the equation by 0.637 and get:

$$E_{peak} = \frac{E_{average}}{0.637}$$

If we assign a value of one (unity) to the average voltage we will get:

$$E_{peak} = \frac{1.0 \ (E_{average})}{0.637} = 1.57 \ E_{average}$$

Peak voltage, then, is 1.57 x the average voltage.

We have been talking about sine waves of voltages. What about sine waves of current? The same formulas apply.

$$I_{average} = 0.637 \times I_{peak}$$

$$I_{peak} = 1.57 \times I_{average} \qquad (2\text{-}7)$$

If we want the average of two halves of the cycle, just multiply by 2. Thus:

$$I_{average} = (0.637 \times 2) \ (I_{peak} \times 2)$$

$$I_{peak} \times 2 = I_{peak\text{-}to\text{-}peak}$$

$$I_{average} = 1.274 \times I_{peak\text{-}to\text{-}peak} \qquad (2\text{-}8)$$

55

To find the average value when given the peak-to-peak, divide peak-to-peak by 2, then multiply by 0.637. Note that:

$$E_{peak} = 0.5\, E_{peak\text{-}to\text{-}peak}$$

or

$$E_{peak\text{-}to\text{-}peak} = 2 \times E_{peak}$$

We can also find the average value, given the peak-to-peak by using this formula:

$$E_{average} = 0.3185 \times E_{peak\text{-}to\text{-}peak} \qquad (2\text{-}9)$$

(0.3185 is simply one-half of 0.637.)

INSTANTANEOUS VALUES

The instantaneous values of a sine wave of voltage or current are values that exist at a particular instant of time, such as any ordinate shown in Fig. 2-2. We use the small letters e and i to represent instantaneous values of voltage and current. How many instantaneous values can we have? As many as we want.

The value of an instantaneous voltage can be calculated by:

$$e = E_{peak} \sin \omega t \qquad (2\text{-}10)$$

ω is an abbreviation for $2\pi f$. π is equal to 3.1416. ωt, then, is 2 x 3.1416 x the frequency (f) x the time (t) in seconds. Table 2-1 gives the sine of angles from zero to 360° in 15-degree steps.

Angle, in degrees	Sine Value	Angle, in degrees	Sine Value
0	0.000	195	−0.259
15	0.259	210	−0.500
30	0.500	225	−0.707
45	0.707	240	−0.866
60	0.866	255	−0.966
75	0.966	270	−1.000
90	1.000	285	−0.966
105	0.966	300	−0.866
120	0.866	315	−0.707
135	0.707	330	−0.500
150	0.500	345	−0.259
165	0.259	360	0.000
180	0.000		

Table 2-1. Sines of angles in steps of 15 degrees.

56

Note that the sine of the angle increases as the angle approaches 90 degrees. Values of the sine above 180° simply repeat values lower than 180°. Thus the sine of 195° is the same as the sine of 180° + 15°.

The base line in Fig. 2-3 is shown in angular degrees. We can select any angle we want and represent it by the letter α. Then:

$$\alpha = \omega t$$

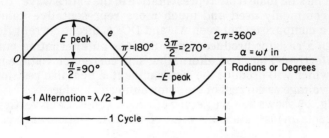

Fig. 2-3. The full length of a wave is the distance from start to finish of one complete cycle of the wave. There are two peaks: one positive; one negative.

We can substitute this in our formula for instantaneous values and get:

$$e = E_{peak} \sin \alpha \qquad (2\text{-}11)$$

Fig. 2-4 shows two instantaneous values of voltage, e1 and e2, selected at random. Note that for a particular sine wave, peak values and average values are fixed. Instantaneous values are fixed only in relationship to a particular instant of time. The same formula can be used for instantaneous values of current:

$$i = I_{peak} \sin \alpha$$

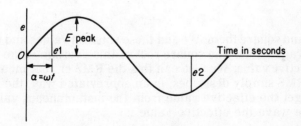

Fig. 2-4. Instantaneous values can be represented by any vertical line, such as e1 or e2.

EFFECTIVE OR RMS VALUES OF A SINE WAVE OF VOLTAGE OR CURRENT

Measuring peak, average and instantaneous voltages or currents of an AC wave are simply attempts to measure a changing waveform. It is true that the peak and average values are fixed, but these are only two points on the waveform, and while valuable, cannot be said to be truly representative of the entire wave. To get a more commonly used and much more representative value, we make a comparison between AC and DC. A direct current flowing through a resistor produces heat. So does an alternating current. The **effective value** of an alternating sine current or voltage is that value which will produce the same amount of heat in a resistor as a direct voltage or current of the same numerical value.

Fig. 2-5 shows how we get the effective value. Each vertical line represents an instantaneous value of current. We take each of these

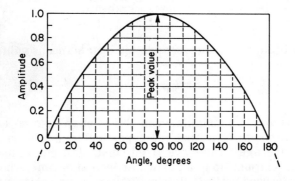

Fig. 2-5. The effective value of a sine wave of voltage or current is obtained from instantaneous values.

values and square them. We add these squared values and then find the average value. The square root of this average value gives us the **effective** value. We also call this the RMS or root-mean-square value. RMS simply describes, in an abbreviated way, the steps we took to get the effective value from the instantaneous values. For any sine wave the effective value is:

$$I_{\text{effective}} = 0.707 \times I_{\text{peak}} \qquad (2\text{-}12)$$

and

$$E_{\text{effective}} = 0.707 \times E_{\text{peak}}$$

If we divide both sides by 0.707, then:

$$E_{\text{peak}} = \frac{E_{\text{eff}}}{0.707} = 1.414 \, E_{\text{effective}}$$

If we assign a value of one (unity) to the effective value, then:

$$E_{\text{peak}} = \frac{1}{0.707} = 1.414 \, E_{\text{effective}}$$

and, in the case of peak-to-peak values:

$$E_{\text{p-p}} = 2 \times 1.414 \, E_{\text{effective}} = 2.828 \, E_{\text{effective}} \qquad (2\text{-}13)$$

(Note that 0.707 is the same as $\frac{1}{2}\sqrt{2}$ and $1.414 = \sqrt{2}$.)

AVERAGE AND EFFECTIVE VALUES

Since:

$$E_{\text{peak}} = \frac{E_{\text{eff}}}{0.707}$$

and

$$E_{\text{peak}} = \frac{E_{\text{avg}}}{0.637}$$

$$\frac{E_{\text{eff}}}{0.707} = \frac{E_{\text{avg}}}{0.637}$$

cross multiplying:

$$0.637 \, E_{\text{eff}} = 0.707 \, E_{\text{avg}}$$

From this relationship we can obtain two new formulas. First, dividing both sides by 0.637:

$$E_{\text{eff}} = \frac{0.707}{0.637} = 1.11 E_{\text{avg}}$$

Then, dividing both sides by 0.707:

$$E_{avg} = \frac{0.637}{0.707} = 0.9E_{eff} \qquad (2\text{-}14)$$

RELATIONSHIPS

We now have four ways to measure or define the value of a sine wave of voltage or current. Table 2-2 summarizes the relationships between these values.

Given This Value	Multiply by this value to get			
	Average	Effective	Peak	P-P
Average	–	1.11	1.57	1.274
Effective	0.9	–	1.414	2.828
Peak	0.637	0.707	–	2.0
P-P	0.3185	0.3535	0.50	–

Table 2-2. Relationships between average, effective, peak and peak-to-peak (p-p) values of sine voltages or currents.

Unless otherwise specified, sinusoidal voltage and currents are in terms of RMS values. There are instruments designed for measuring peak or average values, but these are identified as such on the meter scale or on the instrument itself.

NONSINUSOIDAL WAVES

Pure sine waves are basic waveshapes. A sine wave of any frequency can also be referred to as a fundamental. Frequency multiples of the fundamental waveshape are called harmonics. The second harmonic of a sine wave is two times the fundamental frequency. The third harmonic is three times the fundamental frequency. A fundamental wave and its harmonics are all sine waves when considered separately or when they exist separately. A combination of a fundamental and its harmonics, however, produces nonsinusoidal waveshapes, such as square waves and sawtooth waves. A square wave is composed of a fundamental plus odd harmonics, such as the 3rd, 5th, 7th, etc. The larger the number of odd-order harmonics, the more closely the resulting wave approaches a square wave shape. The wave shape also depends on the amplitudes of the harmonics. A sawtooth waveform is produced by combining a fundamental sine wave with both even and odd order harmonics.

For a square wave:

$$\text{Square wave} = f + 3f + 5f + 7f \dots$$

where f is the fundamental frequency.

For a sawtooth wave:

$$\text{Sawtooth wave} = f + 2f + 3f + 4f + 5f + 6f + 7f \dots$$

Fig. 2-6 shows some preliminary steps in the formation of a square wave. A is the fundamental sine wave; B is the third harmonic. Wave B has three cycles for every complete single cycle of wave A. Wave C is the result of combining wave A and wave B. As more odd harmonics of the correct amplitude are added, the resulting waveshape will gradually approach the appearance of the square wave shown in the illustration.

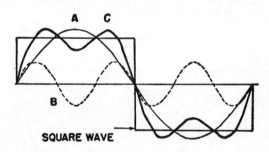

Fig. 2-6. Steps in the formation of a square wave.

Fig 2-7 shows steps in the formation of a sawtooth wave. As in the case of a square wave, the sawtooth starts with a fundamental sine wave. To this sine wave are added both even and odd harmonics. The larger the number of harmonics, the more closely the wave approaches a sawtooth waveform.

61

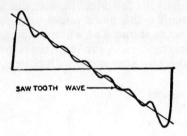

SAW TOOTH WAVE

Fig. 2-7. Steps in the formation of a sawtooth wave.

WAVESHAPE SYMMETRY

A sine wave or its harmonics (when not combined) are symmetrical waves, since each positive alternation is equal to each negative alternation. However, square waves and other waveforms, may or may not be symmetrical. The waves shown in Fig. 2-8 are non-symmetrical. The rounding of the top part of the waveform in wave (3) indicates that it does not contain as many harmonics as wave (1).

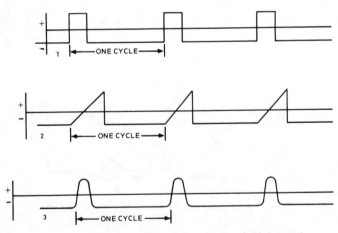

Fig. 2-8. In these waveforms, the negative half does not resemble the positive half.

RISE TIME AND FALL TIME

Theoretically, a square wave (Fig. 2-9) will have a zero rise and fall time—that is, it will rise from its maximum negative to its maximum positive value instantaneously. In practice, it takes the wave a certain amount of time to rise and fall. The wave in Fig. 2-9 is symmetrical since it has equal alternations.

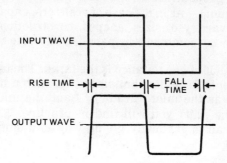

Fig. 2-9. An ideal square wave has zero rise and fall times.

Similarly, the fall time of a sawtooth waveform (Fig. 2-10) is the time required to drop from one amplitude to the other—in this case from maximum positive to maximum negative. Ideally, the rise time of a sawtooth should be linear. The amount of rise time required depends on the application of the sawtooth.

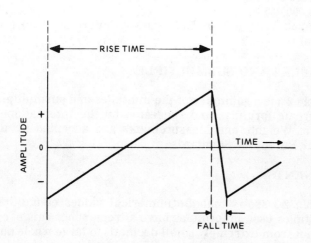

Fig. 2-10. Rise and fall times of a sawtooth wave.

CAPACITORS

A capacitor is a device for storing an electrostatic charge and in its elementary form may consist of a pair of metal plates separated by a gas (such as air), a solid material (such as mica) or by space (vacuum). As in the case of resistors, capacitors come in a tremendous variety of sizes, shapes, construction and also like resistors, may be combined in parallel, in series, or in series-parallel.

The basic unit of capacitance is the farad. The farad is the unit used in electronic formulas, but since it is such a large unit, submultiples such as the microfarad (μf) and the micromicrofarad ($\mu\mu f$) are the units you will find in practice. The submultiple micromicrofarad is gradually giving way to a simpler term, the picofarad (pf).

CONVERSIONS

In practical work, capacitors are rated in terms of microfarads (uf) and picofarads (pf). However, electronic formulas may require conversion of these units to farads.

1 farad = 10^6 microfarads = 1,000,000 microfarads
1 farad = 10^{12} picofarads = 1,000,000,000,000 picofarads
1 microfarad = 10^{-6} farad = 0.000001 farad = 1/1,000,000 farad
1 microfarad = 10^6 picofarads = 1,000,000 picofarads
1 picofarad = 10^{-12} farad = 0.000000000001 farad = 1/1,000,000,000,000 farad
1 picofarad = 10^{-6} microfarad = 0.000001 microfarad = 1/1,000,000 microfarad

MULTIPLES AND SUBMULTIPLES

Table 2-3 is a summary of the multiples and submultiples used in electronic formulas and suggested by the International Committee of Weights and Measurements and accepted by the U.S. National Bureau of Standards.

EXPONENTS

Table 2-3 shows that the numerical values of multiples and submultiples used in formulas have a tremendous range, covering the gamut from extremely small decimals to large whole numbers. Working with such numbers is awkward, time consuming and subject to error. Knowing how to use exponents is essential.

Prefix	Symbol	Numerical Value	Exponential Value
tera	T	1,000,000,000,000	10^{12}
giga	G	1,000,000,000	10^9
mega	M	1,000,000	10^6
kilo	K	1,000	10^3
hecto	H	100	10^2
deka	dk	10	10^1 or 10
deci	d	0.1	10^{-1}
centi	c	0.01	10^{-2}
milli	m	0.001	10^{-3}
micro	μ	0.000,001	10^{-6}
nano	n	0.000,000,001	10^{-9}
pico	p	0.000,000,000,001	10^{-12}

Table 2-3. Electronic prefixes, symbols and multiples.

Table 2-4 shows how to convert from any one of these values to another.

As an example, suppose you want to convert 300 picofarads to farads. The farad is a basic unit. Locate the prefix pico in the left-hand column. Move directly to the right and find the units column. In this column you will see 10^{-12}. Thus, to convert 300 picofarads to farads, multiply it by 10^{-12}.

$$300 \text{ picofarads} = 300 \times 10^{-12} \text{ farad}$$

As another example, convert 3 megaHertz to kiloHertz. Locate the prefix mega in the left-hand column. Move directly across until you find the kilo column. You will see the number 1,000. Thus, to convert 3 megaHertz to kiloHertz, multiply the value in megaHertz by 1,000.

$$3 \text{ megaHertz} = 3 \times 1,000 \text{ kiloHertz} = 3,000 \text{ kHz}$$

CAPACITORS IN PARALLEL

The total capacitance of these components connected in shunt is equal to the sum of the individual capacitances. See Fig. 2-11.

$$C_t = C1 + C2 + C3 \ldots \tag{2-15}$$

Before using the formula, convert the capacitances to identical submultiples of a farad.

TO CONVERT THESE TO → | THESE, MULTIPLY BY THE FIGURES BELOW

	Pico—	Nano—	Micro—	Milli—	Centi—	Deci—	Units	Deka—	Hekto—	Kilo—	Myria—	Mega—	Giga—	Tera—
Pico—		0.001	10^{-6}	10^{-9}	10^{-10}	10^{-11}	10^{-12}	10^{-13}	10^{-14}	10^{-15}	10^{-16}	10^{-18}	10^{-21}	10^{-24}
Nano—	1000		0.001	10^{-6}	10^{-7}	10^{-8}	10^{-9}	10^{-10}	10^{-11}	10^{-12}	10^{-13}	10^{-15}	10^{-18}	10^{-21}
Micro—	10^{6}	1000		0.001	0.0001	10^{-5}	10^{-6}	10^{-7}	10^{-8}	10^{-9}	10^{-10}	10^{-12}	10^{-15}	10^{-18}
Milli—	10^{9}	10^{6}	1000		0.1	0.01	0.001	0.0001	10^{-5}	10^{-6}	10^{-7}	10^{-9}	10^{-12}	10^{-15}
Centi—	10^{10}	10^{7}	10,000	10		0.1	0.01	0.001	0.0001	10^{-5}	10^{-6}	10^{-8}	10^{-11}	10^{-14}
Deci—	10^{11}	10^{8}	10^{5}	100	10		0.1	0.01	0.001	0.0001	10^{-5}	10^{-7}	10^{-10}	10^{-13}
Units	10^{12}	10^{9}	10^{6}	1000	100	10		0.1	0.01	0.001	0.0001	10^{-6}	10^{-9}	10^{-12}
Deka—	10^{13}	10^{10}	10^{7}	10,000	1000	100	10		0.1	0.01	0.001	10^{-5}	10^{-8}	10^{-11}
Hekto—	10^{14}	10^{11}	10^{8}	10^{5}	10,000	1000	100	10		0.1	0.01	0.0001	10^{-7}	10^{-10}
Kilo—	10^{15}	10^{12}	10^{9}	10^{6}	10^{5}	10,000	1000	100	10		0.1	0.001	10^{-6}	10^{-9}
Myria—	10^{16}	10^{13}	10^{10}	10^{7}	10^{6}	10^{5}	10,000	1000	100	10		0.01	10^{-5}	10^{-8}
Mega—	10^{18}	10^{15}	10^{12}	10^{9}	10^{8}	10^{7}	10^{6}	10^{5}	10,000	1000	100		0.001	10^{-6}
Giga—	10^{21}	10^{18}	10^{15}	10^{12}	10^{11}	10^{10}	10^{9}	10^{8}	10^{7}	10^{6}	10^{5}	1000		0.001
Tera—	10^{24}	10^{21}	10^{18}	10^{15}	10^{14}	10^{13}	10^{12}	10^{11}	10^{10}	10^{9}	10^{8}	10^{6}	1000	

Table 2-4. Conversion factors for electronic multiples and submultiples.

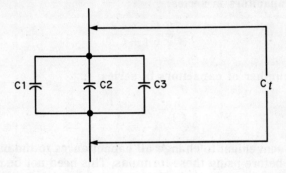

Fig. 2-11. Capacitors in parallel or shunt.

CAPACITORS IN SERIES

All of the formulas for resistors in parallel can be used for capacitors in series. (See Fig. 2-12.) Simply substitute the symbol **C** for **R**.

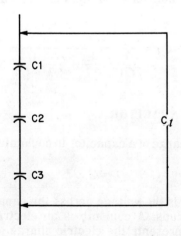

Fig. 2-12. Capacitors in series. The total capacitance is always less than that of the smallest capacitor.

For two capacitors in series:

$$C_t = \frac{C1 \times C2}{C1 + C2} \qquad (2\text{-}16)$$

For any number of capacitors in series:

$$\frac{1}{Ct} = \frac{1}{C1} + \frac{1}{C2} + \frac{1}{C3} \cdots \qquad (2\text{-}17)$$

It is often convenient to change all capacitances to the basic unit, the farad, before using these formulas. This need not be done, but the capacitances must be in the same submultiples.

Formulas are seemingly permissive, that is, having a variety of capacitors on hand we can apparently use any combination to get a desired amount of capacitance. But the formulas for series and parallel capacitors are concerned solely with how capacitors may be connected to get a particular value. The formulas assume perfect capacitors, identical in all respects except capacitance. From a practical viewpoint we may also need to consider working voltage, leakage, tolerance, temperature coefficient, physical size, cost, availability.

CAPACITORS IN SERIES-PARALLEL

Capacitors connected in series-parallel just require a combination of the formulas for capacitors in series and in parallel. See Fig. 2-13.

$$Ct = \frac{1}{\dfrac{1}{C1} + \dfrac{1}{C2} + \dfrac{1}{C3 + C4}}$$

CHARGE OF A CAPACITOR

The electric charge of a capacitor in coulombs (Q) is:

$$Q = C \times E \qquad (2\text{-}18)$$

In this formula, **E** is the voltage across the capacitor and **C** is the capacitance in farads. A coulomb is an electrical charge and a single coulomb represents the electric charge of 6.28×10^{18} electrons. A flow past a given point of one coulomb per second is an ampere.

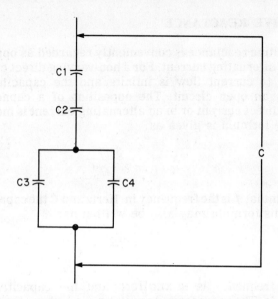

Fig. 2-13. Series-parallel network. The parallel capacitances, C3 and C4, are added, forming an equivalent single capacitor which is then considered in series with C1 and C2.

ENERGY STORED IN A CAPACITOR

In the following formula, the energy, **W**, is given in joules. A joule is the energy used in passing one coulomb through a resistance of 1 ohm.

$$W = \frac{1}{2} C \times E^2 \qquad (2\text{-}19)$$

C is the capacitance in farads and **E** is the voltage across the capacitor.

WORKING VOLTAGE OF A CAPACITOR

While sine wave AC voltages are often designated in terms of their effective or RMS values, the working voltage of a capacitor is the peak or maximum. Thus:

$$E_{\text{working}} = E_{\text{rms}} \times 1.414 \qquad (2\text{-}20)$$

This formula is obtained from Table 2-2, given earlier.

CAPACITIVE REACTANCE

Capacitive reactance is conveniently regarded as opposition to the flow of alternating current. For a non-varying direct current the opposition to current flow is infinite and the capacitor can be viewed as an open circuit. The opposition of a capacitor to a pulsating direct current or to an alternating current is measured in ohms. The formula is given as:

$$X_c = \frac{1}{2\pi \times f \times C} \qquad (2\text{-}21)$$

In this formula, f is the frequency in Hertz and C the capacitance in farads. This formula may also be written as:

$$X_c = \frac{159.2}{f \times C}$$

Here the frequency is in kiloHertz and the capacitance is in microfarads. The same formula may be used where the frequency is in megaHertz and C is in millimicrofarads or nanofarads (thousandths of a microfarad). 1 millimicrofarad (1 nanofarad)= 0.001 μf. On occasion you may see a minus sign preceding the right-hand side of the above formulas. The negative sign simply means that this type of reactance always opposes another type of reactance known as inductive reactance.

CAPACITORS AS VOLTAGE DIVIDERS

Like resistors, capacitors can be used as voltage dividers in AC circuits. Fig. 2-14 shows three capacitors in a voltage divider arrangement. The applied voltage (or source voltage) is distributed among the capacitors in inverse proportion to their capacitance. That is, the largest amount of voltage will be across the unit having the smallest capacitance. For each of the capacitors shown in Fig. 2-14:

$$E1 = \frac{\text{total capacitance}}{C1} \times \text{applied voltage}$$

$$E2 = \frac{\text{total capacitance}}{C2} \times \text{applied voltage}$$

$$E3 = \frac{\text{total capacitance}}{C3} \times \text{applied voltage}$$

$$E \text{ (applied voltage)} = E1 + E2 + E3$$

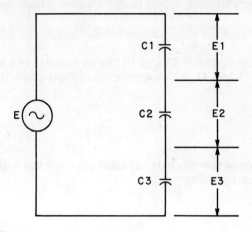

Fig. 2-14. Capacitors used as a voltage divider in an AC circuit.

In a capacitive voltage divider (Fig. 2-15):

$$E_{C1} : E_s = X_{C1} : X_t \qquad (2\text{-}22)$$

X_t is the total reactance. $\mathbf{X_t = X_{C1} + X_{C2}}$.
Through transposition the formula can be arranged in terms of selected unknowns.

$$E_s = \frac{(E_{C1})\,(X_t)}{X_{C1}}$$

$$X_{C1} = \frac{(E_{C1})(X_t)}{E_s}$$

$$X_t = \frac{(E_s)(X_{C1})}{E_{C1}}$$

$$E_{C1} = \frac{(E_s)(X_{C1})}{X_t}$$

Since $\mathbf{I} \times \mathbf{X_{C1}} = \mathbf{E_{C1}}$, the formula for $\mathbf{E_s}$ can be written as:

$$E_s = \frac{(I \times X_{C1})(X_t)}{C1}$$

71

X_{C1} in numerator and denominator cancel. Then:

$$Es = I \times X_t$$

The net reactance of C1 and C2 can be found in two ways:
1) Combine C1 and C2 into a single equivalent capacitor using the formula:

$$C_t = \frac{C1 \times C2}{C1 + C2}$$

The reactance of the single equivalent capacitance will be X_t. Find the reactance by using:

$$X = \frac{1}{6.28 \times f \times C_t} \qquad (2\text{-}23)$$

2) Find the reactance of C1 by using:

$$X = \frac{1}{6.28 \times f \times C1}$$

Find the reactance of C2 the same way. Then add the reactance of C1 to C2 to get X_t.

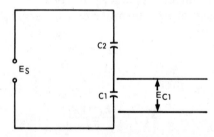

Fig. 2-15. Capacitive voltage divider.

In the network of Fig. 2-15, you can avoid some arithmetic by working directly with voltages and capacitances instead of voltages and reactances.

$$\frac{EC1}{Es} = \frac{C2}{C1 + C2}$$

Transposing:

$$Es = \frac{(E_{C1})(C1 + C2)}{C2}$$

and

$$E_{C1} = \frac{(Es)(C2)}{C1 + C2}$$

OHM'S LAW FOR A CAPACITIVE CIRCUIT

Although reactance and resistance have the same basic unit—the ohm—they are not the same. Resistance does not store electrical energy. In the resistor, electrical energy is changed to heat energy which is then given off or dissipated. A capacitor stores electrical energy—receives it during one part of the AC cycle, returns it during the next. However, we can use capacitive reactance in an Ohm's law formula:

$$E_c = I \times X_c \tag{2-24}$$

The voltage across a capacitor (E_c) is equal to the alternating current multiplied by the capacitive reactance. The voltage is in volts, the current in amperes, and the reactance in ohms. And, like Ohm's law for resistive circuits, the formula can be rearranged to read:

$$I = E_c/X_c = \frac{E_c}{\dfrac{1}{6.28 \times f \times C}}$$

and

$$X_c = E_c/I \tag{2-25}$$

IMPEDANCE OF AN R-C CIRCUIT

In a series R-C circuit (see Fig. 2-16) the total opposition to the flow of current, consisting of the resistance of the resistor and the reactance of the capacitor, is known as impedance. Impedance is represented by the letter Z and is always in ohms. The addition of the resistance and capacitive reactance is done vectorially.

$$Z = \sqrt{R^2 + X_c^2} \tag{2-26}$$

X_C is the capacitive reactance, in ohms. This formula was supplied previously as:

$$X_c = \frac{1}{6.28 \times f \times C}$$

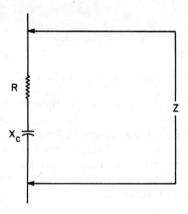

Fig. 2-16. Series R-C circuit. The impedance is the vector sum of the resistance and the capacitive reactance.

This can now be substituted in the impedance formula and so we have:

$$Z = \sqrt{R^2 + \left(\frac{1}{6.28 \times f \times C}\right)^2} \qquad (2\text{-}27)$$

The basic impedance formula,

$$Z = \sqrt{R^2 + X_c^2}$$

involves three quantities, **R**, **Z** and X_C. The formula can be arranged, by transposition, to enable you to solve for any of the three. Thus:

$$Z = \sqrt{R^2 + X_c^2}$$

Squaring both sides we have:

$$Z^2 = R^2 + X_c^2 \qquad (2\text{-}28)$$

or

$$R^2 = Z^2 - X_c^2$$

Taking the square root of both sides:

$$R = \sqrt{Z^2 - X_c^2}$$

Similarly, we can solve for X_C

$$X_c^2 = Z^2 - R^2$$

Taking the square root of both sides:

$$X_c = \sqrt{Z^2 - R^2} \qquad (2\text{-}29)$$

Z, R and X_C are in ohms.

VOLTAGES IN A SERIES R-C CIRCUIT

Whether AC or DC (Fig. 2-17) the current flowing in a series R-C circuit is the same in all parts of the circuit. If we multiply each

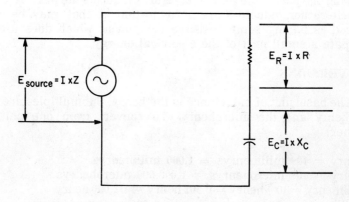

Fig. 2-17. Voltage distribution in a series R-C circuit. The source voltage is equal to the vector sum of the voltages across the resistor and capacitor.

75

of the terms in the formula by **I** (representing the current in the circuit) we will have:

$$IZ = \sqrt{I^2R^2 + I^2X_c^2} \text{ or } E_{source} = \sqrt{E_R^2 + E_c^2}$$

What do these terms signify? **IZ** is the generator or source voltage. That is:

$$E = I \times Z \tag{2-30}$$

By transposing, we can obtain two other forms of this formula:

$$I = E/Z$$

and

$$Z = E/I$$

INDUCTORS (COILS)

Like resistors and capacitors, inductors can be connected in series, in parallel and in series-parallel. However, with inductors there is an additional factor to consider—the magnetic field surrounding the coil. The magnetic fields around two or more inductors can act to aid or oppose each other. Inductors can be mounted sufficiently far apart, or at right angles or covered completely on all sides by some shielding material so that the magnetic fields can be ignored.

Like a capacitor, an inductor stores electrical energy—receives it during one part of the AC cycle, returns it during the next. Neither capacitors nor inductors are perfect—that is, they may be considered as having some resistive component which does use or dissipate a small part of the electrical energy.

CONVERSIONS

The basic unit of inductance is the henry. Submultiples are the millihenry and the microhenry. To convert from one unit to another:

1 henry = 10^3 millihenrys = 1,000 millihenrys
1 henry = 10^6 microhenrys = 1,000,000 microhenrys
1 millihenry = 10^{-3} henry = 0.001 henry = 1/1,000 henry
1 millihenry = 10^3 microhenrys = 1,000 microhenrys
1 microhenry = 10^{-6} henry = 0.000001 henry = 1/1,000,000 henry
1 microhenry = 10^{-3} millihenry = 0.001 millihenry = 1/1,000 millihenry

SINGLE-LAYER AIR-CORE COILS

The inductance of a coil can be accurately measured on a suitable bridge or can be approximated from the physical dimensions of the inductor.

$$L = \frac{(n \times r)^2}{9r + 10_L} \qquad (2\text{-}31)$$

This formula supplies the inductance in microhenrys. To convert the answer to millihenrys, divide by 10^3 and to convert to henrys, divide the answer by 10^6. N = number of turns of wire; L = the length of the coil in inches measured from the outside of the first turn to the outside of the last turn; r is the radius of the coil form plus the radius of the wire (both in inches). The radius of the wire is one half its thickness.

INDUCTANCE OF AIR-CORE MULTI-LAYER COIL

If an inductor has more than a single layer, its inductance can be approximated by:

$$L = \frac{0.8(n \times r)^2}{6r + 9_L + 10_a}$$

L is the inductance in microhenrys; n is the total number of turns (the total number of turns in a single layer multiplied by the number of layers); a is the depth of the coil winding—that is, the distance from the upper side of the top layer to the lower side of the bottom layer; r = radius of the coil + ½ a; L = length of the coil. All dimensions are in inches.

INDUCTORS IN SERIES

For inductors in series (no magnetic interaction):

$$L_t = L1 + L2 + L3 \ldots \qquad (2\text{-}32)$$

INDUCTORS IN PARALLEL

For inductors in parallel (no magnetic interaction)

for two coils
$$L_t = \frac{L1 \times L2}{L1 + L2}$$
(2-33)

for three or more coils
$$L_t = \frac{1}{\frac{1}{L1} + \frac{1}{L2} + \frac{1}{L3} \cdots}$$
(2-34)

Note that formulas for inductors having no magnetic field interaction are the same as for resistors in series or parallel.

COEFFICIENT OF COUPLING AND MUTUAL INDUCTANCE

The inductance of a coil (more properly called self-inductance) is that property of a coil which causes a voltage to be produced across it when the current through the coil is changed. But a coil can have a voltage induced across it, not because of its own varying current, but because of the changing current in a varying magnetic field of some adjacent coil. This property is called mutual inductance, and like self-inductance, is measured in henrys.

The magnetic fields between a pair of coils may aid each other, or oppose each other, depending on their relative polarities (Fig. 2-18). If they aid, the mutual inductance is added to the self-inductance of the coils. If they oppose, the total self-inductance is reduced by the mutual inductance.

The mutual inductance depends upon how closely the coils are coupled and upon the self inductance of the coils. The coefficient of coupling is a measure of how substantially the magnetic flux of one coil links with the turns of an adjacent coil. 100% linkage is known as unity coupling and while it is not reached because there is always some leakage flux, values close to unity coefficient of coupling are often obtained.

The mutual inductance of two coils can be calculated from:

$$M = k\sqrt{L1 \times L2}$$
(2-35)

k is the coefficient of coupling and is a decimal. L1 and L2 represent the self-inductance (in henrys or some submultiple) of two coils.

The formula for mutual inductance can easily be rearranged to supply the coefficient of coupling:

$$k = \frac{M}{\sqrt{L1 \times L2}}$$
(2-36)

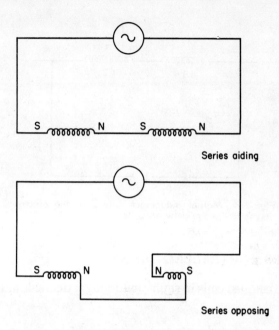

Series aiding

Series opposing

Fig. 2-18. If coils are coupled so that their magnetic fields interact, the overall inductance is dependent upon the coupling arrangement. In the upper drawing, the current flows in the same direction through each coil; the magnetic fields reinforce each other. In the lower circuit, they oppose.

INDUCTORS IN SERIES AIDING

Where the mutual inductance aids the total inductance of two coils connected in series:

$$L_t = L1 + L2 + 2M \qquad (2\text{-}37)$$

Lt is the total inductance; L1 and L2 are the two coils and M is the mutual inductance existing between them. See Fig. 2-19.

INDUCTORS IN SERIES OPPOSING

Where two coils are connected in series and are magnetically coupled but with magnetic fields opposing each other, the total inductance is:

$$L_t = L1 + L2 - 2M \qquad (2\text{-}38)$$

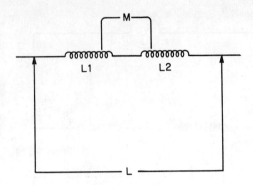

Fig. 2-19. Mutual inductance refers to the electro-magnetic linkage between coils.

INDUCTORS IN PARALLEL AIDING

For two coupled coils in shunt, with magnetic fields aiding:

$$L_t = \frac{1}{\dfrac{1}{L1 + M} + \dfrac{1}{L2 + M}} \qquad (2\text{-}39)$$

INDUCTORS IN PARALLEL OPPOSING

For two coupled coils in shunt, with magnetic fields opposing:

$$L_t = \frac{1}{\dfrac{1}{L1 - M} + \dfrac{1}{L2 - M}} \qquad (2\text{-}40)$$

REACTANCE OF AN INDUCTOR

The inductance of a coil opposes the flow of a varying current through it. This opposition is known as inductive reactance, and like its counterpart, capacitive reactance, is measured in ohms:

$$X_L = 2\pi f \times L \qquad (2\text{-}41)$$

X_L is the inductive reactance in ohms, 2π equals 6.28, f is the frequency in Hertz and L is the inductance of the coil in henrys.

When ω is used to represent $2\pi f$ (as indicated earlier) the formula simplifies to:

$$X_L = \omega L \qquad \text{(2-42)}$$

Note that inductive reactance varies directly with frequency while capacitive reactance varies inversely.

The reactance of a coil is a function of frequency. However, a coil will also have a certain amount of DC resistance, depending on the number of turns, gauge of the wire, resistance of the solder joints at the terminals of the coil, and, in the case of stranded wire, the number of broken strands. Whether a coil will be effective in a circuit is often dependent on how successfully these factors have been considered or kept under control.

OHM'S LAW FOR AN INDUCTIVE CIRCUIT

Inductive reactance, measured in ohms, can be substituted directly into the Ohm's law formula:

$$E_L = I \times X_L \qquad \text{(2-43)}$$

The voltage across a coil is equal to the alternating current through it multiplied by the inductive reactance. To find the current through the coil, we can rearrange the formula to read:

$$I = E_L/X_L = E_L/6.28 \times f \times L$$

and

$$X_L = E_L/I \qquad \text{(2-44)}$$

INDUCTIVE VOLTAGE DIVIDER

When two coils are connected in series and there is no interaction betweeen their magnetic fields, the voltage division of the source voltage is:

$$E2 = E1 \times \frac{L1}{L1 + L2}$$

The voltage is in volts and the inductance is in henrys. The arrangement of the voltage divider is shown in Fig. 2-20.

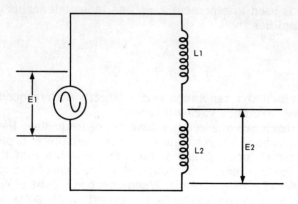

Fig. 2-20. Inductive voltage divider.

RESISTIVE-INDUCTIVE VOLTAGE DIVIDER

If L1 in Fig. 2-20 is replaced by a resistor, the voltage across L2 becomes:

$$E2 = E1 \times \frac{X_l}{\sqrt{R^2 + X_l{}^2}}$$

The circuit is shown in Fig. 2-21.

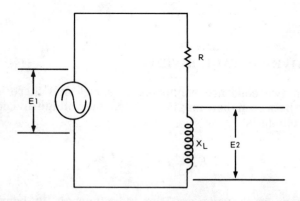

Fig. 2-21. R-L voltage divider.

CAPACITIVE-INDUCTIVE VOLTAGE DIVIDER

Fig. 2-22 shows a capacitive-inductive voltage divider. The voltage across the coil is:

$$E2 = E1 \times \frac{X_L}{X_L - X_c}$$

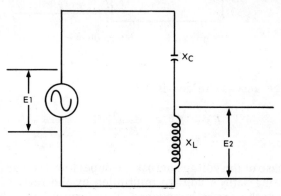

Fig. 2-22. L-C voltage divider.

RESISTIVE-CAPACITIVE-INDUCTIVE VOLTAGE DIVIDER

In a series circuit (Fig. 2-23), the voltages across the individual reactances and also the total reactive voltage is expressed in these formulas:

$$E2 = E1 \times \frac{X_c}{\sqrt{R^2 + (X_L - X_c)^2}}$$

Note that the denominator of this expression is the impedance of the series circuit and so this formula can be simplified to:

$$E2 = E1 \times \frac{X_c}{Z}$$

Thus, the voltage across the capacitor is equal to the source voltage, E1, multiplied by the ratio of the capacitive reactance to the impedance.

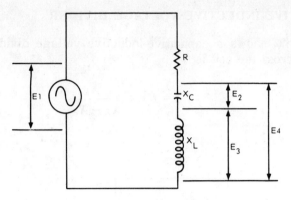

Fig. 2-23. R-C-L voltage divider.

The voltage across the coil is **E3**.

$$E3 = E1 \times \frac{X_L}{\sqrt{R^2 + (X_L - X_c)^2}}$$

As in the case of the voltage across the capacitor, the voltage across the coil is the source voltage multiplied by the ratio of inductive reactance to the series impedance. This formula can also be simplified to:

$$E3 = E1 \times \frac{X_L}{Z}$$

The voltage, **E4**, across the two reactances, the coil and the capacitor is:

$$E4 = E1 \times \frac{X_L - X_c}{\sqrt{R^2 + (X_L - X_c)^2}}$$

$X_L - X_C$ is the net reactance. If the capacitive reactance is greater than the inductive reactance the numerator becomes **$X_C - X_L$**. In either case the net reactance is represented by X. The formula simplifies to:

$$E4 = E1 \times \frac{X}{Z}$$

L-C VOLTAGE DIVIDER

In an **L-C** voltage divider (Fig. 2-24) a proportion can be set up between voltages and reactances.

$$E_c : Es = X_c : X_t$$

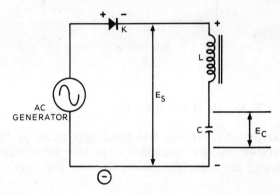

Fig. 2-24. Application of L-C voltage divider in rectifier circuit.

Es is the voltage from the cathode (**K**) of the rectifier to the minus (—) bus. The voltage is DC with an AC component. X_t is the total reactance. $X_t = X_L - X_C$. The ripple frequency in H_Z from K to the minus bus is the same as the AC generator frequency.

R-C VOLTAGE DIVIDER

Fig. 2-25 shows an **R-C** voltage divider. In this arrangement, the formula for the voltage across the capacitor is:

$$E2 = \frac{X_c}{\sqrt{R^2 + X_c{}^2}} \times E1$$

The denominator is the impedance of this circuit and so this formula can be simplified to:

$$E2 = \frac{X_c}{Z} \times E1$$

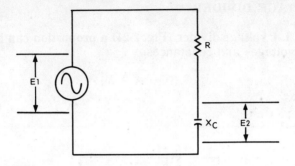

Fig. 2-25. R-C voltage divider.

IMPEDANCE IN AN R-L CIRCUIT

In a series **R-L** circuit, the total opposition to the flow of current, known as the impedance, is the vector sum of the resistance and the inductive reactance. See Fig. 2-26.

$$Z = \sqrt{R^2 + X_L^2} \qquad (2\text{-}45)$$

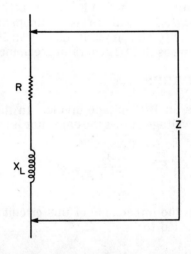

Fig. 2-26. Series R-L circuit. The impedance is the vector sum of the resistance and inductive reactance.

X_L, the inductive reactance of the coil in ohms, isn't always supplied directly, but may be given in terms of inductance and frequency. Thus:

$$X_L = 6.28 \times f \times L$$

f is in Hertz and L is in henrys. The formula for the impedance of an R-L circuit then becomes:

$$Z = \sqrt{R^2 + (6.28 \times f \times L)^2}$$

In other instances, the circuit impedance may be known and also the resistance, in which case it may be necessary to calculate X_L. Or, the impedance and value of X_L may be supplied, with R as the unknown. Either R or X_L can be found by using the original formula.

$$Z = \sqrt{R^2 + X_L^2}$$

squaring both sides:

$$Z^2 = R^2 + X_L^2$$

transposing:

$$Z^2 - R^2 = X_L^2$$

and taking the square root of both sides:

$$X_L = \sqrt{Z^2 - R^2}$$

This will supply the value of X_L when Z and R are given.
   To find the value of R:

$$Z^2 = R^2 + X_L^2$$

transposing

$$R^2 = Z^2 - X_L^2$$

taking the square root of both sides:

$$R = \sqrt{Z^2 - X_L^2} \tag{2-46}$$

Basic units are used in all these formulas. **R** and **Z** are in ohms; **L** is in henrys.

VOLTAGES IN A SERIES R-L CIRCUIT

Since the current is the same in all parts of a series **R-L** circuit, we can multiply each of the terms in the formula and get:

$$IZ = \sqrt{I^2R^2 + I^2X_L^2}$$

or

$$E_{source} = \sqrt{E_R^2 + E_L^2} \tag{2-47}$$

Since the resistance and reactance are added vectorially, the voltages involved as a result of these components are also added vectorially. See Fig. 2-27.

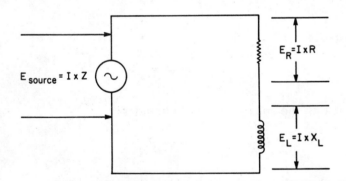

Fig. 2-27. The source voltage in this series R-L circuit is equal to the vector sum of the voltages across the resistor and the coil.

EFFECTIVE RESISTANCE

The resistance of a coil as measured with an ohmmeter, is its DC resistance—that is, this is the resistance the coil would have to the flow of an unvarying direct current. For an alternating current, the resistance (known as effective or AC resistance) will not only be due to the inherent DC resistance but will be somewhat higher because of such factors as hysteresis loss, eddy currents, magnetic skin effect. The effective resistance acts like a resistor in series with the coil.

Q OF A COIL

It is frequently desirable to make coils having as low an effective resistance as possible. The ratio of the inductive reactance of a coil to its effective resistance is known as the figure of merit or quality of the coil (Q). Stated as a formula, we have:

$$Q = \frac{X_L}{R} \text{ or } Q = \frac{\omega L}{R} \qquad (2\text{-}48)$$

R is considered as being in series with the coil.

Q OF A CAPACITOR

The Q of a capacitor is the ratio of its reactance to its effective resistance. Expressed as a formula:

$$Q = \frac{X_c}{R}$$

In an L-C circuit, we are usually concerned only with the Q of the coil, since the Q of the capacitor is ordinarily much higher. However, if the dielectric of the capacitor is such that there are losses in it, power will be dissipated in the dielectric and the capacitor will have a large effective resistance, lowering the Q.

VOLTAGE TRANSFORMERS, STEP UP AND STEP DOWN

The ratio of secondary turns (Ns) to the primary turns (Np) of a transformer is known as the turns ratio Tr. In terms of a formula:

$$T_r = \frac{Ns}{Np} \qquad (2\text{-}49)$$

The voltage step up or step down (Fig. 2-28) of a transformer depends on this turns ratio.

$$\frac{Es}{Ep} = \frac{Ns}{Np} = T_r \qquad (2\text{-}50)$$

89

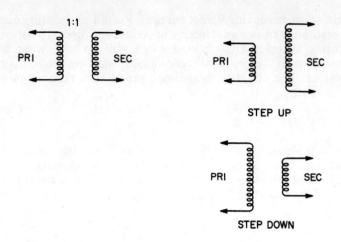

Fig. 2-28. Voltage and current transformation depends on the turns ratio.

Ep is the primary voltage: **Es** the secondary voltage; **Np** the number of primary turns; **Ns** the number of secondary turns. A formula of this type can be arranged in six different ways (including the one shown above).

$$Ep \times Ns = Np \times Es$$

$$Ep = \frac{Np \times Es}{Ns}$$

$$Es = \frac{Ep \times Ns}{Np}$$

$$T_r = \frac{Ep \times Ns}{Es} \qquad (2\text{-}51)$$

$$Ns = \frac{Np \times Es}{Ep}$$

If information concerning the turns ratio is known, the actual number of primary and secondary turns isn't required. Thus:

$$Es = \text{turns ratio} \times Ep$$

or

$$Es = T_r \times Ep$$

This formula can be rearranged to read:

$$Ep = \frac{Es}{Tr}$$

CURRENT TRANSFORMERS, STEP UP AND STEP DOWN

In transformers, the effects on current and voltage are inverse. A transformer will step down current by the same ratio that it steps up voltage.

$$\frac{Ip}{Is} = \frac{Ns}{Np}$$

Ip and Is represent primary and secondary currents. The current formula can be rearranged in the same manner as the voltage formula, and in as many different ways. As in the case of voltage transformation, Ns/Np is the turns ratio. Since:

$$Ip \times Np = Is \times Ns$$

then:

$$Ip = \frac{Is \times Ns}{Np}$$

$$Is = \frac{Ip \times Np}{Ns}$$

(2-52)

$$Np = \frac{Is \times Ns}{Ip}$$

$$Ns = \frac{Ip \times Np}{Is}$$

IMPEDANCE TRANSFORMERS

The ratio of secondary to primary impedance of a transformer varies as the square of the turns ratio.

$$\frac{Zs}{Zp} = \frac{Ns^2}{Np^2} = T_r^{\,2}$$

By taking the square root of both sides, this formula can be stated directly in terms of the turns ratio.

$$\frac{Ns}{Np} = \sqrt{\frac{Zs}{Zp}}$$

$$T_r = \sqrt{\frac{Zs}{Zp}}$$ (2-53)

POWER TRANSFORMER COLOR CODE

Primary (not tapped)	two black leads
Primary (tapped)	black (common)
	black-red
	black-yellow (tap)
Secondary (high voltage)	red
	red
	red-yellow (tap)
Secondary (rectifier filament)	yellow
	yellow
	yellow-blue (tap)
Secondary (amplifier filament)	green
	green
	green-yellow (tap)
Secondary (amplifier filament)	brown
	brown
	brown-yellow (tap
Secondary (amplifier filament)	slate
	slate
	slate-yellow (tap)

In power transformers (Fig. 2-29) a tapped lead always has two colors and yellow is always one of these colors.

The tap on power transformer windings is a center tap. The connection for the tap is made at the electrical center, not the physical center, of the winding. The AC voltage measured from either lead to the tap should be the same.

The color coding of the leads simply indicates lead connections and has no relationship to the amount of voltage or current delivered by the windings. Power transformers may be of the type shown in Fig. 2-29, equipped with high-voltage and various filament windings, or may be a high-voltage type only, or just have filament

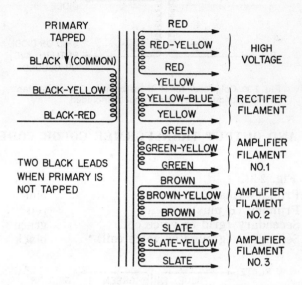

Fig. 2-29. Color code for power transformers.

windings. High-voltage transformers often (but not always) have a low-voltage winding for connection to a rectifier filament (if a tube is to be used as a rectifier). For solid-state rectifiers, no filament winding is needed.

IF TRANSFORMER COLOR CODE

See Fig. 2-30.

Primary (plate)	blue
Primary (B-plus)	red
Secondary (grid or diode)	green
Secondary (grid or diode return, AVC, or ground)	black
Secondary (full-wave diode)	green-black (tap)

93

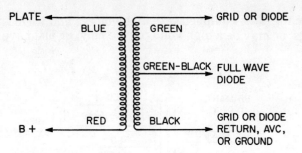

Fig. 2-30. Color code for IF transformers. The center tap on the secondary may or may not be included.

AUDIO AND OUTPUT TRANSFORMER COLOR CODE (Single Ended)

See Fig. 2-31.

Primary (plate)	blue
Primary (B plus)	red
Secondary (grid or voice coil)	green
Secondary (ground or voice coil)	black

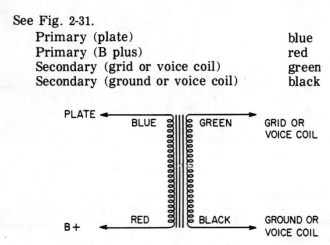

Fig. 2-31. Color code for audio transformers. They may be step up or step down, depending on use.

AUDIO AND OUTPUT TRANSFORMER COLOR CODE (Push-pull)

See Fig. 2-32.

Primary (plate)	blue
Primary (B plus)	red (tap)
Primary (plate)	blue or brown
Secondary (grid or voice coil)	green
Secondary (grid return or voice coil)	black
Secondary (grid)	green or yellow

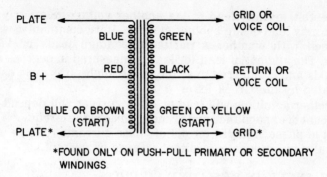

Fig. 2-32. Color code for push-pull audio transformers.

PHASE ANGLE

A pair of voltages, a voltage and a current, or a pair of currents need not necessarily be in step with each other. (These voltages and currents are all AC.) And, since we are talking about a periodic waveform such as a sine wave, we can conveniently measure their relationships between the points at which they cross the X-axis. An example is shown in Fig. 2-33.

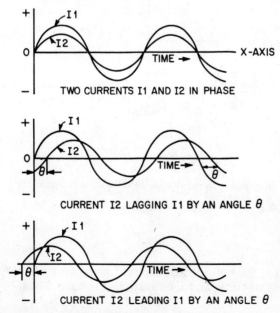

Fig. 2-33. A pair of alternating currents may be in step or phase, or one current may lead or lag the other.

One voltage may lead or lag another voltage. Similarly, one current may lead or lag another current. More commonly, we are concerned with whether a particular voltage leads or lags a current. The amount of lead (or lag) is measured in degrees along the X-axis and is referred to as the phase angle. It is most usually designated by the Greek letter θ

Whether a voltage will lead or lag a current will depend upon the amount of capacitance and/or inductance in the circuit.

Out of phase voltages (or out of phase currents) can be added vectorially to produce a resultant voltage or current.

PHASE ANGLE IN RESISTIVE CIRCUITS

For a resistive circuit consisting of a single resistor (Fig. 2-34), a number of resistors in series, in parallel, or in a series-parallel

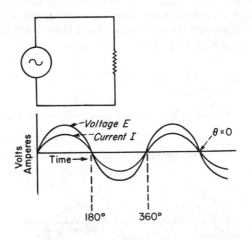

Fig. 2-34. In a resistive circuit, the voltage and current are in phase.

combination, the voltage and current are always in step, rise and fall at the same time, and are said to be in phase. Thus,

$$\theta = 0°$$

PHASE ANGLE IN INDUCTIVE CIRCUITS

For an inductive circuit, consisting of a single or any combination of inductors, the current lags the voltage by a maximum of 90°. Thus,

$$\theta = +90°$$

If the inductor contains resistance, and in practice it always does, then the phase angle is less than 90°, depending upon the amount of resistance compared to inductive reactance. (Fig. 2-35).

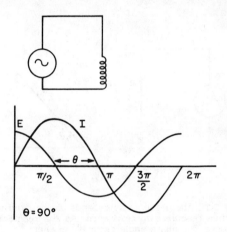

Fig. 2-35. In an inductive circuit, the current may lag the voltage by as much as 90 degrees. The amount of lag decreases as the resistance in the circuit increases.

PHASE ANGLE IN CAPACITIVE CIRCUITS

In a capacitive circuit, consisting of any combination of capacitors, the current leads the voltage by a maximum 90°. Thus:

$$\theta = -90°$$

The plus and minus signs preceding the phase angles may be omitted. They are just convenient reminders that inductors and capacitors have directly opposite effects in AC circuits.

Depending upon the resistance inherent in a particular type of capacitor, the phase angle may be somewhat less than 90°.

PHASE ANGLE OF A SERIES R-L CIRCUIT

For a circuit (see Fig. 2-36) consisting of an inductor in series with a resistor, the phase angle:

$$\theta = \text{arc tan } \frac{X_L}{R}$$

(read this as "theta is the angle whose tangent is X_L' divided by R").

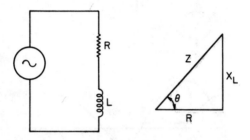

Fig. 2-36. The phase angle depends on the ratio of inductive reactance to resistance. As the reactance is reduced, the phase angle becomes smaller.

PHASE ANGLE OF A SERIES R-C CIRCUIT

For a circuit (see Fig. 2-37) consisting of a capacitor in series with a resistor, the phase angle:

$$\theta = \text{arc tan } \frac{X_c}{R}$$

IMPEDANCE AND PHASE ANGLE OF SINGLE RESISTOR

When a circuit (Fig. 2-38) consists of a single resistor only:

$$Z = R$$
$$\theta = 0°$$

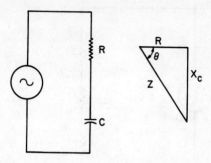

Fig. 2-37. The phase angle depends on the ratio of capacitive reactance to resistance. Note the triangle is drawn upside-down (compare with Fig. 2-36) emphasizing that inductive and capacitive reactances are opposing vectors.

IMPEDANCE AND PHASE ANGLE OF SERIES RESISTORS

When a circuit (Fig. 2-39) consists of two or more resistors in series:

$$Z = R1 + R2 + R3 \ldots$$

$$\theta = 0°$$

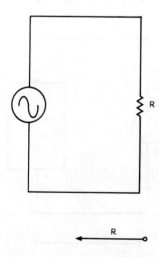

Fig. 2-38. Circuit and vector for resistive circuit.

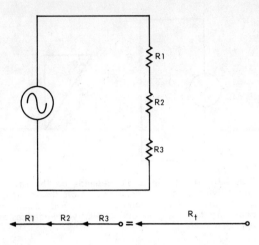

Fig. 2-39. Circuit and vectors for series R circuit.

IMPEDANCE AND PHASE ANGLE OF PARALLEL RESISTORS

When a circuit (Fig. 2-40) consists of two or more resistors in parallel:

$$Z = \frac{R1 \times R2}{R1 + R2}$$

$$\theta = 0°$$

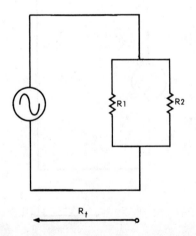

Fig. 2-40. Circuit and vector for parallel R circuit.

100

For all resistive networks, whether single resistors, parallel or series-parallel, the assumption is made that the resistors are non-inductive and that capacitance effects associated with wiring and the resistors are negligible. This is generally true at low frequencies, but wiring and component capacitances become increasingly important with increases in frequency. For DC and low frequencies the formulas are valid. They may not be so for UHF or VHF.

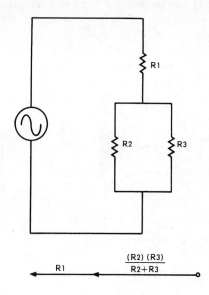

Fig. 2-41. Circuit and vectors for series-parallel R circuit.

IMPEDANCE AND PHASE ANGLE OF SERIES-PARALLEL RESISTORS

When a circuit (Fig. 2-41) consists of resistors wired in series-parallel:

$$Z = R1 + \frac{R2 \times R3}{R2 + R3}$$

$$\theta = 0°$$

IMPEDANCE AND PHASE ANGLE OF SINGLE INDUCTOR

When a circuit consists of a single coil:

$$Z = X_L = 6.28 \times f \times L$$

$$\theta = 90°$$

The assumption is made that the resistance of the coil (Fig. 2-42) is negligible. This may not be true for very low frequencies or when

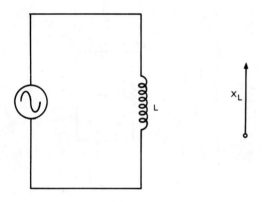

Fig. 2-42. Circuit and vector for L circuit.

the coil has a large number of turns, or both. When the resistance of a coil is a factor to be considered, the resistance is considered as a separate component and the coil is then a series arrangement of R and L. The phase angle becomes less than 90° depending on the amount of resistance present.

IMPEDANCE AND PHASE ANGLE OF COILS IN SERIES

For two or more coils in series:

$$Z = X_{L1} + X_{L2}$$

$$\theta = 90°$$

The reactances of the individual coils (Fig. 2-43) can be calculated separately and then added to get **Z**, as indicated in the formula.

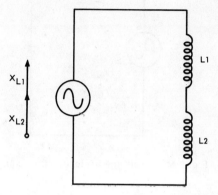

Fig. 2-43. Circuit and vectors for series L circuit.

Alternatively, the total reactance X_{L1} plus X_{L2} can be obtained by:

$$X_t = 6.28 \times f(L1 + L2)$$

The assumption is made that there are no flux linkages between coils. If the coils are wired in series aiding or series opposing, the mutual inductance must be added to or subtracted from the total inductance.

IMPEDANCE AND PHASE ANGLE OF A SINGLE CAPACITOR

When a circuit (Fig. 2-44) consists of a single capacitor:

$$Z = X_c = \frac{1}{6.28 \times f \times C}$$

$$\theta = -90°$$

IMPEDANCE AND PHASE ANGLE OF SERIES CAPACITORS

When two or more capacitors are connected in series (Fig. 2-45):

$$Z = X_{c1} + X_{c2}$$

$$\theta = -90°$$

103

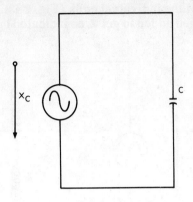

Fig. 2-44. Circuit and vector for C circuit.

The reactance of each individual capacitor can be found from the formula:

$$X_c = \frac{1}{6.28 \times f \times C}$$

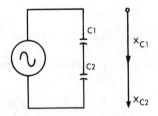

Fig. 2-45. Circuit and vectors for series C circuit.

Or, the individual capacitors can be added to find the total capacitance, using the formula:

$$Ct = \frac{C1 \times C2}{C1 + C2}$$

The reactance can then be calculated for **Ct.**

104

IMPEDANCE AND PHASE ANGLE OF PARALLEL CAPACITORS

When capacitors are wired in parallel (Fig. 2-46).

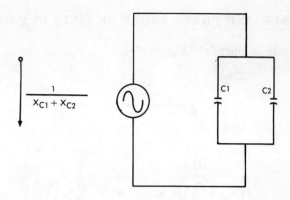

Fig. 2-46. Circuit and vector for parallel C circuit.

$$Z = \frac{1}{X_{c1} + X_{c2}}$$

The individual reactances can be found and then the total impedance can be calculated with the above formula. Or, the total capacitance can be found from:

$$C_t = C_1 + C_2$$

The reactance can then be calculated for Ct. This will then be the impedance.

The formula for the impedance of two parallel capacitors can also be written as:

$$Z = \frac{1}{(6.28 \times f \times C1) + (6.28 \times f \times C2)}$$

105

The terms in the denominator can be collected so that the formula looks like this:

$$Z = \frac{1}{6.28 \times f\,(C1 + C2)}$$

$$\theta = -90°$$

IMPEDANCE AND PHASE ANGLE OF COILS IN PARALLEL

For coils in parallel (Fig. 2-47).

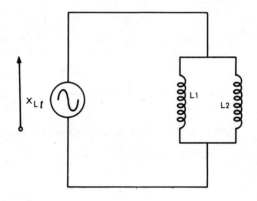

Fig. 2-47. Circuit and vector for parallel L circuit.

$$Z = 6.28 \times f \times \frac{L1 \times L2}{L1 + L2}$$

This formula is valid only if there are no flux linkages between the two coils. If there are such linkages, the mutual inductance must be included as part of the inductance of the coils.

$$\theta = +90°$$

IMPEDANCE AND PHASE ANGLE OF A SERIES L-C CIRCUIT

$$Z = X_L - X_c \qquad \theta = +90°$$

106

or

$$Z = X_c - X_L$$

$$\theta = -90°$$

Either formula may apply, depending on which reactance is larger. Simply subtract the smaller reactance from the larger to obtain the net reactance. In this circuit the resistance is so small compared to the reactances that it may be disregarded. Impedance, resistance, inductive and capacitive reactances are always in ohms.

IMPEDANCE AND PHASE ANGLE OF A SERIES R-L-C CIRCUIT

When the resistance is a factor that must be considered, then the impedance (Fig. 2-48):

(if X_L is larger than X_C)

$$Z = \sqrt{R^2 + (X_L - X_c)^2}$$

$$\theta = \text{arc tan } \frac{X_L - X_c}{R}$$

(if X_C is larger than X_L)

$$Z = \sqrt{R^2 + (X_c - X_L)^2}$$

$$\theta = \text{arc tan } \frac{X_c - X_L}{R}$$

In a series R-L-C circuit four quantities are involved: Z, R, X_L and X_C. All of these are in ohms. The basic formula is:

$$Z = \sqrt{R^2 + (X_L - X_c)^2}$$

Squaring both sides:

$$Z^2 = R^2 + (X_L - X_c)^2$$

Transposing:

$$R^2 = Z^2 - (X_L - X_c)^2$$

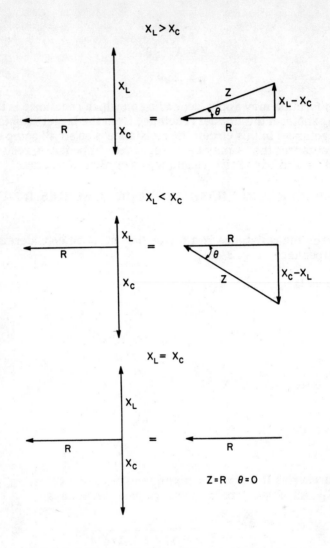

Fig. 2-48. Various conditions that may exist in a series R-L-C circuit.

Taking the square root of both sides:

$$R = \sqrt{Z^2 - (X_L - X_c)^2} \qquad (2\text{-}54)$$

and:

$$X_L = \sqrt{Z^2 - R^2} + X_c$$

$$X_c = X_L - \sqrt{Z^2 - R^2}$$

COMPLEX SERIES CIRCUIT

When a series R-L-C circuit (Fig. 2-49) consists of a number of resistors, capacitors and inductors, various techniques are

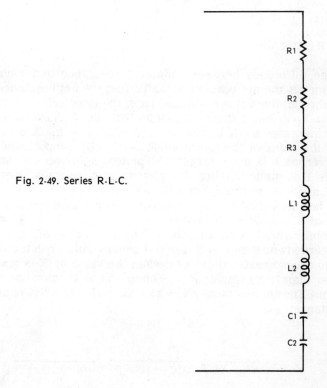

Fig. 2-49. Series R-L-C.

available for calculating the impedance. 1) Combine the resistors into a single unit using the formula $Rt = R1 + R2 + R3$, etc. Next, combine the capacitors into a single unit using the formula $1/C_t = 1/C1 + 1/C2 + 1/C3$, etc. Finally, combine the inductors, using the formula $Lt = L1 + L2 + L3$, assuming no flux linkages between the coils. If there are flux linkages, the mutual inductance must be considered. The mutual inductance will add to or subtract from the overall inductance, Lt, depending on whether the coils are in series aiding or opposing. 2) Combine the resistances into a single unit, using the series resistances formula. Find the inductive reactance of each coil and then add the individual reactances. Find the capacitive reactance of each capacitor and then add the individual reactances. The values of R, X_L and X_C can then be substituted directly into the formula:

$$Z = \sqrt{R^2 + (X_L - X_c)^2} \qquad (2\text{-}55)$$

NET REACTANCE

The difference between inductive reactance and capacitive reactance is the net reactance, X. To find the net reactance, subtract the smaller value reactance from the larger. The vectors for X_L and X_C in Fig. 2-48 are shown as 180° out of phase. The phase angle increases as X increases, and decreases as X decreases. Thus, the value of the phase angle is directly proportional to X. However, as R is made larger, the phase angle becomes smaller, and as R is made smaller, the phase angle becomes larger. The phase angle is inversely proportional to R.

When the value of R becomes very large with respect to X, the value of X may be disregarded and then $Z=R$. When R becomes extremely small with respect to X, the value of R may be disregarded and then $Z = X$. Use this general rule when the value of R is 10 times greater than X or when the value of X is ten times greater than R. Example: $R = 10$ ohms, $X_L = 110$ ohms and $X_C = 10$ ohms. The net reactance, $X = X_L - X_C = 110 - 10 = 100$ ohms. The impedance,

$$Z = \sqrt{R^2 + X^2} = \sqrt{10^2 + 100^2} = \sqrt{100 + 10000}$$

$$= \sqrt{10,100} = 100.5 \text{ ohms.}$$

Note how close the impedance is to the actual value of X.

If the inductive and capacitive reactances are equal, we have a condition of resonance and:

$$Z = R \text{ and } \theta = 0$$

IMPEDANCE AND PHASE ANGLE OF A PARALLEL R-L CIRCUIT

(Fig. 2-50)

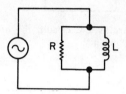

Fig. 2-50. In a parallel R-L circuit, the phase angle is determined by the ratio of resistance to inductive reactance.

$$Z = \frac{R \times X_L}{\sqrt{R^2 + X_L{}^2}} \qquad (2\text{-}56)$$

$$\theta = \text{arc tan } \frac{R}{X_L}$$

IMPEDANCE AND PHASE ANGLE OF A PARALLEL R-C CIRCUIT

(Fig. 2-51)

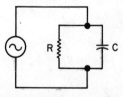

Fig. 2-51. In this circuit, as in the parallel R-L circuit, the impedance is affected by the frequency.

$$Z = \frac{R \times X_c}{\sqrt{R^2 + X_c{}^2}} \qquad (2\text{-}57)$$

$$\theta = -\text{arc tan } \frac{R}{X_c}$$

111

IMPEDANCE AND PHASE ANGLE OF PARALLEL L-C CIRCUIT

(Fig. 2-52)

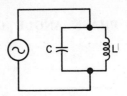

Fig. 2-52. In a parallel L-C circuit, the impedance is
maximum at resonance.

When X_L is larger than X_C

$$Z = \frac{X_L \times X_c}{X_L - X_c} \qquad (2\text{-}58)$$

When X_C is larger than X_L

$$Z = \frac{X_c \times X_L}{X_c - X_L} \qquad (2\text{-}59)$$

At resonance, $X_L = X_C$ and the denominator becomes zero. The impedance reaches an extremely large value. At resonance the phase angle is zero. In this arrangement, R was considered negligible and so does not enter into the calculations.

The coil, capacitor, connecting wires and physical connections can contribute to the total circuit resistance of a parallel L-C circuit. At resonance:

$$X_L = X_c = X$$

$$Z = \frac{X^2}{R} \qquad (2\text{-}60)$$

Z is the impedance in ohms; X is the reactance of either the coil or capacitor at the resonant frequency, and R is the total circuit resistance.

The impedance of a parallel L-C tank at resonance can also be determined by:

$$Z = \frac{L}{R \times C} \qquad (2\text{-}61)$$

Z is the impedance in ohms; **L** the inductance in henrys, **R** the resistance in ohms and **C** is the capacitance in farads.

The impedance of a parallel resonant circuit is also related to **Q**.

$$Z = 2\pi f L Q = Q \times X_L \qquad (2\text{-}62)$$

f is the frequency in Hertz, **L** the inductance in henrys. The **Q** of the circuit is determined by the ratio of inductive reactance to resistance.

$$Q = X_L/R$$

IMPEDANCE AND PHASE ANGLE OF A PARALLEL R-L-C CIRCUIT

(Fig. 2-53)

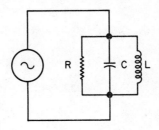

Fig. 2-53. Parallel R-L-C circuit.

$$Z = \frac{R \times X_L \times X_c}{\sqrt{X_L^2 \times X_c^2 + R^2(X_L - X_c)^2}}$$

$$\theta = \text{arc tan} \; \frac{R(X_c - X_L)}{X_L \times X_c} \qquad (2\text{-}63)$$

IMPEDANCE AND PHASE ANGLE OF SERIES R-L SHUNTED BY R

(Fig. 2-54)

113

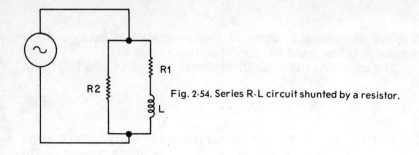

Fig. 2-54. Series R-L circuit shunted by a resistor.

$$Z = R2 \sqrt{\frac{R1^2 + X_L^2}{(R1 + R2)^2 + X_L^2}}$$

$$\theta = \text{arc tan} \frac{X_L R2}{R1^2 + X_L^2 + R1\,R2}$$

(2-64)

IMPEDANCE AND PHASE ANGLE OF SERIES R-L SHUNTED BY C

(Fig. 2-55)

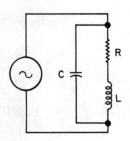

Fig. 2-55. Series R-L circuit shunted by a capacitor.

$$Z = X_c \sqrt{\frac{R^2 + X_L^2}{R^2 + (X_L - X_c)^2}}$$

$$\theta = \text{arc tan} \frac{X_L (X_c - X_L) - R^2}{R X_c}$$

(2-65)

114

IMPEDANCE AND PHASE ANGLE OF R-C IN PARALLEL WITH R-L

In Fig. 2-56, **R1** is the total resistance of all other series or parallel resistors in branch 1, and also includes wiring and con-

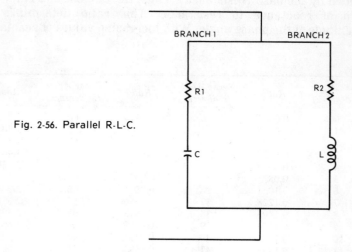

BRANCH 1   BRANCH 2

R1   R2

Fig. 2-56. Parallel R-L-C.

C   L

nection resistances, and any resistance of **C**. **R2** is the total resistance of all other series or parallel resistances in branch 2, including wiring and connection resistances and any resistance associated with **L**. **R** is in ohms; **C** is the total capacitance of all other series, parallel or series-parallel capacitors. **C** is in farads. **L** is the total inductance of all other series, parallel or series-parallel inductors and also includes mutual inductance, if present. **L** is in henrys.

$$Z = \sqrt{\frac{(R_1{}^2 + X_L{}^2)R_2{}^2 + X_c{}^2)}{(R1 + R2)^2 + (X_L - X_c)^2}}$$

(2-66)

$$\theta = \text{arc tan} \frac{X_L\ (R_2{}^2 + X_c{}^2) - X_c(\ R1^2 + X_L{}^2)}{R1(R_2{}^2 + X_c{}^2)\ + R^2(R1^2 + X_L{}^2)}$$

Note, in the formula given here for the impedance, that it resembles the general formula for finding the total resistance of two resistors

115

in parallel, and that it also resembles the impedance of an **R-L** circuit and an **R-C** circuit.

REACTANCE-RESISTANCE RATIO

The tangent of an angle (theta) is the altitude (reactance) divided by the base (resistance). Thus, the tangent is a ratio—the ratio of reactance to resistance. This ratio determines the magnitude of the phase angle. With increasing values of reactance,

Phase Angle (in degrees)	Ratio	Phase Angle (in degrees)	Ratio	Phase Angle (in degrees)	Ratio
0	0.0000	30	0.5774	60	1.7321
1	0.0175	31	0.6009	61	1.8040
2	0.0349	32	0.6249	62	1.8807
3	0.0524	33	0.6494	63	1.9626
4	0.0699	34	0.6745	64	2.0503
5	0.0875	35	0.7002	65	2.1445
6	0.1051	36	0.7265	66	2.2460
7	0.1228	37	0.7536	67	2.3559
8	0.1405	38	0.7813	68	2.4751
9	0.1584	39	0.8098	69	2.6051
10	0.1763	40	0.8391	70	2.7475
11	0.1944	41	0.8693	71	2.9042
12	0.2126	42	0.9004	72	3.0777
13	0.2309	43	0.9325	73	3.2709
14	0.2493	44	0.9657	74	3.4874
15	0.2679	45	1.0000	75	3.7321
16	0.2867	46	1.0355	76	4.0108
17	0.3057	47	1.0724	77	4.3315
18	0.3249	48	1.1106	78	4.7046
19	0.3443	49	1.1504	79	5.1446
20	0.3640	50	1.1918	80	5.6713
21	0.3839	51	1.2349	81	6.3138
22	0.4040	52	1.2799	82	7.1154
23	0.4245	53	1.3270	83	8.1443
24	0.4452	54	1.3764	84	9.5144
25	0.4663	55	1.4281	85	11.43
26	0.4877	56	1.4826	86	14.30
27	0.5095	57	1.5399	87	19.08
28	0.5317	58	1.6003	88	28.64
29	0.5543	59	1.6643	89	57.29

Table 2-5. The ratio tan X/R and corresponding values of phase angle, Θ.

the phase angle increases. Table 2-5 gives this ratio (tangent) for phase angles ranging from zero to 89 degrees.

ADMITTANCE OF A SERIES CIRCUIT

Admittance is the reciprocal of impedance. Since impedance is measured in ohms, admittance is in mhos.

$$Y = \frac{1}{Z} \tag{2-67}$$

and:

$$Z = \frac{1}{Y}$$

but since Z is $\sqrt{R^2 + X^2}$, then:

$$Y = \frac{1}{\sqrt{R^2 + X^2}}$$

$$= \sqrt{G^2 + B^2} \tag{2-68}$$

SUSCEPTANCE

Susceptance is the reciprocal of reactance, and is given in mhos. Just as we can have resistive ohms (due to a resistor) and reactive ohms (due to a coil or capacitor) so too do we have resistive and reactive mhos. In a series circuit, the susceptance is:

$$B = \frac{X}{R^2 + X^2} \tag{2-69}$$

B is the susceptance in mhos, R is resistive ohms, and X is reactive ohms. The reactive component may be either a coil or a capacitor.

We usually consider inductive reactance as positive and capacitive reactance as negative. These polarities are purely conventional and indicate the 180° out-of-phase relationships of these units. But since we now have an inverse condition, the susceptance is considered positive when X is predominantly capacitive and negative when X is inductive.

If the resistance is made zero, then the susceptance is simply the reciprocal of reactance. Thus:

$$B = \frac{1}{X} \tag{2-70}$$

While impedance is often indicated in terms of resistance (R) and reactance (X), it can also be expressed in their reciprocals.

The reciprocal of **R** is $1/R = G$. The reciprocal of **X** is $1/X = B$. **G** is conductance and **B** is susceptance. Both are in mhos.

For parallel circuits:

$$Z = \frac{1}{\sqrt{G^2 + B^2}}$$

(2-71)

CONDUCTANCE

Conductance, previously given as the reciprocal of resistance in a DC circuit, can thus be considered as resistive mhos while susceptance is reactive mhos.

We can regard a wire (or any other component) as being either resistive or conductive. While the terms are reciprocals (or opposites) they are simply two different ways of describing the same thing. Here are the corresponding terms:

	Symbol		Symbol
Resistance	R	Conductance	G
Reactance	X	Susceptance	B
Impedance	Z	Admittance	Y

In an AC circuit, the conductance (resistive mhos) is:

$$G = \frac{R}{R^2 + X^2}$$

(2-72)

Resistance can be given in terms of conductance and susceptance:

$$R = \frac{G}{G^2 + B^2}$$

(2-73)

Reactance can also use these terms:

$$X = \frac{B}{G^2 + B^2}$$

(2-74)

OHM'S LAW FOR AC

Ohm's law is as applicable for alternating-current circuits as it is for DC. Other than the substitution of impedance (Z) for resistance (R), the formulas are identical.

$$E = I \times Z$$

$$I = \frac{E}{Z} \qquad (2\text{-}75)$$

$$Z = \frac{E}{I}$$

Z is in ohms, E is in volts and I in amperes. Z, however, is more complex than the simple R used in Ohm's law for DC.

POWER IN AC CIRCUITS

Since power is the product of voltage and current the phase angle between voltage and current is a factor that must enter such calculations. In a DC circuit power, is simply E × I. Similarly, in a purely resistive AC circuit power, is also E × I since the phase angle, θ , is zero.

In an AC circuit containing a reactive element (a coil or a capacitor),

$$P = E \times I \times \cos \theta \qquad (2\text{-}76)$$

The cosine (or cos) is the ratio of the resistance to the impedance, or:

$$\cos \theta = \frac{R}{Z}$$

P is the power in watts; E and I are the voltage and current, respectively.

There are two conditions in an AC circuit when the phase angle is zero. These are a purely resistive circuit and a resonant circuit (either series or parallel type). Under these conditions:

$$\theta = 0$$

$$\cos \theta = 1$$

and

$$P = E \times I$$

No power is expended in a purely reactive circuit. In such a circuit, the power is returned to the source. Under these conditions:

$$\theta = 90°$$

$$\cos \theta = 0$$

and

$$P = 0$$

In any AC circuit the power ranges somewhere between these two extremes and so cos θ is generally some value less than one and greater than zero.

APPARENT POWER

If the power factor in a reactive AC circuit is disregarded, that is, if we say that $P = E \times I$, then the amount of power calculated in this way is larger than its true value. Known as apparent power or reactive power, it can be stated as:

$$\text{Apparent power} = E \times I$$

Multiplying apparent power ($E \times I$) by the cosine of the phase angle will produce a number representing the true power in the circuit, or; $P = E \times I \times \cos \theta$. This can also be written as:

$$\text{True power } (P) = E \times I \times \cos \frac{R}{Z}$$

POWER FACTOR

The ratio between the true power (also known as real power) and the apparent power is a value less than one since the true power is always less than the apparent power. This ratio is referred to as the power factor and is often abbreviated as **pf**. Stated as a formula we have:

$$pf = \frac{\text{true power}}{\text{apparent power}}$$

True power

$$= E \times I \times \cos R/Z$$

Apparent power

$$= E \times I$$

Hence:

$$pf = \frac{E \times I \times R/Z}{E \times I}$$

And: $pf = R/Z$; $R/Z = \cos \theta$ where θ is the phase angle

$$pf = \cos \theta$$

Power factor is applicable to series and parallel R-C, R-L, and L-C circuits. However, it is also a factor to be considered in the use of electrical devices, such as motors. Also, coils and capacitors, used alone, can have a power factor.

POWER FACTOR OF COILS

The power factor of a coil is:

$$pf = \cos \theta_L = \frac{R_L}{Z_L} \qquad (2\text{-}77)$$

Z_L is the impedance of the coil and can be calculated by:

$$Z_L = \sqrt{R_L{}^2 + X_L{}^2}$$

R_L is the winding resistance of the coil and X_L is the reactance of the coil at a particular frequency.
The formula for the impedance of a coil can be substituted for Z_L in the power factor formula.

$$pf = \frac{R_L}{\sqrt{R_L{}^2 + X_L{}^2}} \qquad (2\text{-}78)$$

Note that the resistance of the coil will remain constant regardless of frequency. However, the reactance of the coil, X_L, which is part of the impedance of the coil, will vary directly with frequency. The lowest frequency limit is 0 Hz or 0 cps. When this happens:

$$pf = \frac{R_L}{\sqrt{R_L{}^2}} = \frac{R_L}{R_L} = 1$$

In a circuit having resistance only, power factor is unity.

POWER FACTOR OF CAPACITORS

Power factor for capacitors follows the same approach used for power factor for coils.

$$pf = \cos \theta_c = \frac{R_c}{Z_c} = \frac{R_c}{\sqrt{R_c{}^2 + X_c{}^2}} \qquad (2\text{-}79)$$

Here the power factor is also dependent on frequency.

In AC circuits where power factor is not a consideration (such as in a purely resistive circuit) the formula for power is identical with that used in DC.

$$P = I^2 \times R$$
$$I = \sqrt{\frac{P}{R}} \qquad (2\text{-}80)$$

Where the relationship between voltage and current (the phase angle) is a factor, Ohm's law for AC circuits can take a variety of forms. These can be expressed in terms of power, current, voltage or impedance.

POWER

$$P = I^2 Z \cos \theta$$
$$P = \frac{E^2 \cos \theta}{Z} \qquad (2\text{-}81)$$

CURRENT

$$I = \frac{P}{E \cos \theta}$$
$$I = \sqrt{\frac{P}{Z \cos \theta}} \qquad (2\text{-}82)$$

Table 2-6 is a summary of Ohm's law and power formulas for AC.

Table 2-6. Summary of power and Ohm's law formulas
for AC.

Watts	Amperes	Volts	Impedance
$P =$	$I =$	$E =$	$Z =$
$I^2 R$	E/Z	IZ	E/I
$EI \cos \theta$	$\dfrac{P}{E \cos \theta}$	$\dfrac{P}{I \cos \theta}$	$\dfrac{E^2 \cos \theta}{P}$
$\dfrac{E^2 \cos \theta}{Z}$	$\sqrt{\dfrac{P}{Z \cos \theta}}$	$\sqrt{\dfrac{PZ}{\cos \theta}}$	$\dfrac{P}{I^2 \cos \theta}$
$I^2 Z \cos \theta$	$\sqrt{\dfrac{P}{R}}$	$\dfrac{\sqrt{PR}}{\cos \theta}$	$\dfrac{R}{\cos \theta}$

VOLTAGE

$$E = \sqrt{\frac{PZ}{\cos \theta}}$$

(2-83)

$$E = \frac{P}{I \cos \theta}$$

IMPEDANCE

$$Z = \frac{E^2 \cos \theta}{P}$$

(2-84)

$$Z = \frac{P}{I^2 \cos \theta}$$

RESONANCE IN A SERIES CIRCUIT

In a series L-C circuit a condition of equal values of inductive and capacitive reactance is known as resonance. The resonant

123

frequency is identified by the letter f and sometimes by f_r.

$$f = \frac{1}{2\pi\sqrt{LC}}$$ (2-85)

or

$$f = \frac{0.159}{\sqrt{LC}}$$ (2-86)

Basic units are used in this formula. f is the frequency in Hertz, L the inductance in henrys, and C the capacitance in farads. For most applications these are not practical values, but the formula is easily modified to:

$$f = \frac{10^6}{2\pi\sqrt{LC}}$$

f is now the frequency in kiloHertz; L is the inductance in microhenrys (μh), and C is the capacitance in picofarads (pf).

The same formula is a reasonable approximation for parallel L-C circuits having a circuit Q of 10 or more.

If the inductance and the capacitance are both in microunits, that is, microhenrys and microfarads (with the frequency, f, in kiloHertz), then the basic resonance formula can be modified to:

$$f = \frac{159.2}{\sqrt{LC}}$$

If the frequency is known, then the basic formula for resonance can be rearranged to find either the inductance, L, or the capacitance C.

$$L = \frac{1}{4\pi^2 f^2 C}$$ (2-87)

and

$$C = \frac{1}{4\pi^2 f^2 L}$$ (2-88)

In both of these formulas L is the inductance in henrys, C is the capacitance in farads, f is the frequency in Hertz. These can be modified to reflect more practical values.

$$L = \frac{25,330}{f^2 C}$$ (2-89)

and

$$C = \frac{25,330}{f^2 L} \qquad (2\text{-}90)$$

Here the inductance is in microhenrys, the capacitance, C, is in microfarads, and the frequency, f, is in kiloHertz.

Q OF A SERIES RESONANT CIRCUIT

The ratio of inductive reactance to the effective resistance of a coil is known as the figure of merit, or Q —a concept that can also be applied to a tuned circuit.

$$Q = \frac{f_r}{f - f_r} \qquad (2\text{-}91)$$

In this formula, f_r is the resonant frequency. The circuit is then detuned until the resonant voltage drops to 0.707 of its peak value (its value at resonance). This supplies the value of f.

The Q of a tuned circuit is also the ratio of reactive power to true power.

$$Q = \frac{I^2 \times X}{I^2 \times R} = \frac{X}{R}$$

X is the net reactance in ohms. When $X_L > X_C$, $X = X_L - X_C$. When $X_L > X_C$, then $X = X_C - X_L$. R is the total circuit resistance. While X and R are both in ohms, Q is not named in units.

For a series R-L circuit:

$$Q = \frac{6.28 \times f \times L}{R} \qquad (2\text{-}92)$$

f is the frequency in Hz, L the inductance in henrys and R the resistance in ohms. The Greek letter omega (ω) can be used to represent $2 \pi f$ (6.28 f), hence:

$$Q = \frac{\omega L}{R}$$

For a series R-C circuit:

$$Q = \frac{1}{\omega R C} \qquad (2\text{-}93)$$

125

For a parallel R-C circuit:

$$Q = \omega RC \qquad (2\text{-}94)$$

R is the resistance in ohms; C is the capacitance in farads.

DECIBELS AND NEPERS

The bel represents the logarithm (to the base 10) of a comparison or ratio of two powers. Expressed as a formula:

$$N_b = \log_{10} \frac{P2}{P1}$$

N_b is the number of bels. P2 and P1 represent the two powers (in watts). P2 is generally used to indicate the output, P1 the input. When P2 is larger than P1, the power gain is positive and the number of bels may be preceded by a plus sign. The plus sign may be omitted, however. If P2 is less than P1, the output is obviously less than the input and we have a loss of power. The answer should then be preceded by a minus sign.

As in the case of other units in electronics formulas (such as the farad for capacitance) the bel is much too large, and so a more convenient unit, the decibel (tenth of a bel) is used. That is:

$$1 \text{ bel} = 10 \text{ decibels}$$

Substituting this information in our formula, we have:

$$N_{db} = 10 \log_{10} \frac{P2}{P1} \qquad (2\text{-}95)$$

Since power (in watts) is the product of current and resistance ($P = I^2 R$), we can modify the formula for decibels:

$$N_{db} = 10 \log_{10} \frac{P2}{P1}$$

$$= 10 \log_{10} \frac{I2^2 \ R2}{I1^2 \ R1}$$

If R2 and R1 are equal (that is, if the input and output resistances are identical) resistance terms cancel:

$$N_{db} = 10 \log_{10} \frac{I2^2}{I1^2} \qquad (2\text{-}96)$$

and since logarithms obey the following relationship:

$$\log x'' = n \log x$$

we have:

$$N_{db} = 20 \log \frac{I2}{I1} \qquad (2\text{-}97)$$

($\log_{10}$ is abbreviated simply as log.)
Also, since power $\mathbf{P} = \mathbf{E^2/R}$, we have

$$N_{db} = \log \frac{E2^2\ R1}{E1^2\ R2}$$

While the resistance terms are inverse of what they were previously, they too cancel if they are equal and the formula is commonly used as:

$$N_{db} = 20 \log \frac{E2}{E1} \qquad (2\text{-}98)$$

A similar group of formulas with the natural base ϵ (2.718281) can also be used. The unit is called the Neper. When working with two power levels:

$$N_n = 1/2 \log \epsilon \frac{P2}{P1} \qquad (2\text{-}99)$$

The relationship between nepers and decibels is such that

$$1 \text{ db} = 0.1151 \text{ neper}$$
$$1 \text{ neper} = 8.686 \text{ db}$$

When using formulas involving decibels, it will be more convenient to have the larger value of power, voltage, or current appearing in the numerator. This will avoid the necessity for working with decimal values.

REFERENCE LEVELS (0 db)

All of these formulas are concerned with power, voltage and current relationships where input and output are clearly specified. However, there are a number of arbitrary reference levels which

127

can be used. 6 milliwatts across 500 ohms is one of these; others are 10 and 100 milliwatts. Still another reference level used in broadcast work to indicate program levels is 1 milliwatt across 600 ohms. This reference level is considered as 0 db. A power higher than the reference level is positive db while any power less than the reference level is negative db. DBM is sometimes used as an abbreviation for decibels referred to 1 milliwatt.

VOLUME UNITS (VU)

A volume unit is one in which the reference level is clearly specified. Thus:

$$N_{vu} = 10 \log_{10} \frac{P2}{.001}$$

$$N_{vu} = 10 \log \frac{P2}{10^{-3}}$$

This can be rearranged to read:

$$N_{vu} = 10 \log 10^3 P2$$

or

$$N_{vu} = 30 \log P2 \qquad (2\text{-}100)$$

(since the log of 10^3 or 1,000 is 3). In all of these formulas, common logs (logs to the base 10) are used.

Table 2-7. Decibel table.

DB	Power Ratio	Voltage or Current Ratio	DB	Power Ratio	Voltage or Current Ratio
0	1.00	1.00	10	10.0	3.2
0.5	1.12	1.06	15	31.6	5.6
1.0	1.26	1.12	20	100	10
1.5	1.41	1.19	25	316	18
2.0	1.58	1.26	30	1,000	32
3.0	2.00	1.41	40	10,000	100
4.0	2.51	1.58	50	10^5	316
5.0	3.16	1.78	60	10^6	1,000
6.0	3.98	2.00	70	10^7	3,162
7.0	5.01	2.24	80	10^8	10,000
8.0	6.31	2.51	90	10^9	31,620
9.0	7.94	2.82	100	10^{10}	10^5

FILTERS

A filter is a combination of resistors, coils, and capacitors to permit the passage of some frequencies (generally a band of frequencies) and to suppress others. The upper and/or lower limit of such a band is known as the cutoff frequency.

While filters range from the extremely simple to the very complex, they can usually be categorized as low pass, high pass, band pass and band elimination types. The input and output connections of filters are terminated in source and load resistances or impedances equal in value to the impedance of the filter.

HIGH-PASS FILTER (Constant K)

A high-pass filter (Fig. 2-57) is one in which frequencies higher

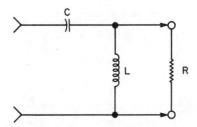

Fig. 2-57. High-pass filter. The inductor bypasses lower frequencies, has increasing reactance as the frequency is increased.

than the cutoff frequency (f) are passed, while frequencies lower than the cutoff frequency are attenuated. For a constant K type:

$$C = \frac{1}{4 \pi f R}$$

$$L = \frac{R}{4\pi f}$$

$$R = \sqrt{\frac{L}{C}}$$

C is the series capacitance in farads; L the shunt inductance in henrys and R is the terminating resistance. The cutoff frequency is f.

The high-pass filter in Fig. 2-57 consists of two elements—a series capacitor and a shunt coil. Filters can be made up of various combinations of series and shunt components. A constant-K filter is so named since the product of its series and shunt impedances is a constant at all frequencies.

Filters of all types take advantage of the fact that coils and capacitors behave inversely in the presence of AC. Thus, in the high-pass filter, the series unit, a capacitor in series with the line, has a decreasing reactance as the frequency is increased. The coil, shunted across the line, acts as a bypass to low frequencies but has an increasing reactance as the frequency is increased.

LOW-PASS FILTER (Constant K)

A low-pass filter (Fig. 2-58) is one which passes all frequencies below a selected value and attenuates higher frequencies. Its ac-

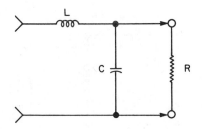

Fig. 2-58. Low-pass filter. As the frequency is increased, the bypassing action of the capacitor becomes more and more effective.

tion, then, is exactly the opposite of a high-pass filter, so it isn't surprising to find that its circuit arrangement is also exactly opposite. For a low-pass filter:

$$C = \frac{1}{\pi f R}$$

$$L = \frac{R}{\pi f}$$

and

$$R = \sqrt{\frac{L}{C}}$$

In this formula, the shunting element is C, L is the series inductance. R is the terminating resistance while f is the cutoff frequency.

130

BAND-PASS FILTER (Constant K)

This type of filter, as its name suggests, permits the passage of a selected band of frequencies while attenuating lower and higher frequencies.

A band-pass filter takes advantage of the differing impedance characteristics of series and parallel-tuned circuits. A series circuit has minimum impedance at its resonant frequency. A parallel circuit has maximum impedance at its resonant frequency. These two circuits are combined in the band-pass filter of Fig. 2-59.

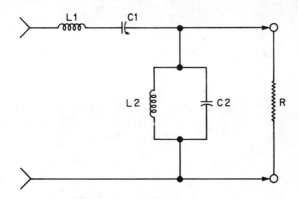

Fig. 2-59. Band-pass filter. A filter of this kind attenuates frequencies above and below the desired band.

The series arm has minimum impedance at the center frequency of the desired band. The impedance increases on either side of resonance. Exactly the opposite behavior is given by the shunt arm—in this case, a parallel tuned circuit.

$$C1 = \frac{f2 - f1}{4 \pi f1 f2 R}$$

$$C2 = \frac{1}{\pi (f2 - f1) R}$$

$$L1 = \frac{R}{\pi (f2 - f1)}$$

$$L2 = \frac{(f2 - f1) R}{4 \pi f1 f2}$$

131

L1 and C1 form the series-tuned circuit inserted in the line; L2 and C2 are the elements of the parallel-tuned circuit shunting the line. $f1$ is the lower cutoff frequency and $f2$ is the upper cutoff frequency.

BAND-ELIMINATION FILTER (Constant K)

Also known as a band-rejection, band-stop or band-suppression filter, it utilizes the particular characteristics of parallel-tuned and series-tuned circuits. As you can see in Fig. 2-60, the arrangement is exactly the opposite of a band-pass filter.

$$C1 = \frac{1}{4\pi(f2 - f1)R}$$

$$C2 = \frac{f2 - f1}{\pi f1 f2 R}$$

$$L1 = \frac{(f2 - f1)R}{\pi f1 f2}$$

$$L2 = \frac{R}{4\pi(f2 - f1)}$$

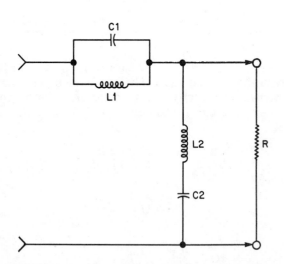

Fig. 2-60. Band-elimination filter. Note that the circuit arrangement is exactly the opposite of that shown in Fig. 2-59.

As in the band-pass filter, f 1 and f 2 represent the lower and upper cutoff frequencies, respectively.

T-TYPE LOW-PASS FILTER (Constant K)

It is difficult to produce sharp frequency cutoff with single section filters. A single coil can be added to the low-pass filter (Fig. 2-61) to produce the T-type (so named because of its appearance).

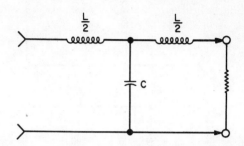

Fig. 2-61. This is an improved version of the low-pass filter. Additional units, inductors and capacitors, can be added to increase the effectiveness of the filtering action.

Two T-type low-pass filters can be combined as shown in Fig. 2-62.

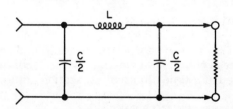

Fig. 2-62. This circuit represents the combination of two T-type low-pass filters into a single unit.

The coils can be combined into a single inductor. Assuming no coupling between these coils, the replacement coil would have a value of $L = L1 + L2$. Because of its appearance the filter is known as a π-type.

A high-pass filter can also be made into a T-type by inserting another series capacitor into the line. A multi-section T-type, made by joining two such units, would have a pair of immediately connected capacitors, (see Fig. 2-63). These capacitors can be replaced by a single unit having an equivalent value.

Multi-section band-pass and band-elimination filters can be made by joining additional sections.

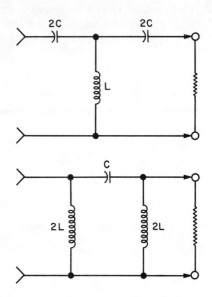

Fig. 2-63. T-type (above) and π-type high-pass filters.

π-TYPE LOW-PASS FILTER

T-type filters are made by putting in additional series elements. A π-type filter is obtained by adding another shunt element. As in the method used in T-type filters, multi-section units can be formed.

π-TYPE HIGH-PASS FILTER

Adding another shunt inductor, as in Fig. 2-63, gives us a single-section, π-type, high-pass filter. A two-section unit can be made by joining two single units. If the two inductors are identical, they can be replaced by a single unit having half the value of either.

The impedance of the circuit or the component connected across the input of a filter is called the source impedance. The circuit or component across the output of the filter is the load impedance.

The filter itself represents an impedance—that is, it has its own input and output impedances. These impedances, at each end of the

134

filter, are known as image impedances. For maximum transfer of energy from the source to the load, the image impedances should be equal to the source and load impedances.

m-DERIVED FILTERS

In Fig. 2-64 we have an elementary low-pass constant **K** type filter. This filter will pass all frequencies below the cutoff frequency, f. That is, the attenuation of all frequencies starting with zero (considering DC as our starting point, or zero frequency) up to the cutoff frequency will be zero. This is just another way of saying that all these frequencies will be passed. But, as shown in the

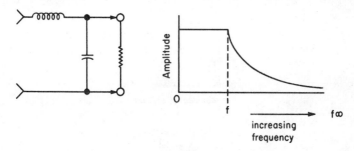

Fig. 2-64. Low-pass constant K type filter. The curve shown at the right is idealized. The cutoff is by no means as sharp, nor is the bandpass as flat as indicated.

graph, attenuation gradually increases with a rise in frequency. At some frequency the attenuation will be so large that we consider it infinite. This frequency is designated as f_∞ .

The ratio of the cutoff frequency, f , to the infinite attenuation frequency, f_∞ , is a factor which is designated by the letter **m**. For a low-pass filter:

$$m = \sqrt{1 - \left(\frac{f^2}{f_\infty}\right)}$$

and for a high-pass filter

$$m = \sqrt{1 - \left(\frac{f_\infty}{f}^2\right)}$$

An **m**-derived filter is one that is derived from or obtained from one of the constant **K** types. m-derived filters have additional impedances and so have a much sharper cutoff. The type of derived filter we get depends on the kind of modification we make to the basic constant **K** type.

If we add an impedance to the shunt arm of the basic filter, we obtain a filter that is known as a series-derived **m**-type filter. If we connect an impedance in the series arm, the modified filter is called a shunt-derived **m**-type. The additional impedances may be coils or capacitors, or series-parallel combinations.

TYPES OF m-DERIVED FILTERS

m-derived filters may be low-pass, high-pass or bandpass. Within these three main categories we will find single- and multi-element and T sections. Fig. 2-65 shows several m-derived filters.

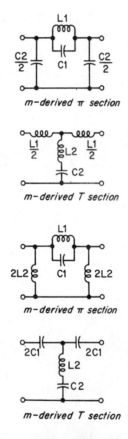

Fig. 2-65. Filters of the m-derived type can be T-type, π-type, or may contain several such sections in the filter.

ATTENUATORS AND PADS

Attenuators and pads are resistive networks used to drop the voltage between a source EMF and a load. Attenuators use variable resistors; pads use fixed resistors.

L-ATTENUATOR

The L-attenuator (Fig. 2-66) so-called because of its fancied resemblance to an upside-down L, has two variable resistors R1 and R2 mounted on a common shaft, so that the values of R1 and R2 are changed simultaneously. The attenuator presents a constant resistance to the source voltage. Since maximum power is transferred when the resistance of the source if equal to the resistance of the load, the attenuator can be adjusted so that its input resistance equals the source resistance. At the same time the attenuator drops the voltage to the amount required by the load, and

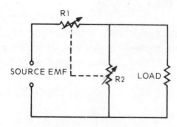

Fig. 2-66. L attenuator.

also matches the resistance of the load. The total resistance of the attenuator and the load presented to the source voltage is:

$$R \text{ presented to the source } = R1 + \frac{(R2)(R_{\text{load}})}{R2 + R_{\text{load}}}$$

L-PAD

When the resistance of the source is greater than the resistance of the load, values for R1 and R2 of the L-pad (Fig. 2-67) can be calculated from:

$$R1 = \sqrt{R_s(R_s - R_L)}$$

and

$$R2 = \frac{R_s \times R_L}{R1}$$

137

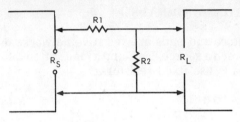

Fig. 2-67. L pad.

The insertion loss, the voltage loss caused by the L pad in db can be calculated from:

$$dB_{\text{loss}} = 20 \log_{10}\left(\sqrt{\frac{R_s}{R_L}} + \sqrt{\frac{R_s}{R_L}-1}\right)$$

NONSINUSOIDAL WAVES

Unless otherwise specified, alternating current formulas are based on the use of pure sine waves of constant frequency and amplitude—that is, waves which follow the equation for a sine curve, whose positive and negative halves are symmetrical and which repeat in a periodic manner (Table 2-8).

Table 2-8. Sine and e values for selected amounts of θ .

θ	0°	30°	60°	90°	120°	150°	180°
$\sin \theta$	0.00	0.500	0.866	1.00	0.866	0.500	0.00
e	0.00	50.0	86.6	100	86.6	50.0	0.00

θ	210	240	270	300	330	360
$\sin \theta$	−0.500	−0.866	−1.00	−0.866	−0.500	0.00
e	−50.0	−86.6	−100	−86.6	−50.0	0.00

While the sine wave is the simplest type of AC waveform, there are many other waveforms that are nonsinusoidal. However, if a wave is a steadily recurring one, it can be resolved into two or more sine waves. Conversely, a pair of pure sine waves can be combined or added to yield either a symmetrical or a nonsymmetrical wave.

Whether the resultant wave, produced by the vector addition of sine waves, is symmetrical or nonsymmetrical, depends on the frequency of the sine waves. If the sine waves consist of a fundamental, plus even-order harmonics (f, 2f, 4f, etc.) the resultant will be a nonsinusoidal wave which will also be asymmetrical (nonsymmetrical). However, if the sine waves are odd-order harmonics (f, 3f, 5f, etc.) the nonsinusoidal resultant waves will be symmetrical.

The sine wave having the lowest frequency (f) is referred to as the fundamental, or is sometimes called the first harmonic. The second harmonic is a wave having twice the frequency of the fundamental (2f); the third harmonic (3f) has three times the fundamental frequency, etc.

As a general rule, the amplitude of a harmonic is less than that of the fundamental. However, it is entirely possible for a harmonic, such as the third, to be stronger (have more amplitude) than a lower-frequency harmonic, such as the second.

FUNDAMENTAL AND HARMONIC RELATIONSHIPS

The instantaneous value of a sine wave of voltage or current was given earlier as:

$$e = E_{\text{peak}} \sin \omega t$$

If we are concerned with a fundamental and a number of harmonics, we can identify the peak voltages by numbering them. Thus, the fundamental would now be:

$$e = E1_{\text{peak}} \sin \omega t$$

The second harmonic would be:

$$e = E2_{\text{peak}} \sin 2 \omega t$$

And the third harmonic:

$$e = E3_{\text{peak}} \sin 3 \omega t$$

Chapter 3

Vacuum Tubes and
Vacuum Tube Circuits

The behavior of a tube can be predicted from a graph of its characteristics. Static characteristics are found by applying only DC voltages to the elements of the tube. A dynamic characteristic is an attempt to obtain information about the tube's behavior under simulated working conditions. A controlled AC signal of a particular frequency is injected into the grid, and the plate of the tube works into its specified load. The DC voltages on the various elements are those which would normally be used.

From the characteristics of a tube, plotted in graph form, we can obtain the tube's constants. These constants are amplification factor (μ), plate resistance (r_p), also known as AC plate resistance or dynamic plate resistance, and the mutual conductance (g_m), also known as the plate conductance.

TUBE CURRENTS AND VOLTAGES

Under conditions of no signal input (Fig. 3-1), the tube voltages are:

Plate voltage = supply voltage$-$(E1 + E2)
Screen voltage = supply voltage$-$(Is x R2)
Bias voltage = I_t x R1.
I_t = total tube current; I_s = screen current; I_p = plate current
E_p = plate voltage; E_s = screen voltage; E_g = bias voltage
Plate current = $I_t - I_s$
Screen current = $I_t - I_p$
Cathode current = I_t = $I_p + I_s$
$E_{plate} = E$ supply $- [(I_t$ x R1) + (I_p x R3)]

AMPLIFICATION FACTOR

Amplification factor is an electronic yardstick, letting us measure how effectively the grid and plate control the flow of tube current.

$$\mu = \frac{\Delta E_p}{\Delta E_g} \qquad (3\text{-}1)$$

(with constant plate current)

141

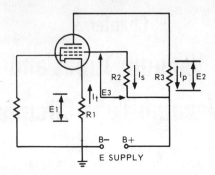

Fig. 3-1. IR drops in pentode circuit.

Δ means "change of". Δ**Ep** and Δ**Eg** refer to changes in plate and grid DC voltages. An increase in plate voltage (Δ**Ep**) increases the plate current. An increase in bias voltage (Δ**Eg**) can be adjusted so that the plate current decreases to its original value. The ratio of the two is the amplification factor of the tube. Amplification factor is simply expressed as a number.

DC PLATE RESISTANCE

Whenever we have a voltage across two points and a current flow produced as a result of this voltage, we have resistance. Ohm's law makes the same statement, but much more concisely, as
$$R = E/I.$$
In a tube, current flows between cathode and plate as a result of the voltage placed across these two elements. This meets the condition established by Ohm's law and so we can consider the space between cathode and plate as a resistor. But this is by no means an ordinary resistor, nor can it be compared to a physical resistor except in a very limited sense. With no signal input to a tube and with the bias kept constant, the DC plate resistance of the tube is:

$$R_p = \frac{E_p}{I_p}$$

Rp is the plate resistance in ohms; **Ep** the voltage between plate and cathode, in volts, and **Ip** is the plate current in amperes.

AC PLATE RESISTANCE

Although the current in a tube is unidirectional—that is, it moves in but one direction—from cathode to plate, we regard it as

AC, not DC, since the current changes with changes in input signal voltage.

The AC plate resistance (r_p) of a tube (also known as the dynamic plate resistance) is the resistance (in ohms) offered by the space between cathode and plate to the flow of a changing current. Its value is obtained by making a **small** change in plate voltage and then dividing this by the resulting change in the plate current. Expressed as a formula, we have:

$$r_p = \frac{\Delta E_p}{\Delta I_p} \qquad (3\text{-}2)$$

The grid voltage is kept constant during any plate resistance measurement.

PLATE EFFICIENCY

Efficiency was previously defined as the ratio of output to input. The plate efficiency of a tube is its power output divided by the power input. All units are in watts, volts and amperes.

$$\text{plate eff} \quad = \quad \frac{\text{power output}}{\text{power input}}$$

Input to a tube is the product of voltage measured between plate and cathode of the tube, and the plate current. The formula becomes:

$$\text{plate eff} \quad = \frac{\text{power output}}{\text{plate voltage x plate current}}$$

MUTUAL CONDUCTANCE

Since conductance is the reciprocal of resistance, we might expect the formula for mutual conductance (g_m) to be the inverse of the formula for plate resistance. It is, with one change. We use the grid (E_g) instead of the plate voltage (E_p). Thus:

$$g_m = \frac{\Delta I_p}{\Delta E_g} \qquad (3\text{-}3)$$

(with plate voltage constant)

This formula is intended to test the effectiveness of a change in grid voltage on plate current. Mutual conductance is measured in mhos, or, more practically, in micromhos.

RELATIONSHIPS OF μ, r_p and g_m

The relationships between these tube constants can be obtained by multiplying the mutual conductance by plate resistance.

$$g_m \times r_p = \frac{I_p}{E_g} \times \frac{E_p}{I_p}$$

Since we have similar terms (Ip) in numerator and denominator, these cancel, and we have:

$$g_m \times r_p = \frac{E_p}{E_g}.$$

But $E_p/E_g = \mu$ Hence, we have: (3-4)

$$\mu = g_m \times r_p$$

We can rearrange this formula in terms of mutual conductance and plate resistance:

$$g_m = \frac{\mu}{r_p} \qquad r_p = \frac{\mu}{g_m}$$

MERIT COEFFICIENT (FIGURE OF MERIT)

In some applications, such as video amplifiers, the tube must be capable of amplifying a wide band of frequencies. For such use the tube should have a high value of mutual conductance compared to the sum of its input and output capacitances. Known as the merit coefficient, m:

$$m = \frac{g_m}{C_i + C_o}$$

Ci is the input capacitance; Co the output capacitance and g_m the mutual conductance. The mutual conductance (transconductance) is in micromhos and the capacitances are in picofarads. The Figure of Merit or the Merit Coefficient is simply a number for use in comparisons between tubes.

VOLTAGE AMPLIFIERS

The voltage amplification of a vacuum-tube stage is the ratio of the output signal voltage to the input signal voltage:

$$\text{voltage amplification} = \frac{e_o}{e_g} \qquad (3\text{-}5)$$

The output voltage can be measured across some value of plate load resistor (R_p) or a reactive element such as a plate load impedance, Z.

The voltage amplification with resistive load is:

$$\text{amplification} = \frac{\mu \times R_L}{r_p + R_L} \qquad (3\text{-}6)$$

The amplification factor is μ, r_p is the plate resistance of the tube and R_L is the plate load resistor. But since the ratio e_o/e_g also represents the amplification of the tube, we can set this up to read:

$$\frac{e_o}{e_g} = \frac{\mu \times R_L}{r_p + R_L}$$

By multiplying both sides by e_g we can have our formula supply us with information in terms of output voltage.

$$e_o = e_g \times \frac{\mu \times R_L}{r_p + R_L}$$

This is quite satisfactory for a triode but tube manuals do not, as a rule, list the amplification factor of tubes other than triodes. But since $\mu = g_m \times r_p$, we can substitute this in our formula:

$$\text{amplification} = \frac{g_m \times r_p \times R_L}{r_p + R_L} \qquad (3\text{-}7)$$

In this formula, g_m is the transconductance and is in mhos. For this purpose the mho is an inconveniently large unit. Tube manuals list transconductance in micromhos. We can conveniently modify our formula this way:

$$\text{voltage amplification} = \frac{g_m \times r_p \times R_L}{10^6 \times (r_p + R_L)}$$

In this formula, g_m is the transconductance in micromhos. Resistance (both plate and load) remains in ohms.

The formula for the output voltage across a load impedance is similar to that given earlier for a resistive load.

$$e_o = e_g \times \frac{\mu \times Z}{Z + r_p} \qquad (3\text{-}8)$$

145

CATHODE FOLLOWERS

The formulas we have given would indicate that the voltage amplification is directly dependent upon the amplification factor, the plate resistance and the value of the load. However, it also depends on how we connect the load. In the cathode follower we transfer the load from the plate to the cathode circuit. In such circuits the voltage amplification is always less than one (unity). However, for this sacrifice in voltage amplification we get a circuit that can be used for impedance transformation—connecting a high impedance circuit at the input to a low impedance circuit at the output of the cathode follower. For triode cathode followers, the voltage amplification is:

$$\text{voltage amplification} = \frac{\mu \times R_L}{r_p + R_L \times (\mu + 1)} \qquad (3\text{-}9)$$

For a pentode used as a cathode follower:

$$\text{voltage amplification} = \frac{g_m \times R_L}{1 + (g_m \times R_L)} \qquad (3\text{-}10)$$

RESISTANCE-COUPLED AUDIO AMPLIFIERS (TRIODES)

For the sake of convenience, audio frequencies can be divided into three ranges—low, medium and high. We can arbitrarily select the center of each range as 100 Hertz for the low-frequency range, 1,000 Hertz for the center of the medium range, and 10,000 Hertz for the high range.

In R-C amplifiers we may consider the resistive elements as constant for the three audio ranges. The frequency-sensitive component is capacitive. Ignoring stray capacitances, such as the capacitance between adjacent wires and wiring and the chassis, the interelectrode capacitances of the tube and the coupling capacitor between the driver and driven tube will affect the gain.

At low frequencies, capacitive reactance is high. Its effect on a circuit will be serious or negligible, depending on how it is connected. For a series arrangement, the high reactance must be considered. Where the capacitance is a shunt element, the high reactance means we may disregard it safely.

For the low-frequency range, the equivalent circuit may be drawn as shown in Fig. 3-2. Note that for the low range we are not concerned with the shunting interelectrode capacitances of the tube. The dominant element is the coupling capacitor C.

For the medium frequency range, the reactance of the coupling capacitor C has such a low value that we may disregard it.

146

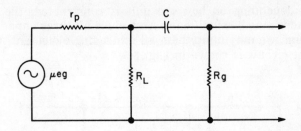

Fig. 3-2. Equivalent circuit for the low-frequency range.

Note, in the equivalent circuit (Fig. 3-3) for the medium frequencies that all capacitances have been omitted.

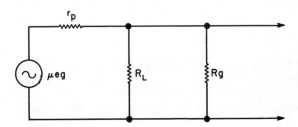

Fig. 3-3. Equivalent circuit for the medium frequency range. The reactance of the coupling capacitor is now low enough so that it may be disregarded.

For the high frequency range, the interelectrode capacitances enter the picture. The capacitance between plate and cathode (Cpk) is now a shunting element across the plate load resistor, R_L. Similarly, the interelectrode capacitance (Cgk) between the grid and cathode of the driven tube is a shunting element across the grid leak Rg (Fig. 3-4).

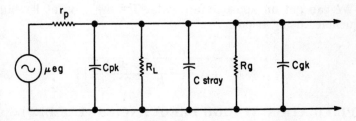

Fig. 3-4. Equivalent circuit for the high-frequency range. The shunting effect of miscellaneous capacitance now becomes important.

147

Now, depending on how the unit is constructed, the wiring capacitances may be significant. And, since all three capacitances are in shunt, we may lump them all into a single element, Ct. The equivalent circuit is shown in Fig. 3-5.

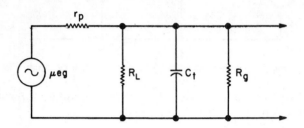

Fig. 3-5. The equivalent circuit for the high-frequency range may be simplified by lumping all the capacitances.

AMPLIFICATION AT MEDIUM FREQUENCIES (TRIODES)

The output impedance for a triode at medium frequencies is:

$$Z_o = \frac{R_L \times R_g}{R_L + R_g} \tag{3-11}$$

(Note that this is the same as our formula for two resistors in parallel.) The impedance is resistive since the capacitive element is disregarded. The amplification at intermediate frequencies is:

$$A = \frac{\mu \times Z_o}{Z_o + r_p} \tag{3-12}$$

AMPLIFICATION AT LOW FREQUENCIES (TRIODES)

We can get an approximate value for the gain at low audio frequencies using triodes by:

$$A = \frac{\mu \times R_g}{\sqrt{R_g{}^2 + X_c{}^2}\left(\dfrac{r_p\ (R_L + R_g)}{R_L \times R_g} + 1\right)} \tag{3-13}$$

AMPLIFICATION AT HIGH FREQUENCIES (TRIODES)

The gain at high frequencies becomes even more complex since the various interelectrode capacitances of both tubes, and the

148

wiring capacitances, now come into play. The value obtained for the gain will just be a reasonable approximation.

$$A = \frac{\mu \times R_g}{\sqrt{R_g{}^2 + X_c{}^2} \left(\dfrac{r_p \, (R_L + R_g)}{R_L \times R_g} + 1 \right)} \qquad (3\text{-}14)$$

RESISTANCE-COUPLED AUDIO AMPLIFIERS (PENTODES)

The equivalent circuits for resistance-coupled pentodes at low, medium, and high frequencies is shown in Fig. 3-6. The plate

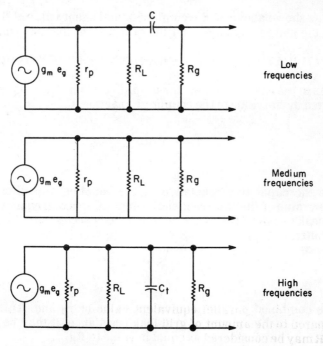

Fig. 3-6. Equivalent circuits for pentodes for low, medium and high frequencies.

resistance is now regarded as a shunt element instead of being in series with the source. Again, at medium frequencies the equivalent circuit may be considered as being purely resistive. The three resistances, the plate resistance (r_p), the load resistance (R_L) and the grid (or grid leak) resistor, R_g, are in shunt. The equivalent value (R_{eq}) of this combination can be obtained by using any one of the various formulas given earlier for combining parallel resistors.

$$\left(R_{eq} = \frac{1}{\dfrac{1}{r_p} + \dfrac{1}{R_L} + \dfrac{1}{R_g}}\right.$$ (3-15)

AMPLIFICATION AT MEDIUM FREQUENCIES (PENTODES)

The gain at medium frequencies is:

$$A = g_m \times R_{eq}$$ (3-16)

R_{eg}, as shown above, is the combined total shunt value of the plate load, the plate resistance, and the grid-leak of the following stage.

AMPLIFICATION AT LOW FREQUENCIES (PENTODES)

As in the case of triodes, the amplification at low frequencies is affected by the value of the coupling capacitor, C.

$$A = \frac{g_m \times R_{eq}}{\sqrt{1 + \left(\dfrac{X_c}{R}\right)^2}}$$ (3-17)

X_C is the capacitive reactance of the coupling capacitor at the center value of the low-frequency range. For low frequencies, the grid-leak resistor (R_g) is considered to be in series with the parallel combination of plate load (R_p) and plate resistance (r_p). That is:

$$R = \frac{r_p \times R_l}{r_p + R_l} + R_g$$ (3-18)

If the combined parallel equivalent value of r_p and R_L is small compared to the amount of grid-leak resistance, it may be ignored and R may be considered as equal in value to R_g.

The formula for pentode amplification at low frequencies has some unusual points of interest. Note that the numerator (g_m x R_{eq}) is identical with our formula for the gain at medium frequencies. And, in the denominator, if the value of R should become exactly equal to the value of X_C, then the numerical amount of the denominator would be the square root of 2 or 1.414. That is, the voltage amplification, under these conditions, will be 70.7 percent of the amplification at medium frequencies. This is a 3 db drop in gain and is noticeable. The change in sound volume becomes even more apparent as the reactance of the capacitor increases. Thus, when $X_C = 2R$, the voltage amplification drops 7 db. The importance of not using too small a value of coupling capacitance becomes obvious.

AMPLIFICATION AT HIGH FREQUENCIES (PENTODES)

For both triodes and pentodes, the shunting capacitances are important, and for both types of tubes, the total shunting capacitance is:

$$C_t = C_{stray} + C_{pk} + C_i \qquad (3\text{-}19)$$

C_{stray} represents the miscellaneous stray wiring capacitances of the circuit. C_{pk} is the interelectrode capacitance between the plate and the cathode of the driver tube. C_i is the input capacitance of the driven tube.

We cannot consider C_i as the sum of the interelectrode capacitances of the driven tube. The value of C_i can be obtained from:

$$C_i = C_{gk} + C_{gp} (1 + A) \qquad (3\text{-}20)$$

C_{gk} is the capacitance between grid and cathode; C_{gp} is the capacitance between grid and plate. A is the amplification of the circuit. A reasonable value for A is to consider it as being equal to one-half the amplification factor of the tube.

For the high-frequency range for pentodes, the voltage amplification is:

$$A = \frac{g_m \times R_{eq}}{\sqrt{1 + (R_{eq}/X_t)^2}} \qquad (3\text{-}21)$$

X_t represents the capacitive reactance of C_i. Note, in this formula, the effect on the gain of R_{eq}, and the reactance of the shunting capacitances. When these two are equal, the denominator will reduce the square root of 2 and the gain will be equal to 70.7 of the gain at the medium frequencies. Under these conditions, the gain at the high frequencies will be 3 db down from the medium frequency gain.

The formula also shows us that if we let C_t (the total shunting capacitance) get out of hand, the gain at higher audio frequencies will suffer.

NEGATIVE FEEDBACK

In audio amplifiers a portion of the output voltage is fed back, out of phase, to the input. Known as negative, inverse, or degenerative feedback, its effect is to reduce distortion at the expense of gain.

For an amplifier without feedback, the amplification A, is:

$$A = \frac{e_o}{e_g}$$

e₀ is the amplified version of the input signal voltage, eg.

We can rearrange this formula to read:

$$e_o = A \times e_g$$

If we now take a fraction of the output voltage (we will call it β) and feed it back to the input, then our output voltage will now be:

$$e_o = A (e_g + \beta e_o)$$

Performing the indicated multiplication, we will get:

$$e_o = A e_g + \beta A e_o$$

If we now transpose βAeo, we will have:

$$e_o - \beta A e_o = A e_g$$

We can simplify the left-hand expression:

$$e_o (1 - \beta A) = A e_g$$

There are two terms in this equation in which we are now interested. One of these is the input voltage, eg, and the other is the output voltage, e₀. We can get their ratio by dividing and transposing:

$$\frac{e_o}{e_g} = \frac{A}{1 - \beta A} = K \qquad (3\text{-}22)$$

This is now our formula for the gain of an amplifier with feedback. K is used to represent a condition of amplification with negative feedback.

POWER AMPLIFIERS

The efficiency of any device is the ratio of what we get out to what we put in. In the case of a power amplifier, the efficiency (η) is the ratio of the AC power output (P₀) to the DC power input. Since

152

this measurement must be taken with an input signal on the grid, the DC power is obtained by multiplying the average DC plate voltage by the average DC plate current.

$$n = \frac{P_o}{E_p \times I_p} \times 100 \qquad (3\text{-}23)$$

Here P_o is the AC output power, E_p is the average plate voltage and I_p is the average plate current. Since the formula is multiplied by 100, the answer is directly in terms of percentage.

POWER SENSITIVITY

We can get a measure of the power sensitivity of a tube by comparing the AC output power (P_o) to the square of the AC input signal.

$$\text{Power sensitivity} = \frac{P_o}{E_g^2} \qquad (3\text{-}24)$$

E_g is the input signal in volts rms. P_o is the AC output power. The power sensitivity is given in mhos.

POWER OUTPUT

We can regard the plate current of a power amplifier tube, when driven by a signal, as varying DC or as DC with an AC component. The output power (P_o) is the product of the AC component (i_p) of the plate current and the effective plate load (R_L). If the load is resistive and distortion is negligible:

$$P_o = (i_p)^2 \times R_L \text{ or } P_o = E_p \times i_p$$

The AC component of the plate current is sometimes referred to as the dynamic plate current. The formula shown here is for rms values of dynamic plate current and voltage. For peak-to-peak values:

$$P_o = \frac{(i_p^2) \times R_L}{2\sqrt{2}} \qquad (3\text{-}25)$$

The rms value of the AC component of the plate current of an audio amplifier power triode can be written in terms of the maximum (or peak) and the peak-to-peak values in this way:

$$i_p = \frac{i_{max}}{\sqrt{2}} = \frac{i_{max} - i_{min}}{2\sqrt{2}} \qquad (3\text{-}26)$$

153

We can handle the AC component of the plate voltage in the same way

$$e_p = \frac{e_{max}}{\sqrt{2}} = \frac{e_{max} - e_{min}}{2\sqrt{2}} \tag{3-27}$$

but, since power is the product of voltage and current, we can get another expression for power (but this time in terms of maximum and minimum values of voltage and current).

$$P_o = \frac{i_{max} - i_{min}}{2\sqrt{2}} \times \frac{e_{max} - e_{min}}{2\sqrt{2}}$$

$$= \frac{(i_{max} - i_{min})(e_{max} - e_{min})}{8} \tag{3-28}$$

In a class-A triode power amplifier working into a resistive load, R_L, the plate current, i_p, is:

$$i_p = \frac{\mu \times e_g}{r_p + R_L}$$

If we substitute this for i_p in our formula for output power, we will get:

$$P_o = \left(\frac{\mu \times e_g}{r_p + R_L}\right)^2 \times R_L \tag{3-29}$$

MAXIMUM TRANSFER OF POWER TO THE LOAD

We will get maximum transfer of power from the source (the tube) to the load (R_L) when the resistance of the source and the load are equal, provided the amplification factor (μ), the plate resistance (r_p) and the signal voltage, e_g, are constant. Thus, when $R_L = r_p$,

$$P_o \text{ max} = \left(\frac{\mu \times e_g}{2 \times r_p}\right)^2 \times r_p$$

(note that r_p has been substituted for R_L)
By squaring and dividing, the formula can be simplified to:

$$P_o \text{ max} = \frac{\mu^2 \times e_g^2}{4 \times r_p} \tag{3-30}$$

154

While the transfer of power to the load is maximum when $R_L = r_p$, the peak transfer is not critical. That is, the value of R_L may be varied as much as 25% above or below its selected value, without seriously affecting the transfer of power from the tube to the load.

POWER IN THE PLATE LOAD

Where the source and load values in a power amplifier are not equal, the transfer of power to the load is:

$$P = \left(\frac{\mu \times e_g}{r_p + R_p}\right)^2 \tag{3-31}$$

UNDISTORTED POWER OUTPUT

The maximum undistorted power output when the plate load resistor (R_p) is twice the value of the plate resistance (r_p) is:

$$P_{\text{undistorted}} = \frac{2(\mu \times e_g)^2}{9 \times r_p} \tag{3-32}$$

SINGLE PENTODE AUDIO POWER OUTPUT

The audio power output of a single pentode may be fairly well approximated by:

$$P = 0.33 \times E_p \times I_p \tag{3-33}$$

The product, E x I, represents the DC power input to the tube, E_p is the DC plate voltage and I_p is the DC plate current.

SECOND-HARMONIC DISTORTION OF A POWER AMPLIFIER

The greatest portion of distortion is due to the second harmonic, but because it is an even-order harmonic, it lends itself nicely to cancellation.

percentage of
second-harmonic distortion $= \dfrac{2\,(i_p\max + i_p\min) - i_p}{(i_p\max - i_p\min)} \times 100$ (3-34)

i_p max is the maximum of the AC component, i_p min is the minimum of the AC component, i_p is the amount of plate current that flows at the operating or quiescent point (the bias point), as shown in Fig. 3-7.

155

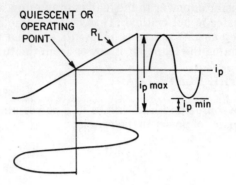

Fig. 3-7. The position of the quiescent or operating point is determined by the amount of bias used. Here the operating point is at the center of the characteristic curve.

Chapter 4

Semiconductors

Compared to a vacuum tube, the impedances associated with the input and output circuits of a transistor are low. We can regard vacuum tubes as voltage operated components; transistors as current operated.

Although triodes are not uncommon, most tubes are multi-element—that is, are usually pentode or beam power. Most transistors, though, are triodes. The elements of the transistor triode are the emitter, base and collector and while, for the sake of analogy, these are often compared to the cathode, grid and plate of a vacuum tube, there is little other similarity. A vacuum tube is a

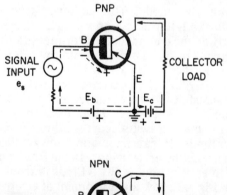

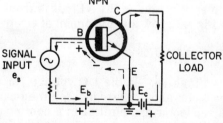

Fig. 4-1. In a vacuum tube, electron current moves only from cathode to plate. In a transistor, current can move to or from the collector, depending on the type of transistor used.

unilaterally conducting device—that is, electron current moves from cathode to plate and in that direction only.

In a transistor, depending on its arrangement, electrons and "holes" can move in either direction, from emitter to collector or collector to emitter (Fig. 4-1).

DIRECTION OF CURRENT FLOW

The direction of current flow through a component, such as a resistor, is usually indicated by an arrow placed above the component with the head of the arrow representing the direction in which the current moves.

The arrows used in connection with diode and transistor symbols point in a direction that is opposite to electron movement. In the diode symbol, Fig. 4-2, the straight line represents the cath-

K OR CATH

Fig. 4-2. Direction of electron current flow through a semiconductor diode.

ode; the arrow the anode. The cathode is sometimes marked "cath" or with the letter K. Some manufacturers print the diode symbol directly on the component. Other manufacturers use a color code to identify the particular diode, with the colors placed near the cathode end of the diode. The arrow above the diode symbol in Fig. 4-2 shows the direction of electron current flow.

Since a transistor may be regarded as a pair of diodes, back-to-back, direction of current flow is the same as through a diode.

In Fig. 4-1 (upper drawing) current flows from the collector to the emitter in the PNP transistor and from emitter to collector in the NPN transistor (lower drawing). In the PNP current movement is from base to emitter and in the NPN it is from emitter to base. The arrows in Fig. 4-1 show the movement of electron current.

ELECTRODE VOLTAGES

Collector voltage (e_c) is the DC voltage (in volts) measured between the collector and the base in a common-base configuration, or between the collector and emitter in a common-emitter circuit.

Emitter voltage (e_e) is the DC voltage (in volts) existing between emitter and base in a common-base circuit or between emitter and ground in common emitter, common collector and common base arrangements.

Base voltage (e_b) is the DC voltage, in volts, measured between base and ground. In unijunction and tetrode transistors, there are two base voltages: base 1 and base 2.

ELECTRODE CURRENTS

The collector current is the direct current flowing to or from the collector. Collector current is i_c.

Emitter current is the direct current flowing to or from the emitter. Emitter current is i_e.

Base current is the direct current flowing to or from the base electrode. Base current is i_b.

In terms of an equation:

$$i_e = i_c + i_b$$

i_e is the emitter current, i_c the collector current and i_b the base current. The collector current is smaller than the emitter current and so any change in the collector current is smaller than a change in emitter current.

$$\Delta i_e = \Delta i_c + \Delta i_b$$

Δ is the Greek letter delta, and means "change of."

CURRENT AMPLIFICATION

Since, the transistor, like the tube, is an amplifying device, we may look for comparable parameters. But because of the completely different nature of tubes and transistors, we cannot apply the analysis used for tubes to transistors.

In a transistor not all of the current carriers injected by the emitter reach the collector. The maximum, approached but not attained, would be 100 percent or 1. The ratio of a change (Δ) in collector current (i_c) to a change in emitter current (i_e) is called current gain and is represented by the Greek lower case letter α (alpha). Thus:

$$\alpha = \frac{\Delta i_c}{\Delta i_e} \qquad (4\text{-}1)$$

If all carriers leaving the emitter reached the collector, the collector current change (Δi_c) would be equal to the emitter current change (Δi_e) and the current amplification, or α, would be 1. For transistors other than point-contact types (forerunners of our present-day transistors) values of alpha are 0.99 or less.

159

RESISTANCE GAIN

The term current amplification or current gain or alpha of a transistor might tend to be misleading since there is no current gain at all, but a loss. However, the amplification possibilities of transistors become evident when we consider the resistance gain—that is, the ratio of the output and the input resistances.

$$\text{Resistance gain} = \frac{r_o}{r_i} \tag{4-2}$$

r_0 is the output resistance and r_i the input resistance. In a representative transistor, the output resistance is much higher than the input resistance, and the word **gain** is used in this sense. Thus, in working with transistors, we can get a rough approximation of the gain by making a comparison of the output and input resistances—that is, by determining their ratio.

VOLTAGE GAIN

As in the case of a tube, the voltage gain of a transistor is the ratio of the output (e_0) to the input voltage (e_i), or:

$$\text{Voltage gain} = \frac{e_o}{e_i}$$

Voltage is the product of current and resistance:

$$\text{Voltage gain} = \frac{e_o}{e_i} = \frac{i_c \times r_o}{i_e \times r_i}$$

But the ratio of i_c to i_e is the current gain or alpha. Thus, we have:

$$\text{Voltage gain} = \alpha \, \frac{r_o}{r_i} \tag{4-3}$$

POWER GAIN

We can get a term for power gain by considering that power is the product of voltage and current.

$$\text{Power gain} = \frac{e_o \times i_c}{e_i \times i_e} \tag{4-4}$$

Note that the voltage gain (e_o/e_i) is part of this formula. But the previous formula shows that voltage gain is equal to α x r_o/r_i. We can substitute this in our formula for power gain:

$$\text{Power gain} = \alpha \, \frac{r_o \times i_c}{r_i \times i_e}$$

We can simplify this power formula by considering that alpha is equal to the ratio i_c to i_e. We now have:

$$\text{Power gain} = \alpha \times \alpha \, \frac{r_o}{r_i} = \alpha^2 \times \frac{r_o}{r_i} \qquad (4\text{-}5)$$

The derivation of the formula for power gain starts with the basic formula for power: $\mathbf{P} = \mathbf{E} \; \mathbf{x} \; \mathbf{I}$. However, the same results can be obtained by utilizing another power formula: $\mathbf{P} = \mathbf{I}^2 \; \mathbf{x} \; \mathbf{R}$. The output power:

$$P_o = i_c{}^2 \times r_o$$

The output power equals the output current (the collector current) squared, multiplied by the output resistance. Similarly, then, the input power is:

$$P_i = i_e{}^2 \times r_i$$

The input power is the emitter current squared multiplied by the amount of input resistance.

The ratio of these two powers supplies the power gain.

$$\frac{P_o}{P_i} = \frac{\Delta \; i_c{}^2 \times r_o}{\Delta \; i_e{}^2 \times r_i}$$

since current amplification,

$$\alpha = \frac{i_c}{i_e},$$

then

$$\frac{i_c{}^2}{i_e{}^2} = \alpha^2$$

Substituting α^2 for i_c^2/i_e^2, the formula for power gain is:

$$\text{Power gain} = \alpha^2 \times \frac{r_o}{r_i}$$

Where alpha is very close to unity, we can disregard it and recognize that the power gain is the ratio of the output impedance to the input impedance.

BASIC CIRCUITS

Commonly, transistor circuits are arranged so that the base and emitter form the input circuit, with collector and emitter as the output circuit. This most nearly resembles a vacuum tube circuit in which the cathode is the common element to input and output circuits. Fig. 4-3 shows three basic arrangements of transistor circuits plus their nearest vacuum-tube equivalents.

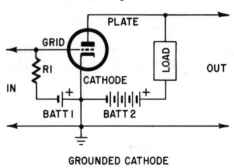

GROUNDED CATHODE

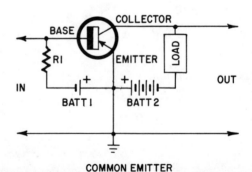

COMMON EMITTER

Fig. 4-3. The common emitter circuit resembles the grounded cathode vacuum tube amplifier.

The circuit shown in Fig. 4-3 is a common emitter, comparable to the grounded cathode vacuum tube circuit. The common emitter (also known as a grounded emitter) has a low input resistance and a fairly high output resistance. The input resistance may range from about 300 ohms to 1,000 or more; output from 5,000 to 50,000 or higher.

The common base (grounded base) in Fig. 4-4 is similar to a grounded grid vacuum tube amplifier. The input resistance is about

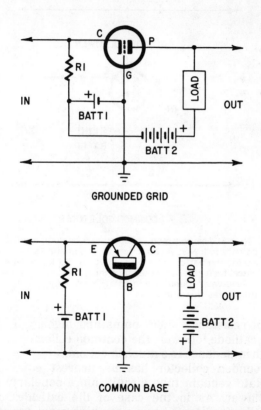

GROUNDED GRID

COMMON BASE

Fig. 4-4. The common base transistor circuit is similar to the grounded grid vacuum tube amplifier.

the same as the common emitter, but the output resistance is much higher, ranging from 100,000 ohms up to and beyond a half megohm.

The common collector (grounded collector) in Fig. 4-5, has a very high input resistance (100,000 ohms or more) and a much

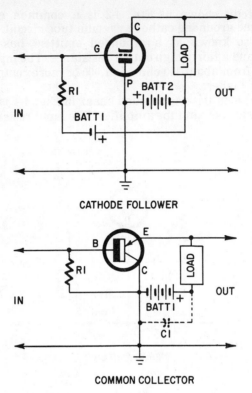

CATHODE FOLLOWER

COMMON COLLECTOR

Fig. 4-5. The common collector can be compared to a cathode follower. A capacitor, C1, is sometimes shunted across the battery to act as a bypass. As batteries get older, their internal resistance increases and they tend to behave as coupling elements. The shunting capacitor minimizes this effect.

lower output resistance (1,000 ohms and higher). Like its counterpart, the cathode follower, the common collector can be used to match a high impedance to a much lower one.

The grounded collector has its nearest equivalent in the grounded plate vacuum tube circuit, more popularly known as a cathode follower. As in the case of the cathode follower, the grounded collector circuit has a very high input resistance and a comparatively lower output resistance.

PHASE REVERSAL

As shown in Fig. 4-6, it is possible to get phase reversal of the input signal with a transistor circuit, just as in the case of a vacuum-tube circuit.

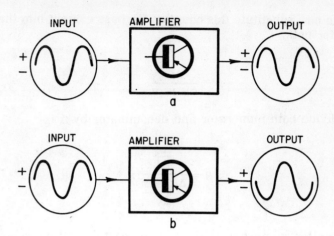

Fig. 4-6. The illustration at the top (A) represents the grounded base and grounded collector circuits. Input-output are in phase. The lower drawing (B) indicates a grounded emitter. This circuit supplies phase reversal.

The grounded-emitter circuit is the only one of the three in which there is phase reversal of the signal. In the grounded base and grounded collector circuits, the output and input signals are in phase.

BASE CURRENT AMPLIFICATION FACTOR

We can get another ratio of current gain by comparing the change in collector current to the change in base current. Known as beta and represented by the Greek letter β it is shown as:

$$\beta = \frac{\Delta i_c}{\Delta i_b} \tag{4-6}$$

However, as indicated earlier, the sum of the collector and base currents is equal to the emitter current.

$$\Delta i_e = \Delta i_c + \Delta i_b$$

transposing:

$$\Delta i_b = \Delta i_e - \Delta i_c$$

165

We can now substitute this equation for base current into the formula for beta.

$$\beta = \frac{\Delta i_c}{\Delta i_e - \Delta i_c}$$

Now divide both numerator and denominator by $\Delta\, i_e$

$$\beta = \frac{\dfrac{\Delta i_c}{\Delta i_e}}{\dfrac{\Delta i_e - \Delta i_c}{\Delta i_e}}$$

Examine the numerator and you will see that it represents the equation for current amplification. (Eq. 4-1).

$$\alpha = \frac{\Delta i_c}{\Delta i_e}$$

and so the formula for beta can be simplified to

$$\beta = \frac{\alpha}{\dfrac{\Delta i_e - \Delta i_c}{\Delta i_e}}$$

Δi_e (in the denominator) divided by itself is equal to 1. And i_c/i_e, also in the denominator is equal to α. Hence the formula for beta is:

$$\beta = \frac{\alpha}{1 - \alpha}$$

Alpha can also be expressed in terms of beta:

$$\alpha = \frac{\beta}{1 + \beta}$$

ALPHA CUTOFF FREQUENCY

The limitation of the use of transistors at high frequencies is the transit time of current from emitter to collector (or collector to emitter). Alpha cutoff frequency is that frequency at which alpha drops to 0.707 (3 db) of its value at lower frequencies.

Alpha cutoff frequency = $0.707 \times \alpha$

Circuit	Input resistance	Output resistance
Common base	$r_e + r_b$	$r_c + r_b$
Common emitter	$r_b + r_e$	$r_c + r_e$
Common collector	$r_b + r_c$	$r_e + r_c$

INTERNAL INPUT AND OUTPUT RESISTANCES

There is no isolation between the output and input circuits of a transistor. The transistor can be looked on as an active resistance network. The input and output circuits are related through their respective resistances, as shown in Fig. 4-7.

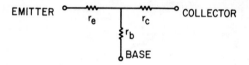

Fig. 4-7. A transistor resembles an active resistive network. This is the equivalent circuit for a grounded-base diagram.

BASE RESISTANCE

With constant emitter current in the grounded-base configuration, a change in collector current results in a change in base current. The base current (Fig. 4-8) is **ib**. The base voltage is:

$$e_b = i_b \times r_b$$

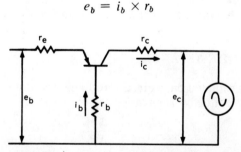

Fig. 4-8. Static leakage current (collector cutoff current) is small in this common base arrangement.

Thus, with a change in collector current, there will be a corresponding change in base voltage. With emitter current kept constant, the base resistance is:

$$r_b = \frac{\Delta e_c}{\Delta i_c}$$

e_b is the voltage between emitter and base. Note in Fig. 4-8 that the emitter-base circuit is open, hence $i_e = 0$.

EMITTER RESISTANCE

In the grounded emitter circuit (Fig. 4-9), with the base current kept constant,

$$r_e = \frac{\Delta e_b}{\Delta i_c}$$

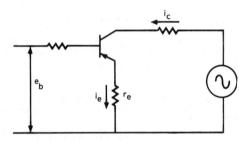

Fig. 4-9. Collector leakage current is also small in common emitter circuit.

e_b is the voltage between base and emitter. r_e is the emitter resistance. Note that the circuit of Fig. 4-9 shows an open arrangement between base and emitter and so the base current is zero.

COLLECTOR RESISTANCE

Using a grounded base circuit and keeping the emitter current constant, the collector resistance is:

$$r_c = \frac{\Delta e_c}{\Delta i_c}$$

e_c is the voltage between collector and base.
The circuit arrangement is the same as that shown earlier in Fig. 4-8. The emitter circuit is open and so the emitter current, i_e, is zero.
The formula for collector resistance isn't quite correct since the collector resistance and the base resistance are in series. However, the base resistance is very small compared to the collector resistance and is disregarded.

STATIC LEAKAGE CURRENT

In a common base arrangement (Fig. 4-8). with no emitter voltage, but with voltage existing between base and collector, there is a very small flow of collector current. This current is small because of the very high value of r_c. The collector current that flows under conditions of no input signal is called static leakage current or cutoff current. It is designated as i_{co}.

In the common emitter circuit (Fig. 4-9), with no base voltage applied but with voltage existing between collector and emitter, there is also a small leakage current, i_{eo}.

POWER DISSIPATION

As in the case of tubes, DC voltages are applied to each of the elements of a transistor—the base, the emitter, and the collector. Because current flows through them, they are called on to dissipate DC power. Power is the product of voltage and current.

$$p_b = e_b \times i_b$$

e_b and i_b are the base voltage and the base current, respectively. Both are in volts. P is in watts. Similarly:

$$P_{\overline{e}} = e_e \times i_e$$

P_e is the power in watts dissipated by the emitter. e_e is the emitter voltage and i_e is the emitter current.

Finally, the power dissipated by the collector is:

$$p_c = e_c \times i_c$$

e_c is the collector voltage and i_c is the collector current.

CIRCUIT EFFICIENCY

The efficiency of a circuit is the ratio of its AC signal power output to its DC power input.

$$\eta = \frac{P_o}{P_i}$$

If the output, for example, is taken from the collector circuit, then the DC collector power is e_c x i_c, and the formula for efficiency becomes:

$$\eta = \frac{P_o}{e_c \times i_c} \times 100$$

$$= \text{Efficiency in percent}$$

P_0 is the AC signal power output.

RISE TIME

When a transistor is used in a switching circuit, rise time is the time it takes for the transistor to go from zero to maximum pulse output (Fig. 4-10). Rise time, though, isn't actually calculated from

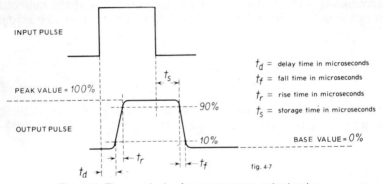

Fig. 4-10. Time analysis of a square wave output pulse.

zero to peak but rather the time it takes to go from 10% above the base line to 10% below maximum level. This is equivalent to 10% of maximum to 90% of maximum. Rise time is designated as t_r, and is specified in microseconds.

FALL TIME

In switching transistor circuits, fall time is the amount of time it takes for a pulse to drop from 90% of peak to 10% of peak. Fall time, specified in microseconds, is designated as t_f.

STORAGE TIME

Storage time (Fig. 4-10) is the amount of time, in microseconds, it takes for an output pulse to fall to 90% of its peak value after the input pulse has dropped to zero.

DELAY TIME

In transistor switching circuits, delay time is the amount of time, in microseconds, it takes for the output pulse to reach 10% of maximum amplitude after the application of the input pulse. In Fig. 4-10, delay time is designated t_d.

Chapter 5

Television

Width of TV broadcast channels for monochrome or color is 6 MHz for all channels. Fig. 5-1 illustrates Channel 2.

TELEVISION WAVEFORMS

Picture carrier = sound carrier − 4.5 MHz
Picture carrier = low end of TV channel + 1.25 MHz
Lower video sideband = 0.75 MHz
Sound carrier = upper end of TV channel − 0.25 MHz
Sound carrier − picture carrier = 4.5 MHz

TELEVISION CHANNELS (VHF)

Channel	Band in MHz	Frequency of Pix Carrier (MHz)	Frequency of Sound Carrier (MHz)
2	54 - 60	55.25	59.75
3	60 - 66	61.25	65.75
4	66 - 72	67.25	71.75
5	76 - 82	77.25	81.75
6	82 - 88	83.25	87.75
7	174 - 180	175.25	179.75
8	180 - 186	181.25	185.75
9	186 - 192	187.25	191.75
10	192 - 198	193.25	197.75
11	198 - 204	199.25	203.75
12	204 - 210	205.25	209.75
13	210 - 216	211.25	215.75

UHF CHANNELS

There are 70 UHF TV channels between 470 and 890 MHz, with each channel 6 MHz wide. The lowest channel frequency is Channel 14 at 470 MHz. To find the lowest frequency of any UHF TV channel:

$$f_L = 6(\text{channel number-14}) + 470$$

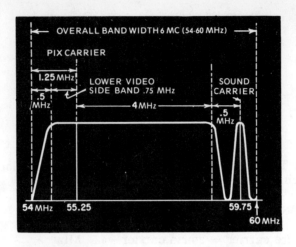

Fig. 5-1. Picture and sound carrier relationships in a 6-MHz television channel.

f_L is the lowest frequency of the unknown channel. Example: The low-frequency end of Channel 40 is:

$$f_L = 6(40-14) + 470$$

$$= (6 \times 26) + 470 = 626 \text{ MHz}$$

Since each channel is 6 MHz wide, 626 + 6 = 632 MHz supplies the high frequency end of Channel 40. Channel 40 extends from 626 to 632 MHz.

FINDING THE CHANNEL NUMBER

If the lowest frequency of the UHF channel is known, you can find the channel number by using this formula:

$$\text{Channel number} = \frac{f_L - 470}{6} + 14$$

If the lowest frequency is 662 MHz, the channel number is:

$$\text{Channel number} = \frac{662 - 470}{6} + 14 = \text{channel } 46$$

TELEVISION CHANNELS (UHF)

Channel	Band in MHz	Frequency of Pix Carrier (MHz)	Frequency of Sound Carrier (MHz)
14	470 - 476	471.25	475.75
15	476 - 482	477.25	481.75
16	482 - 488	483.25	487.75
17	488 - 494	489.25	493.75
18	494 - 500	495.25	499.75
19	500 - 506	501.25	505.75
20	506 - 512	507.25	511.75
21	512 - 518	513.25	517.75
22	518 - 524	519.25	523.75
23	524 - 530	525.25	529.75
24	530 - 536	531.25	535.75
25	536 - 542	537.25	541.75
26	542 - 548	543.25	547.75
27	548 - 554	549.25	553.75
28	554 - 560	555.25	559.75
29	560 - 566	561.25	565.75
30	566 - 572	567.25	571.75
31	572 - 578	573.25	577.75
32	578 - 584	579.25	583.75
33	584 - 590	585.25	589.75
34	590 - 596	591.25	595.75
35	596 - 602	597.25	601.75
36	602 - 608	603.25	607.75
37	608 - 614	609.25	613.75
38	614 - 620	615.25	619.75
39	620 - 626	621.25	625.75
40	626 - 632	627.25	631.75
41	632 - 638	633.25	637.75
42	638 - 644	639.25	643.75
43	644 - 650	645.25	649.75
44	650 - 656	651.25	655.75
45	656 - 662	657.25	661.75
46	662 - 668	663.25	667.75
47	668 - 674	669.25	673.75
48	674 - 680	675.25	679.75
49	680 - 686	681.25	685.75

Channel	Band in MHz	Frequency of Pix Carrier (MHz)	Frequency of Sound Carrier (MHz)
50	686 - 692	687.25	691.75
51	692 - 698	693.25	697.75
52	698 - 704	699.25	703.75
53	704 - 710	705.25	709.75
54	710 - 716	711.25	715.75
55	716 - 722	717.25	721.75
56	722 - 728	723.25	727.75
57	728 - 734	729.25	733.75
58	734 - 740	735.25	739.75
59	740 - 746	741.25	745.75
60	746 - 752	747.25	751.75
61	752 - 758	753.25	757.75
62	758 - 764	759.25	763.75
63	764 - 770	765.25	769.75
64	770 - 776	771.25	775.75
65	776 - 782	777.25	781.75
66	782 - 788	783.25	787.75
67	788 - 794	789.25	793.75
68	794 - 800	795.25	799.75
69	800 - 806	801.25	805.75
70	806 - 812	807.25	811.75
71	812 - 818	813.25	817.75
72	818 - 824	819.25	823.75
73	824 - 830	825.25	829.75
74	830 - 836	831.25	835.75
75	836 - 842	837.25	841.75
76	842 - 848	843.25	847.75
77	848 - 854	849.25	853.75
78	854 - 860	855.25	859.75
79	860 - 866	861.25	865.75
80	866 - 872	867.25	871.75
81	872 - 878	873.25	877.75
82	878 - 884	879.25	883.75
83	884 - 890	885.25	889.75

ASPECT RATIO

The aspect ratio is the ratio of picture width to height. The ratio is 4 : 3.

SCANNING FREQUENCIES FOR MONOCHROME TV

One complete picture, or frame, consists of 525 horizontal sweeps or lines. These lines are divided into two equal groups called fields. The frame repetition rate is 30 frames/second. Since there are two fields/frame, the field repetition rate is 30 x 2 = 60 fields per second.

Each frame has 525 lines and since each frame has a repetition rate of 30 frames/second, the horizontal line frequency is 525 x 30 15,750 Hz.

FREQUENCY RESPONSE

The relationship between the number of lines on a TV screen and frequency is:

$$N = 80F$$

N is the number of lines and F is the frequency response in MHz. If the response is 3 MHz, then the number of lines will be 80 x 3 = 240.

HORIZONTAL SWEEP FREQUENCY (MONOCHROME)

A raster is composed of 525 lines at a rate of 30 times per second. The horizontal scanning frequency is:

$$525 \times 30 = 15,750 \, Hz$$

Since this means there are 15,750 lines per second, the time duration of a single line is:

$$\frac{1 \text{ second}}{15,750} = 63.5 \times 10^{-6} \text{ second or } 63.5 \text{ microseconds}$$

A single line requiring 63.5 microseconds (Fig. 5-2) for full forward sweep and return is set up as follows:

forward sweep (visible trace)	=	53.3 microseconds
return sweep (blanked return)	=	10.2 microseconds
		63.5 microseconds

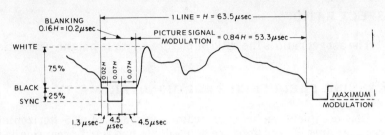

Fig. 5-2. Single line of modulated picture waveform plus blanking.

The vertical sawtooth period is 33,333 microseconds and the horizontal sawtooth period is 63.5 microseconds. The number of lines swept out on the face of the picture tube is the ratio of these two periods.

$$\frac{\text{vertical sawtooth period}}{\text{horizontal sawtooth period}} = \text{number of horizontal lines}$$

$$= \frac{33,333}{63.5} = 525 \text{ horizontal lines}$$

The vertical sawtooth period mentioned above is for two fields or a complete frame. Vertical sweep is 60 Hz or 60 cps. The time of one complete sweep sawtooth is 1/60 second = 16,667 microseconds.

COMPOSITION OF A SINGLE LINE

A single line has a time duration-H of 63.5 microseconds. Of this 63.5 microseconds, 53.3 microseconds is used by picture modulation. Modulation is 84% of the time duration of a single line.

modulation = 0.84H = 0.84 x 63.5 microseconds = 53.3 microseconds

A single complete line (H) consists of modulation plus a blanking pulse.

Modulation	= 0.84H	= 53.3 microseconds
Blanking pulse	= 0.16H	= 10.2 microseconds
	= 1.00H	= 63.5 microseconds

The forward sweep of a single line across the face of the picture tube, then, requires 84% of the time of a single sweep (H), while the return (horizontal blanking) requires 16%.

The horizontal sync pulse is positioned on the blanking pulse.

HORIZONTAL BLANKING PULSE COMPOSITION

Front porch	= .02 H	= 1.3 microseconds
Back porch	= .07 H	= 4.445 microseconds
Hor. sync pulse	= .07 H	= 4.445 microseconds
	= .16 H	= 10.2 microseconds

VERTICAL BLANKING

Each field has a total time duration of 16,667 microseconds (Fig. 5-3). Vertical blanking is equivalent in time to the sweep of 15 horizontal lines.

vertical blanking $= 15H = 15 \times 63.5 = 952.5$ microseconds

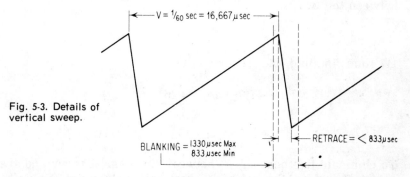

Fig. 5-3. Details of vertical sweep.

This value isn't fixed, since FCC standards call for a vertical blanking period between 13H and 21H. Hence, up to 21 lines/field do not assist in picture formation.

Each vertical sync pulse has a time duration of 3H = 3 x 63.5 = 190 microseconds.

DEFLECTION FREQUENCIES

For monochrome television, the vertical deflection frequency is 60 Hz, and 15,750 Hz for horizontal deflection.

For color television, the vertical deflection frequency is 59.95 Hz, and 15,734.264 Hz for horizontal deflection.

COLOR SUBCARRIER

The frequency of the color subcarrier is: 455 times one-half the horizontal line frequency:

$$\frac{H}{2} \times 455 = 3.579545 \text{ MHz}$$

H is the horizontal sweep frequency (15,734.264 Hz).
The chrominance subcarrier (or color subcarrier) is frequently rounded off to 3.58 MHz.

BEAT INTERFERENCE

In color transmission, as in black and white, the sound carrier is 4.5 MHz away from the picture carrier. The beat frequency between the color subcarrier and the sound carrier is:

$$4.5 \text{ MHz} - 3.579545 \text{ MHz} = 0.920455 \text{ MHz} = 920 \text{ kHz}$$

Since the sound carrier is 575 times the half line frequency and the color subcarrier is 455 times the half line frequency, the separation between the two is:

$$575 - 455 = 117$$

117 times the half line frequency is:

$$117 \times H/2 = 117 \times \frac{15,734.264}{2}$$

$$= 117 \times 7867.132 = 920.45 \text{kHz}$$

To eliminate this beat signal between the sound carrier and the color subcarrier, the color subcarrier is suppressed. Only the sidebands are transmitted, and the upper sideband is kept to 0.5 MHz.

REVERSAL OF PICTURE AND SOUND SIGNALS

The effect of the heterodyning action of the local oscillator or converter signal (Fig. 5-4) is to transpose the relative positions of the picture and sound signals. At the antenna the sound signal is higher in frequency than the picture signal by 4.5 MHz. Using Channel 2 as an example, the sound signal is 59.75 MHz and the picture signal is 55.25 MHz. Following the mixer or converter the IF signal has a sound IF of 41.25 MHz and a picture IF of 45.75 MHz. The separation between sound and picture remains 4.5 MHz. Thus, the sound signal which was originally higher in frequency than the picture signal is now lower.

Assume a local oscillator signal of 101 MHz. For the sound signal:

$$101 - 59.75 = 41.25 \text{MHz}$$

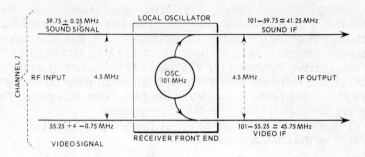

Fig. 5-4. Local oscillator in TV receiver transposes signal frequencies.

and for the picture signal:

$$101 - 55.25 = 45.75 \text{ MHz}$$

VIDEO IF

Fig. 5-5 shows an ideal IF response curve. Normally, a carrier would have equal sidebands above and below the carrier frequency. To save channel space, part of one picture sideband is suppressed. One picture sideband is transmitted in full and extends to 4 MHz. The other sideband is cut off at 0.75 MHz. This means that all parts of the picture modulation extending from 0 to 0.75 MHz are transmitted as two sidebands, or double strength. The higher frequency

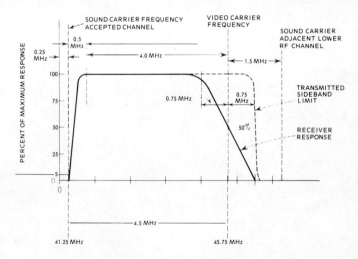

Fig. 5-5. Position of video and sound carriers in video IF waveform.

components—those above 0.75 MHz—are transmitted single sideband, and thus have only half the strength of modulation components below 0.75 MHz. To compensate for this, the video IF response is made to drop off from about 0.75 MHz on one side of the picture carrier. Note that the video carrier frequency is at the 50% point on the response curve. There is an equal drop off or loss of gain above this point compared to the gain below this point. Thus, the overall gain from 0-0.75 MHz is equalized.

The sound IF signal is at about the 5% point, that is, at 5 percent of maximum response.

Chapter 6

Antennas and Transmission Lines

The length of a radio wave or the distance occupied by one complete cycle of a radio wave, or its wavelength (in meters) is its velocity in free space divided by the frequency in Hertz.

$$\lambda = \frac{300,000,000}{f}$$

In free space the velocity of a radio wave is 300,000,000 meters per second. To express this formula in terms of kiloHertz, divide numerator and denominator by 1,000. Hence:

$$\lambda = \frac{300,000}{f}$$

where f is the frequency in kiloHertz.
The original formula can be expressed in terms of megaHertz by dividing numerator and denominator by 1,000,000.

$$\lambda = \frac{300}{f}$$

where f is the frequency in megaHertz. In all of the formulas shown above, λ is the wavelength in meters. 1 meter = 3.28 ft. = 39.37 ins.

PHYSICAL LENGTH OF AN ANTENNA

The formulas showing the inverse relationship of wavelength and frequency are predicated on the velocity of radio waves in free space. If these formulas are used directly for the calculation of antenna length, the antenna will be cut for resonance at a slightly lower frequency. To have the antenna resonate at the correct frequency its length should be about 95% (k) of a theoretical antenna in free space. Thus, the preceding formulas convert to:

$$\lambda = \frac{300 \times 0.95}{f}$$

183

where f is the frequency in megaHertz.

The 95% factor is caused by: 1) the slower velocity of radio waves along the conductor or conductors comprising the antenna and 2) end effect or stray capacitance near the antenna supports.

Since λ and f are inverse, the preceding formulas can be rearranged as:

$$f = \frac{300{,}000{,}000}{\lambda}$$

where f is the frequency in Hertz.

An approximation of antenna length in feet can be had by dividing 492 by the frequency (in megaHertz) of the wave being transmitted. The relationship between the wavelength, λ, (in feet) and the frequency, f, (in megaHertz) is:

$$\lambda = \frac{984}{f} \qquad (6\text{-}1)$$

Since we are seldom concerned with full-wave antennas, we can divide both sides of the equation by 2 (for a half-wave antenna):

$$\frac{\lambda}{2} = \frac{492}{f}$$

The length obtained will be somewhat longer than practical as mentioned earlier. A more accurate figure can be obtained by multiplying the answer by a correction factor, k, depending on the frequency. For frequencies of 3 megaHertz or less, k is 0.96. For 3 to 30 megaHertz, k drops to 0.95 and for frequencies above 30 megaHertz, k is 0.94. We can thus modify our formula for the length of an antenna in feet to read:

$$l = \frac{492 \times k}{f} \qquad (6\text{-}2)$$

For UHF, where wavelengths are very short, it is more practical to work in inches, rather than in fractions of a foot. The length of a half-wave antenna (l) in inches is:

$$l = \frac{5906}{f} \qquad (6\text{-}3)$$

The value of f is still in megaHertz. Note that without the correction factor, reference is to the electrical length of the antenna rather than its actual physical length. End effects, or capacitance effects at the ends of the antenna, require that we reduce the actual length of the antenna. A 4 to 6 percent reduction (k ranges between 0.96 and 0.94) is typical.

To find the length of a half-wave antenna in **meters**:

$$l = 1/2 \times \frac{3 \times 10^8}{f} \qquad (6\text{-}4)$$

The length, l, is in meters. The frequency, f, is in Hertz.

FULL WAVE ANTENNAS

For a full-wave antenna or for an antenna having a multiple amount of half waves the formula for antenna length is somewhat modified because of the lesser influence of end effects.

$$l = \frac{492 \ (n - 0.05)}{f} \qquad (6\text{-}5)$$

l is the length in feet; f the frequency in megaHertz; n is the number of half wave sections comprising the antenna. For a full-wave antenna, n would have a value of 2.

The formula shown above and the one given earlier for a half-wave antenna indicate that an antenna operated on some harmonic of its fundamental frequency will not be cut exactly right for that harmonic.

ANTENNA IMPEDANCE

The impedance of an antenna is the ratio of the voltage to the current—that is, $Z = E/I$. Fig. 6-1 shows the relationship between the current and the voltage along the length of a half-wave antenna. The current is maximum at the center and zero at the ends. The voltage is zero at the center and maximum at the ends. This means that the impedance is not constant along the length of antenna but varies from a maximum at the ends (maximum voltage, minimum current) to a minimum at the center.

The drawing in Fig. 6-1 shows that the impedance at the center should be zero. Practically, the impedance is about 72 ohms.

RADIATION RESISTANCE

What is this impedance? Since we try to cut our antenna length so that the antenna will be resonant at the transmission frequency,

185

we can consider this impedance as resistive—that is, it contains no reactive component such as inductance or capacitance. The ohmic

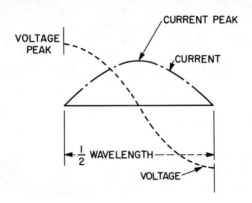

Fig. 6-1. Voltage and current distribution along the length of a half-wave antenna. The impedance is minimum at the center; maximum along the ends.

or DC resistance of the antenna is usually very small in comparison with the impedance and so may be disregarded.

Ignoring the ohmic resistance, then, the impedance may be regarded as the radiation resistance of the antenna.

RADIATED POWER

For the power (P_r) in watts radiated by the antenna, we have:

$$P_r = I_a{}^2 \times R_r \qquad (6\text{-}6)$$

Ia is the antenna current, in amperes and Rr is the radiation resistance in ohms.

POWER GAIN

The field strength of an antenna is directly related to the amount of current flowing in it. A comparison between a standard antenna and the antenna being used is called the power gain and is given in **db**. The standard or comparison antenna has the same height, length and polarization (that is, vertical or horizontal) as the antenna being tested. Thus, if the gain of the antenna being tested has a field intensity in microvolts per meter that is three times that of a standard antenna, the antenna gain is:

$$db = 20 \log \frac{3}{1}$$

the log of 3 is 0.4771

$$db = 20 \times 0.4771 = 9.5$$

A standard antenna isn't required for making antenna comparisons to determine antenna gain. Instead, a reference field strength may be used. Thus, a reference could be 186 microvolts per meter at a distance of 1 mile for a transmitter input of 1 kw. The antenna under test is then situated a similar distance with the same amount of power input to its transmitter. The db gain of the antenna being tested utilizes the same formula except that the ratio is a comparison with field strength. If the antenna has a field strength of 900 microvolts per meter compared to the standard of 186 microvolts per meter, the db gain of the antenna is:

$$db = 20 \log \frac{900}{186} = 20 \log 4.8378$$

$$= 20 \times 0.68458 = 13.6916 \, db$$

However, as long as a reference field strength is known, the transmitter for the antenna being tested need not have the same input power as the reference antenna. Thus, if the transmitter has an input of 2 kw compared to 1 kw for the reference transmitter, the reference field becomes $\sqrt{2}\ / 1$ multiplied by the reference field strength.

If the reference field for 1 kw input is 186 uv/m, it will be $\sqrt{2}\ /1$ x 186 = 263 uv for a 2 kw input.

Example: Reference field strength is 186 uv/m at a distance of 1 mile for an input of 1 kw. What is the gain of an antenna set up under identical physical conditions but whose input is 2 kw? The test antenna shows a field strength of 1100 microvolts/meter.

$$\sqrt{\frac{2}{1}} \times 186 = 1.414 \times 186 = 263\text{u v} / \text{meter}$$

$$\text{antenna gain} = 20 \log \frac{1100}{263} = 20 \log 4.1825$$

$$= 20 \log \times 0.62143 = 12.4286 \text{ db}$$

The elevation of an antenna (height above ground) has a pronounced effect on its gain, as shown in the graph, Fig. 6-2.

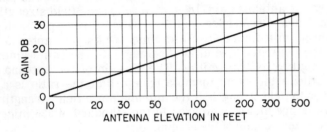

Fig. 6-2. Antenna gain is increased with height.

WAVE ANGLE

The angle between the conducting element of an antenna and the axis of any main lobe is the wave angle, ϕ (Fig. 6-3).

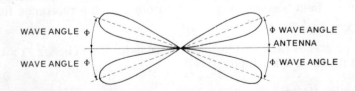

Fig. 6-3. Determination of the wave angle of an antenna.

TRANSMISSION LINES

The purpose of a transmission line is to deliver maximum power from the transmitter to the antenna. Ideally, such a line would have no losses (that is, would consume no power), would match the impedance of the output tank of the transmitter to the impedance of the antenna; would be perfectly "flat"—that is, would have no reflections along its length.

The impedance of a transmission line, known as surge or characteristic impedance, is a function of the inductance and capacitance of the line and may be approximately represented by:

$$Z = \sqrt{L/C} \qquad (6\text{-}7)$$

There is a certain amount of DC resistance in the transmission line but this is generally negligible. The inductance and capacitance of the line depends on the amount of spacing between the wires of the line and the size of the wires (Fig. 6-4).

Thus, the impedance is determined by the conductor size and spacing as shown in Fig. 6-4.

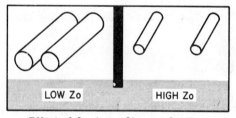

Effect of Conductor Size and Spacing

Fig. 6-4. Impedance of a transmission line is controlled by spacing and wire thickness.

TWO-WIRE OPEN TRANSMISSION LINE

Where the impedance of the transmission line matches that of the antenna, energy delivered by the line is absorbed by the load (the antenna). No energy, under these conditions, is reflected to the source. For a two-wire, open line (Fig. 6-5) using air insulation:

$$Z = 276 \log \frac{s}{r} \qquad (6\text{-}8)$$

Reference here (and in other formulas, unless otherwise stated, is

189

to common logs—base 10). **Z** is the surge impedance (in ohms); **s** is the spacing between the wire centers in inches and **r** is the radius of the wire (in inches). (This formula is not applicable to a two-wire line using a continuous solid dielectric along the entire length of the transmission line as a means of separating the two wires.)

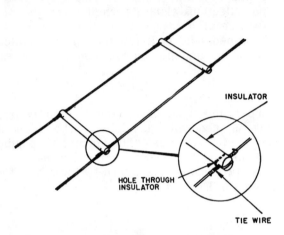

Fig. 6-5. Two-wire open transmission line.

ATTENUATION

The attenuation of a line is directly proportional to the DC resistance of the line and inversely proportional to the impedance. Obviously, the lower the resistance of the line, the smaller will be the power losses.

$$A = 4.35 \frac{R}{Z} \qquad (6\text{-}9)$$

A is the attenuation in **db** (per 100 feet of transmission line); **R** is the resistance in ohms (per 100 feet) and **Z** is the surge impedance (in ohms).

CONCENTRIC TRANSMISSION LINE

A concentric transmission line (also known as a coaxial line) has a center conductor, either solid or stranded wire. The outer conductor completely surrounds the center conductor and is concentric to it. The space between the two conductors may be any insulator, but is usually air or some form of polyethylene dielectric. The impedance:

$$Z = 138 \log \frac{D}{d} \qquad (6\text{-}10)$$

Z is the characteristic impedance, in ohms; D is the inside diameter of the outside conductor, in inches; d is the outside diameter of the inside conductor in inches.

The above formula can be used where the substance in the space between the two conductors has a dielectric constant, k, of 1. For dry air, k = 1. When k ≠ 1, the formula becomes:

$$Z = \frac{138}{\sqrt{k}} \log \frac{D}{d}$$

The dielectric constant for various materials is:

Material	k
dry air	1.
glass	4.2
mica	5.5
porcelain	5.5
pure water	81.
polystyrene	2.5

k will vary depending on substance purity, temperature, moisture in the substance and the EMF across it. The values given in the above table are approximations.

RESISTANCE OF COAXIAL TRANSMISSION LINE

$$R = 0.1 \left(\frac{1}{d} + \frac{1}{D} \right) \sqrt{f} \qquad (6\text{-}11)$$

R is the resistance, in ohms, per 100 feet of line; f is the frequency in megaHertz; d is the outside diameter of the inside conductor, in inches; D is the inside diameter of the outside conductor, in inches.

RESISTANCE OF OPEN TWO-WIRE COPPER LINE

$$R = \frac{\sqrt{f}}{5 \times d} \qquad (6\text{-}12)$$

R is the resistance, in ohms, per 100 feet of line; f is the frequency in megaHertz; d is the diameter of the copper line, in inches.

STANDING WAVE RATIO (SWR)

The SWR of a transmission line is an excellent indicator of the effectiveness of the impedance match between the transmission line and the antenna. The SWR is the ratio of the maximum to the minimum current along the length of the transmission line, or the ratio of the maximum to the minimum voltage. When the line is absolutely matched the SWR is unity. In other words, we get unity SWR when there is no variation in voltage or current along the transmission line. The greater the number representing SWR, the larger is the mismatch. Also, I^2R losses increase with increasing SWR.

For a purely resistive load:

$$SWR = \frac{Z_r}{Z_o} \qquad (6\text{-}13)$$

Z_0 is the characteristic impedance of the transmission line; Z_r is the impedance of the load.

SWR is optimum when Z_r is equal to Z_0. It is unimportant as to which of these terms is in the numerator. Since SWR cannot be a decimal, it is advisable to put the larger of the two numbers in the numerator.

CHARACTERISTIC IMPEDANCE

Characteristic impedance can be determined in a number of ways:

$$Z_0 = \sqrt{\frac{R + j\,2\pi f\,L}{G + j\,2\pi f\,C}} \qquad (6\text{-}14)$$

The numerator $(R + j2\pi f L)$ represents the series impedance while the denominator $(G + j2\pi f C)$ is the shunt conductance.

MATCHING IMPEDANCES

We can match two different values of impedances by connecting them with a quarter-wave section of transmission line, provided the matching section has an impedance equal to the square root of the two impedances to be matched. In terms of a formula, we have:

$$Z_o = \sqrt{Z1 \times Z2} \qquad (6\text{-}15)$$

(text continues on p. 205)

TABLE OF ANTENNA TYPES

Type of Antenna	Description	Application
PARABOLIC REFLECTOR ANTENNAS	A radiator placed at the focus of a parabola which forms a reflecting surface. Variations in the shape of the parabola provide changes in the shape of the beam produced.	Used for radar.
COSECANT-SQUARED REFLECTOR	A reflector shaped to produce a beam pattern in which signal strength is proportional to the square of the cosecant of the angle between the horizontal and the line to the target.	Used for surface search by airborne radar sets.
HORN ANTENNAS	Consists of a waveguide with its mouth flared into a horn or funnel-like shape. The horn usually radiates into a reflector to provide the required beam shape.	Widely used for radar applications.

TABLE OF ANTENNA TYPES—Continued

Type of Antenna	Description	Application
END-FED HERTZ (Zepp)	Half wavelength voltage-fed radiator fed at one end with tuned, open-wire feeders. (Fig. 6-6).	For receiving and transmitting in the 1.6- to 30-MHz range. Most useful for multiband operation where space is limited. Use for fixed-station installations.
CENTER-FED HERTZ (tuned doublet or center-fed Zepp)	A center-fed, half-wave doublet usually employing spaced feeders. Current fed on fundamental and voltage fed on all even harmonics. (Fig. 6-7)	For receiving and transmitting in the 1.6- to 30-MHz range. Can be used on any frequency if the system as a whole can be tuned to that frequency.
FUCHS ANTENNA	Long-wire, voltage-fed radiator an even number of quarter waves long. One end of radiator brought directly to the transmitter or tuning unit without using a transmission line.	For transmitting and receiving on any frequency where simplicity and convenience are desired.
CORNER REFLECTOR	A half-wave radiator with two large metal sheets or screws arranged so their surfaces meet at an angle whose apex lies behind the radiator.	Used in the VHF and UHF ranges to provide directivity in the plane which bisects the angle formed by the reflector.

TABLE OF ANTENNA TYPES—Continued

Type of Antenna	Description	Application
MARCONI	A vertical radiator approximately one-quarter wavelength long at operating frequency. One end is grounded or worked against ground. May be fed at or near base with low-impedance line. Electrical length may be increased by using loading coil in series with base or near center of radiator or by using capacitive loading at the top. The length, **L**, in feet can be computed by: $L = \frac{234}{f}$ f is in megahertz. **L** is the overall length, in feet, from the top of the antenna to the point where it connects to ground or counterpoise. The total power dissipated in and radiated from a Marconi antenna can be calculated by: $P_t = I^2 (R_g + R_r)$ **I** is the antenna current measured at the antenna base, **R_r** is the radiation resistance and **R_g** is the ground resistance. The useful radiated power is the difference between the total power consumed and the power lost in the ground resistance. Radiated power, **P_r** is: $P_r = P_t - I^2 \times R_g$ Fig. 6-8 shows the current and voltage waveforms of a Marconi.	Widely used for medium- and low-frequency receiving and transmitting where vertical polarization is desirable.

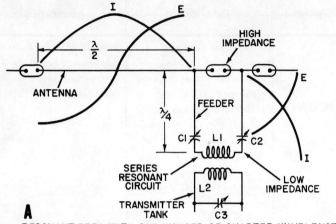

A

RESONANT FEED WITH ODD NUMBER OF QUARTER WAVELENGTHS

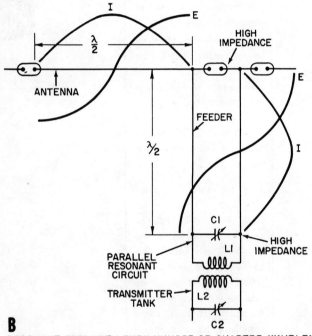

B

RESONANT FEED WITH EVEN NUMBER OF QUARTER WAVELENGTHS

Fig. 6-6. Methods of feeding an end-fed half-wave Hertz.

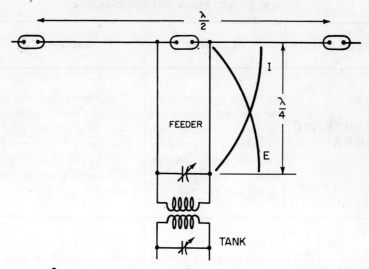

A ODD NUMBER OF QUARTER-WAVELENGTHS

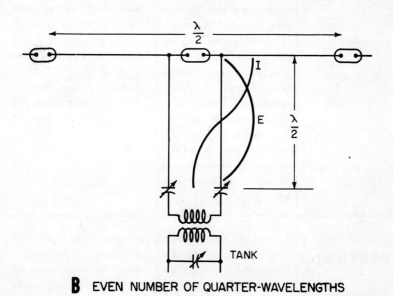

B EVEN NUMBER OF QUARTER-WAVELENGTHS

Fig. 6-7. Methods of feeding a center-fed half-wave Hertz.

TABLE OF ANTENNA TYPES—Continued

Type of Antenna	Description	Application
PARASITIC ARRAY	Consists of a radiator with a reflector behind and/or one or more directors in front. Produces a unidirectional radiation pattern. May be either vertically or horizontally polarized.	Used to develop high gain in one direction with little or no radiation or pickup in other directions. Used on all frequencies where these characteristics are desired and space is available.
RHOMBIC ANTENNA	A system consisting of four long-wire radiators arranged in the form of a diamond and fed at one end. If the corner opposite the feed point is open, response is bidirectional in a line running through these two corners. If the open end is terminated with the proper resistance, response is unidirectional in the direction of the terminated end. Gain may vary from 20 to 40 times that of a dipole, depending on the number of wavelengths in each leg.	Widely used where high gain and directivity is required. Can be used over a wide range of frequencies and is particularly useful when each leg is two or more wavelengths long on lowest frequency. Angle of radiation is lowered and vertical directivity narrowed by increasing length of legs and/or increasing operating frequency.
VERTICAL J	A one-half wavelength vertical radiator fed at the bottom through a quarter-wave matching stub. It is omnidirectional, produces vertical polarization, and can be fed conveniently from a wide range of feed-line impedances.	Practical for use at frequencies above about 7 MHz. Normally used for fixed-frequency applications because of its extreme sensitivity to frequency changes. Efficiency falls off as frequency is raised.

Type of Antenna	Description	Application
COAXIAL ANTENNA (sleeve antenna)	Vertical radiator one-half wavelength long. Upper half consists of a relatively thin radiator and the bottom half a large diameter cylinder. Fed at the center from coaxial cable of 70 to 120 ohms.	Practical for frequencies above about 7 MHz. Normally used for fixed frequency applications. Changes in frequency require that the antenna be retuned by varying length of the two halves of the radiator. Practical for operation up to about 100 MHz.
GROUND-PLANE ANTENNA	Omnidirectional quarter-wave vertical radiator mounted above a horizontal reflecting surface. Its impedance is approximately 36 ohms or less.	Practical for producing vertically polarized waves at frequencies above about 7 MHz and frequently used at frequencies as high as 300 MHz.
CROW-FOOT ANTENNA	A low-frequency antenna consisting of comparatively short vertical radiator with a 3-wire V-shaped flat top and a counterpoise having the same shape and size as the flat top. (Fig. 6-9)	Normally used where it is impractical to erect a quarter-wave vertical radiator. Used most frequently for reception and transmission in the 200 to 500 kHz range.

TABLE OF ANTENNA TYPES—Continued

Type of Antenna	Description	Application
TURNSTILE ANTENNA	An omnidirectional, horizontally polarized antenna consisting of two half-wave radiators mounted at right angles to each other in the same horizontal plane. They are fed with equal currents 90 degrees out of phase. Gain is increased by stacking. Dipoles may be simple, folded, or special broadband types.	Normally used for transmission and reception of FM and television broadcast signals.
SKIN ANTENNAS	Usually consist of an insulated section of the skin of an aircraft. Its radiation pattern varies with frequency, size of the radiating section, and position of the radiator on the aircraft.	Used for VHF and UHF reception and transmission in high-speed aircraft. Often used to replace fixed-wire antennas used in the 2 to 2.5 MHz range.
ILAS ANTENNAS	Localizer antennas are of several different types. One type consists of two or more square loops. Glide path is usually produced by two stacked antennas. The lower antenna is usually a horizontal loop bisected by a metal screen and supported about 6 feet off the ground. The upper antenna is a V-shaped dipole radiator with a parasitic element. Marker beacon antennas may consist of colinear dipoles or arrays.	Used to enable pilots to locate the airport and to land the plane on the desired runway when weather conditions would prohibit a landing under visual flight reference.

TABLE OF ANTENNA TYPES—Continued

Type of Antenna	Description	Application
OMNI-RANGE (VOR)	Consists of two pairs of square-loop radiators surrounding a single square-loop radiator.	Use to provide navigation signals for aircraft in all directions from the range station.
ADCOCK ANTENNA	Consists of vertical radiators which produce bidirectional vertically polarized radiation.	Used in low-frequency radio ranges and for direction finding.
LOOP ANTENNAS	A loop of wire consisting of one or more turns arranged in the shape of a square, circle, or other convenient form. It produces a bidirectional pattern along the plane of the loop.	Normally used for direction-finding applications, particularly in ships and aircraft.
STUB MAST	A quarter-wave vertical radiator consisting of a metal sheath over a hard-wood supporting mast. Fed with 50-ohm line with the outer conductor connected to a large metal ground surface.	Used for wide-band reception and transmission of frequencies above 100 MHz. Normally used in aircraft installations.

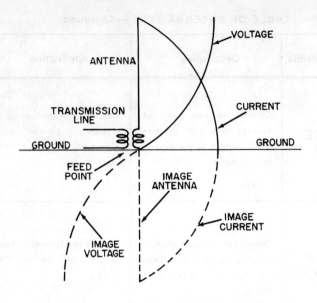

Fig. 6-8. Current and voltage distribution of a Marconi.

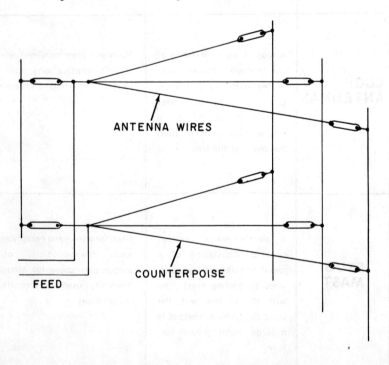

Fig. 6-9. Arrangement of a crow-foot antenna.

Type of Antenna	Description	Application
HALF RHOMBIC (inverted V or tilted wire)	A two-wire antenna with the legs in a vertical plane and in the shape of an inverted V. Directivity is in the plane of the legs. Feeding one end and leaving the other open results in bidirectivity. Terminating the free end with a suitable resistor produces unidirectional radiation in the direction of the termination. Gain and angle between legs depend on frequency and the number of wavelengths in each leg.	Used to provide high gain. Used where low angle of radiation is desirable. Usable over a wide frequency range. Bandwidth is greatest for terminated type. Angle of radiation is lowered as leg length and/or operating frequency is increased.
BEVERAGE ANTENNA	A directional long-wire horizontal antenna, two or more wavelengths long. The end nearest the distant receiving station is terminated with a 500-ohm resistor connected to a good counterpoise. The antenna, generally suspended 10 to 20 feet above ground, is non-resonant.	Used for transmitting and receiving vertically polarized waves. Often used for long-wave transoceanic broadcasts. Its input impedance is fairly constant so it can be used over a wide frequency range. Useful for frequencies between 300 kHz and 3 MHz. Highly suitable for use over dry, rocky soil. Never use over salt marshes or water.
FOLDED DIPOLE	A simple center-fed dipole with a second half-wave conductor connected across its ends. Spacing between the conductors is a very small fraction of a wavelength.	Its impedance is higher than that of a simple dipole. Applications same as simple dipole. Often used in parasitic arrays to raise the feedpoint impedance to a value which can be conveniently matched to transmission line.

TABLE OF ANTENNA TYPES—Continued

Type of Antenna	Description	Application
V ANTENNA	Bidirectional antenna made of two long-wire antennas in the form of a V and fed 180 degrees out of phase at its apex (points A - C in Fig. 6-3E). The V antenna is a combination of two long-wire antennas. As the length is increased, more power is concentrated near the axis of the wire. The length of each leg of a V antenna can be found by: $$L = \frac{492\,(N - 0.05)}{f}$$ **N** is the number of half wavelengths in each leg, and **f** is the frequency in megahertz. More gain can be obtained by stacking a second V, one-half wavelength above the first.	Used in military and commercial applications.

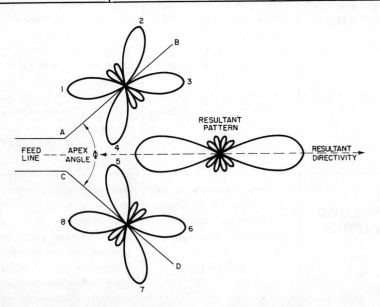

Fig. 6-10. Lobes of a V antenna.

VELOCITY FACTOR

The velocity of a wave along a conductor, such as a transmission line, is not the same as the velocity of that wave in free space. The ratio of the two (actual velocity vs velocity in space) is known as the velocity factor. Obviously, velocity factor must always be less than 1, and, in typical lines varies from 0.6 to 0.97.

Type of Line	Velocity factor (V)
Two-wire open line (wire with air dielectric)	0.975
Parallel tubing (air dielectric)	0.95
Coaxial line (air dielectric)	0.85
Coaxial line (solid plastic dielectric)	0.66
Two-wire line (wire with plastic dielectric)	0.68-0.82
Twisted-pair line (rubber dielectric)	0.56-0.65

LENGTH OF TRANSMISSION LINE

Specification of the length of a transmission line in terms of quarter wave, half wave, etc. is a reference to electrical, not physical length. The physical length of a transmission line can be determined from:

$$L = \frac{984}{f} \times V \qquad (6\text{-}16)$$

L is the length of the transmission line, in feet; f the frequency in megaHertz and V is the velocity factor.

The above formula is for a full wavelength long. For a half wavelength:

$$L = \frac{492}{f} \times V$$

and for a quarter wavelength:

$$L = \frac{246}{f} \times V$$

Chapter 7

Measurements

While many types of instruments are used in electronics, one of the most popular is the d'Arsonval or moving-coil meter. Basically a current-measuring device, it can be easily adapted for the measurement of voltage and resistance.

HOW TO DETERMINE THE RESISTANCE OF A d'ARSONVAL METER MOVEMENT

The d'Arsonval meter movement is shown as M in Fig. 7-1. Adjust potentiometer R1 for full scale deflection of the meter pointer, with R2 disconnected. Then connect R2 in parallel with M and adjust R2 until the meter pointer is at half scale. The scale selected must be linear. Disconnect R2 and measure its resistance across a bridge. The slide arm of R2 must not be moved during this test. The value of R2 is the resistance of the moving coil of the meter.

The values of R1 and R2 will depend on meter sensitivity and the value of E. Assume M requires 1 ma for full scale when $E = 1$ volt. $R = E/I = 1/0.001 = 1,000$ ohms. To limit I to 1 ma, the sum of R1 plus the meter resistance must equal 1,000 ohms. If R1 = 1,000 ohms it will be close to the end of its range. R1 having a value of 2,000 ohms will be at about center setting.

The value of R2 will be small, possibly less than 10 ohms. It will be necessary to find its value experimentally. If meter M is a 1 ma movement, when R2 is adjusted for half-scale setting, ½ ma will

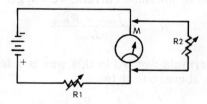

Fig. 7-1. Technique for measuring meter resistance.

207

flow through **M** and ½ ma through **R2**. Therefore, at this adjustment, **R2 = R_m**.

SHUNT RESISTANCE

The range of a current-measuring meter—microammeter, milliammeter or ammeter—can easily be extended by shunting the meter (Fig. 7-2) so that a large proportion of the current to be measured is bypassed around the meter.

$$R = \frac{R_m}{n - 1} \tag{7-1}$$

R is the value of shunt resistance; **R_m** the internal resistance of the meter, **n** is the multiplication factor of the original scale.

Since the shunt and the meter are in parallel, the same voltage drop must appear across both. That is:

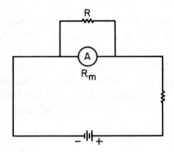

Fig. 7-2. The range of an ammeter can be extended by using shunts.

$$E_{\text{shunt}} = E_{\text{meter}}$$

Considering this voltage as an **IR** drop, we can express the same thought as:

$$I_{\text{shunt}} \times R_{\text{shunt}} = I_{\text{meter}} \times R_{\text{meter}}$$

Dividing both sides by the shunt current, we will get:

$$R_{\text{shunt}} = \frac{I_{\text{meter}} \times R_{\text{meter}}}{I_{\text{shunt}}}$$

And, because a formula worded in this way is a bit awkward, we can conveniently abbreviate it to:

$$R = \frac{I_m \times R_m}{I_{sh}} \tag{7-2}$$

MULTIPLIER RESISTANCE

Both shunts and multipliers are resistors. The nature of a shunt is such that it must carry a large current load, hence its resistance value is low. A shunt, as its name implies, is put in parallel with the meter. A multiplier is put in series with it. Multipliers have large values of resistance compared to shunts. The purpose of a shunt is to extend the current-reading range of the meter. That of the multiplier (Fig. 7-3) is to permit the use of the ammeter as a voltage measuring device.

$$R = R_m \ (n - 1) \qquad (7\text{-}3)$$

R is the value of multiplier resistance; R_m is the total resistance of the meter; and n is the multiplication factor (factor by which the scale reading is to be multiplied).

The required value of multiplier for a milliammeter can easily be found from:

$$R = \frac{1{,}000 \times E}{I}$$

I represents the full scale current reading of the meter (in milliamperes); E is the full-scale voltage-reading that is required.

Alternatively, the multiplying value of a resistor can be found from:

$$M = \frac{R + R_m}{R_m} \qquad (7\text{-}4)$$

Here M is the multiplication that will result from using the resistor; R is the resistance of the multiplier resistor, and R_m is the resistance of the meter. All resistance values are in ohms.

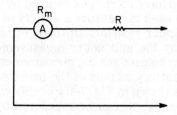

Fig. 7-3. Current-reading meter is changed to voltmeter by using series multiplier.

METER SENSITIVITY

The sensitivity of a meter is the load, or amount of current it draws from a source voltage, for full scale deflection of the meter pointer. The smaller the amount of current required by the meter for full-scale deflection the greater the sensitivity of the meter. To determine meter sensitivity:

$$\text{meter sensitivity} = \frac{\text{meter resistance} + \text{multiplier resistance}}{\text{full scale reading in volts}}$$

In this formula we have resistance (ohms) divided by volts, hence the sensitivity of a meter is in terms of ohms/volt. If the resistance of a meter is 50 ohms and its multiplier is 149,950 ohms, the total resistance is 50 + 149,950 = 150,000 ohms. If the full scale reading is 150 volts:

$$\text{meter sensitivity} = \frac{150,000 \text{ ohms}}{150 \text{ volts}} = 1,000 \text{ ohms per volt}$$

The current drawn by such a meter movement can be calculated using Ohm's law:

$$I = \frac{E}{R} = \frac{150}{150,000} = \frac{1}{1,000} = 0.001 \text{ ampere} = 1 \text{ milliampere}$$

One milliampere of current through this meter movement will produce full scale deflection. A more sensitive meter having a sensitivity of 20,000 ohms per volt, will have a current requirement of:

$$I = \frac{E}{R} = \frac{1}{20,000} = 0.00005 \text{ ampere} = 50 \text{ microamperes}$$

RESISTANCE MEASUREMENTS

An ammeter can have its range extended by using one or more shunts and it can be used to measure a variety of voltages by using a selection of multiplier resistors. In both instances, the voltage source is supplied by the unit under measurement.

An ammeter can be used for the measurement of resistance by including a cell or battery as part of the instrument. The simplest type of ohmmeter is shown in Fig. 7-4. For this circuit, the value of the unknown resistance, R, can be measured by:

$$R = \frac{R_m \times e}{E} - R_m \qquad (7\text{-}5)$$

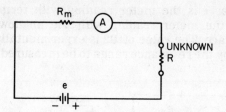

Fig. 7-4. Current-reading meter can be used for the measurement of resistance.

R is the unknown whose value is being checked; e is the voltage supplied by the battery; R_m is the resistance of the meter and E is the voltage indicated by the meter with R connected.

The circuit is not suited for the measurement of low values of resistance.

Fig. 7-5 shows another ohmmeter circuit. In this arrangement, the formula for finding the value of the unknown resistor is:

$$R = \frac{R_m \times I2}{I1 - I2}$$ (7-6)

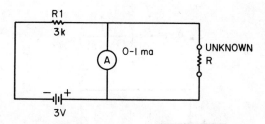

Fig. 7-5. Simple ohmmeter circuit. The resistance to be measured is in shunt with the milliammeter.

If a meter having a full-scale deflection of 1 milliampere is used, then the battery can be 3 volts and R1 can be 3,000 ohms.

I1 is the open circuit current—that is, with the unknown resistor disconnected. I2 is the current with the unknown resistor in place.

For use with a higher sensitivity meter, the circuit of Fig. 7-6 is preferable.

$$R = \frac{R2 \times e}{E} - R2$$ (7-7)

In this formula, **e** is the meter reading with terminals 1 and 2 shorted; **E** is the meter reading with the unknown resistor **R**, connected in place. The value of **R2** is experimentally selected and is determined by the resistance range to be measured.

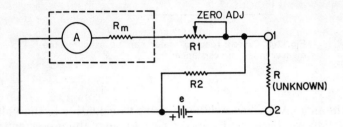

Fig. 7-6. More elaborate ohmmeter circuit using meter having a higher sensitivity.

SHUNT OHMMETER FOR LOW RESISTANCE MEASUREMENTS

The circuit in Fig. 7-7 has its zero adjust control in series with the ohmmeter voltage source. This series combination is shunted across the meter. The functioning of the meter is based on this formula:

$$R_x = R_m \left(\frac{I1}{I2 - I1} \right)$$

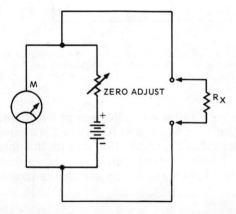

Fig. 7-7. Shunt ohmmeter for low resistance measurements.

R_X is the small-value unknown resistor being checked; R_m is the resistance of the moving coil of the d'Arsonval meter; I1 is the current with R_X connected; I2 is the current with R_X disconnected. In use the zero adjust control is set for full-scale deflection with R_X disconnected.

This circuit can also be used for measuring the resistance of a d'Arsonval meter movement. Set the zero-adjust control for full-scale deflection. Use a small-value potentiometer for R_X (10 ohms or less) and adjust it until pointer of M is at halfway point on linear scale. Remove the potentiometer and measure its resistance on a bridge. The value is the resistance of the moving coil of the meter.

BRIDGES

Bridges are resistive networks, or networks consisting of combinations of resistance, capacitance and inductance. Bridge circuits are used for making more precise measurements of resistance than is possible with an ohmmeter. Bridge circuits are also used for making measurements of inductance and capacitance.

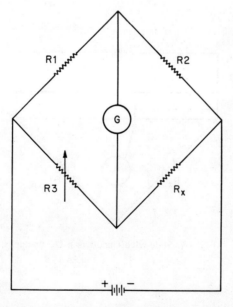

Fig. 7-8. When the Wheatstone bridge is balanced, the voltage across the galvanometer is zero.

WHEATSTONE BRIDGE

Bridges can be conveniently arranged into two major groups: those using DC as the source voltage and those using AC. A greater number of bridges, by far, use AC.

Probably the best known of all DC bridges is the Wheatstone, shown in Fig. 7-8. The indicating meter is a galvanometer. R3 is adjusted until the galvanometer (a zero-center reading type) is at zero. The value of the unknown is then read from a scale or a calibrated dial. In Fig. 7-8, R3 is a calibrated resistor.

$$R_x = R3 \times \frac{R2}{R1} \qquad (7\text{-}8)$$

SLIDE WIRE BRIDGE

The slide-wire bridge (Fig. 7-9) makes use of a resistance on which is mounted a slider. The slider is adjusted until the galvanometer reads zero. The value of the unknown resistance is then computed by:

$$R_x = \frac{l}{L - l} \times R1 \qquad (7\text{-}9)$$

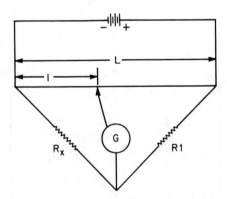

Fig. 7-9. Slide-wire circuit is a DC bridge.

THE SCOPE

The scope can be used for the measurement of spot frequencies by using the test setup shown in Fig. 7-10. The unknown frequency, in

214

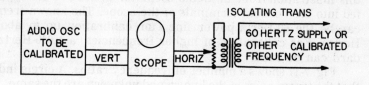

Fig. 7-10. Scope setup for the calibration of unknown frequencies.

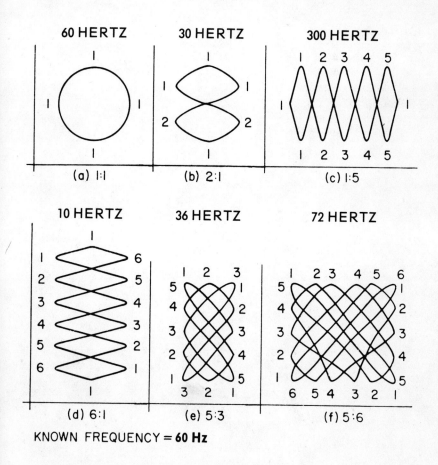

KNOWN FREQUENCY = **60 Hz**

Fig. 7-11. Lissajous patterns obtained by comparing 60 Hertz with various other frequencies.

this illustration from an audio oscillator in need of calibration, is fed into the vertical terminals of the scope. The known frequency can be the 60-Hertz power line (for calibration up to about 500 Hertz). For calibration of higher frequencies, a 1,000-Hertz standard can be used.

Fig. 7-11 shows a number of frequency ratios. A circle indicates that the frequencies of the known and unknown are the same.

To calculate the frequency ratio, count all the loops along the horizontal and vertical edges. To find the ratio, divide the number of vertical edge loops by the number of horizontal edge loops. This will give you the ratio of the standard to the unknown frequency. Thus, in Fig. 7-11B, the unknown frequency is 30 Hz.

Chapter 8

Tables and Data

Conversion Factors

To Change			To Change Back		
Units	Multiplied by	Yields	Units	Multiplied by	Yields
LENGTH			*LENGTH*		
Mils	.0254	Mm.	Mm.	39.37	Mils
Mils	.001	In.	In.	1,000.	Mils
Mm.	.03937	In.	In.	25.4	Mm.
Cm.	.3937	In.	In.	2.54	Cm.
Cm.	.03281	Ft.	Ft.	30.48	Cm.
In.	.0254	M.	M.	39.37	In.
Ft.	.3048	M.	M.	3.2808	Ft.
Yds.	.9144	M.	M.	1.0936	Yds.
Kilometer	.6214	Miles	Miles	1.6093	Kilometer
AREA			*AREA*		
Cir. Mils	.0000007854	Sq. In.	Sq. In.	1,273,240.	Cir. Mils
Cir. Mils	.7854	Sq. Mils	Sq. Mils	1.2732	Cir. Mils
Cir. Mils	.0005066	Sq. Mm.	Sq. Mm.	1,973.51	Cir. Mils
Sq. Mm.	.00155	Sq. In.	Sq. In.	645.16	Sq. Mm.
Sq. Mils	.000001	Sq. In.	Sq. In.	1,000,000.	Sq. Mils
Sq. Cm.	.155	Sq. In.	Sq. In.	6.4516	Sq. Cm.
Sq. Ft.	.0929	Sq. M.	Sq. M.	10.764	Sq. Ft.
VOLUME			*VOLUME*		
Cu. In.	.01639	Liters	Liters	61.023	Cu. In.
Cu. In.	.004329	Gals.	Gals.	231.	Cu. In.
Liters	.26417	Gals.	Gals.	3.7854	Liters
Cu. Cm.	.06102	Cu. In.	Cu. In.	16.387	Cu. Cm.
Cu. Cm.	.000264	Gal.	Gal.	3,785.4	Cu. Cm.
POWER			*POWER*		
Ft.-Lbs. per Min.	.0000303	H.P.	H.P.	33,000.	Ft.-Lbs. per Min.
Ft.-Lbs. per Sec.	.001818	H.P.	H.P.	550.	Ft.Lbs. per Min.
Ft.-Lbs. per Min.	.0226	Watts	Watts	44.25	Ft.-Lbs. per Min.
Ft.-Lbs. per Sec.	1.356	Watts	Watts	.7373	Ft.-Lbs. per Sec.
Watts	.001341	H.P.	H.P.	746.	Watts
B.T.U. per Hr.	.000393	H.P.	H.P.	2,545.	B.T.U. per Hr.

Conversion Factors

To Change			To Change Back		
ENERGY			**ENERGY**		
Ergs	.0000001	Joules	Joules	10,000,000.	Ergs
Joules	.2388	Gram-Calories	Gram-Calories	4.186	Joules
Joules	.10198	Kg.-M.	Kg.-M.	9.8117	Joules
Joules	.7375	Ft.-Lbs.	Ft.-Lbs.	1.356	Joules
Ft.-Lbs.	.1383	Kg.-M.	Kg.-M.	7.233	Ft.-Lbs.
Gram-Calories	.003968	B.T.U.	B.T.U.	252.	Gram-Calories
Joules	.000947	B.T.U.	B.T.U.	1,055.	Joules
Ft.-Lbs.	.001285	B.T.U.	B.T.U.	778.	Ft.-Lbs.
B.T.U.	.293	Watt-Hrs.	Watt-Hrs.	3.416	B.T.U.
WEIGHTS			**WEIGHTS**		
Lbs. (Avdp.)	.4536	Kgs.	Kgs.	2.2046	Lbs. (Avdp.)
Oz. (Avdp.)	.0625	Lbs. (Avdp.)	Lbs. (Avdp.)	16.	Oz. (Avdp.)
Oz. (Troy)	.0833	Lbs. (Troy)	Lbs. (Troy)	12.	Oz. (Troy)
Oz. (Avdp.)	.9115	Oz. (Troy)	Oz. (Troy)	1.097	Oz. (Avdp.)
Lbs. (Troy)	.82286	Lbs. (Avdp.)	Lbs. (Avdp.)	1.2153	Lbs. (Troy)
Oz. (Avdp.)	.0759	Lbs. (Troy)	Lbs. (Troy)	13.166	Oz. (Avdp.)
Oz. (Troy)	.0686	Lbs. (Avdp.)	Lbs. (Avdp.)	14.58	Oz. (Troy)
Grains	.00209	Oz. (Troy)	Oz. (Troy)	480.	Grains
Grains	.002285	Oz. (Avdp.)	Oz. (Avdp.)	437.5	Grains
Milligrams	.005	Carats	Carats	200.	Milligrams
MISCELLANEOUS			**MISCELLANEOUS**		
Ohms per Ft.	.3048	Ohms per Meter	Ohms per Meter	3.2808	Ohms per Ft.
Ohms per Kilometer	.3048	Ohms per 1000 Ft.	Ohms per 1000 Ft.	3.2808	Ohms per Kilometer
Ohms per Kilometer	.9144	Ohms per 1000 Yds.	Ohms per 1000 Yds.	1.0936	Ohms per Kilometer
Kg. per Kilometer	.6719	Lbs. per 1000 Ft.	Lbs. per 1000 Ft.	1.488	Kg. per Kilometer
Lbs. per 1000 Yds.	.4960	Kg. per Kilometer	Kg. per Kilometer	2.016	Lbs. per 1000 Yds.

Equivalents

Unit	Equivalents	Unit	Equivalents
1 H.P.	746 Watts	1 Kw.	1,000 Joules per Sec.
1 H.P.	0.746 Kw.	1 Kw.	1.34 H.P.
1 H.P.	33,000 Ft.-Lbs. per Min.	1 Kw.	44,250 Ft.-Lbs. per Min.
1 H.P.	550 Ft.-Lbs. per Sec.	1 Kw.	737.3 Ft.-Lbs. per Sec.
1 H.P.	2,545 B.T.U. per Hr.	1 Kw.	3,412 B.T.U. per Hr.
1 H.P.	0.175 Lbs. Carbon oxidized per Hr.	1 Kw.	0.227 Lbs. Carbon oxidized per Hr.
1 H.P.	17 Lbs. Water per Hr. heated from 62-212° F.	1 Kw.	22.75 Lbs. Water per Hr. heated from 62-212° F.
1 H.P.	2.64 Lbs. Water per Hr. evaporated from and at 212° F.	1 Kw.	3.53 Lbs. Water per Hr. evaporated from and at 212° F.

This is a list of abbreviations used in the formulas and data presented in this book. Of necessity, letters may often represent various (and quite unrelated) ideas.

Electronic Abbreviations		Electronic Abbreviations	
R	resistance	pf	power factor
G	conductance	N_b	bels
ρ	specific resistance or resistivity	db	decibels
$°F$	degrees Fahrenheit	N_n	nepers
$°C$	degrees Celsius	ϵ	natural base (2.718281)
E	voltage	vu	volume unit
I	current	E_p	plate voltage
P	power	E_g	grid voltage
P_o	output power	Δ	change of
P_i	input power	μ	amplification factor
η	efficiency	r_p	plate resistance
dc	direct current	g_m	mutual conductance
ac	alternating current	I_p	plate current
L	inductance	C_i	input capacitance
C	capacitance	C_{pk}	interelectrode capacitance, plate to cathode
t	time constant		
T	time	C_{gk}	interelectrode capacitance, grid to cathode
λ	wavelength		
f	frequency	A	amplification
f_r	resonant frequency	β	feedback voltage
cps	cycles per second (Hz)	K	amplification with negative feedback
Hz	Hertz (cps)		
kHz	Kilohertz (kc)	i_c	collector current
MHz	megahertz (mc)	i_e	emitter current
μf	microfarad	α	current gain
pf	picofarad (same as micromicrofarad)	β	current gain
		k	correction factor
$E_{p\text{-}p}$	peak-to-peak voltage	SWR	standing wave ratio
V	velocity	j	-1 (j-operator)
D	distance	R_m	meter resistance
π	3.1416	n	multiplication factor
ω	$2 \times \pi \times f$		
α	ωt		
Q	coulomb		
RMS	root-mean-square		
Z	impedance		
X_L	inductive reactance		
X_c	capacitive reactance		
M	mutual inductance		
k	coefficient of coupling		
N_p	primary turns		
N_s	secondary turns		
N_s/N_p	turns ratio		
θ	phase angle		
B	susceptance		
Y	admittance		

Decimal Equivalents of Fractions of an Inch

	Fractions of an Inch				
Decimal	64th	32nd	16th	1/8th	1/4th
.015625	1				
.031250	2	1			
.046875	3				
.062500	4	2	1		
.078125	5				
.093750	6	3			
.109375	7				
.125000	8	4	2	1	
.140625	9				
.156250	10	5			
.171875	11				
.187500	12	6	3		
.203125	13				
.218750	14	7			
.234375	15				
.250000	16	8	4	2	1
.265625	17				
.281250	18	9			
.296875	19				
.312500	20	10	5		
.328125	21				
.343750	22	11			
.359375	23				
.375000	24	12	6	3	
.390625	25				
.406250	26	13			
.421875	27				
.437500	28	14	7		
.453125	29				
.468750	30	15			
.484375	31				
.500000	32	16	8	4	2
.515625	33				
.531250	34	17			
.546875	35				
.562500	36	18	9		
.578125	37				
.593750	38	19			
.609375	39				
.625000	40	20	10	5	

Decimal Equivalents of Fractions of an Inch — Continued

	Fractions of an Inch				
Decimal	64th	32nd	16th	1/8th	1/4th
.640625	41				
.656250	42	21			
.671875	43				
.687500	44	22	11		
.703125	45				
.718750	46	23			
.734375	47				
.750000	48	24	12	6	3
.765625	49				
.781250	50	25			
.796875	51				
.812500	52	26	13		
.828125	53				
.843750	54	27			
.859375	55				
.890625	57	28	14	7	
.906250	58	29			
.921875	59				
.937500	60	30	15		
.953125	61				
.968750	62	31			
.984375	63				
1.000000	64	32	16	8	4

$$\text{Percentage } (\%) = \text{decimal x } 100$$

$$\text{Decimal} = \frac{\text{Percentage}}{100}$$

Wavelength and Frequency Bands

Frequency	Description	Abbreviation
Below 30 kHz	very-low frequency	VLF
30 to 300 kHz	low frequency	LF
300 to 3,000 kHz	medium frequency	MF
3,000 to 30,000 kHz	high frequency	HF
30 to 300 MHz	very-high frequency	VHF
300 to 3,000 MHz	ultra-high frequency	UHF
3,000 to 30,000 MHz	super-high frequency	SHF
30,000 to 300,000 MHz (30 gHz to 300 gHz)*	extremely-high frequency	EHF

* gHz=gigaHertz. A gigaHertz (formerly gigacycle, gc) is 10^9 cycles (common usage in microwave work). Formerly also called kilomegacycles.

Math Symbols

× or ·	Multiplied by
÷ or :	Divided by
+	Positive. Plus. Addition
−	Negative. Minus. Subtraction
±	Positive or negative. Plus or minus
∓	Negative or positive. Minus or plus
= or ::	Equals
≡	Identical to or identical with
≅	Is approximately equal to
≠	Does not equal
>	Is greater than
≫	Is much greater than
<	Is less than
≪	Is much less than
≧	Greater than or equal to
≦	Less than or equal to
∴	Therefore
∠	Angle
∡	Angles
Δ	Change. Increase or decrease
⊥	Perpendicular to
∥	Parallel to
$\|n\|$	Absolute value of n
$\sqrt{\quad}$	Square root
$\sqrt[3]{\quad}$	cube root

∠ or ∢	Angle
∠θ	Angle theta
∠a	Angle a
$X^{1/2}$	X to the ½ power or square root of X ($\sqrt{X}$)
$\sqrt{X}$ or $\sqrt[2]{X}$ or $X^{1/2}$	Square root of X
$\sqrt[3]{X}$ or $X^{1/3}$	Cube root of X

MATH DATA

π = 3.14159265	$\sqrt{2}$ = 1.4142	log 1 = 0.000000
2π = 6.28318530	$\sqrt{3}$ = 1.7321	log 2 = 0.301030
$(2\pi)^2$ = 39.476089	$\sqrt{4}$ = 2.0000	log 3 = 0.477121
4π = 12.5663706	$\sqrt{5}$ = 2.2361	log 4 = 0.602060
π^2 = 9.8690440	$\sqrt{6}$ = 2.4495	log 5 = 0.698970
$\pi/2$ = 1.57079633	$\sqrt{7}$ = 2.6458	log 6 = 0.778151
$\pi/3$ = 1.04719755	$\sqrt{8}$ = 2.8248	log 7 = 0.845098
$\pi/4$ = 0.78539816	$\sqrt{9}$ = 3.0000	log 8 = 0.903090
$1/\pi$ = 0.31830989	$\sqrt{10}$ = 3.1623	log 9 = 0.954243
$1/\pi^2$ = 0.10132118	$1/\sqrt{2}$ = 0.707	log 10 = 1.000000
$1/\sqrt{\pi}$ = 0.56418958	$1/\sqrt{3}$ = 0.577	(logs are to base 10)
$\sqrt{\pi}$ = 1.77245385	$1/\sqrt{4}$ = 0.500	1 radian = 180°/π = 57° 17' 45''
$4/3\pi$ = 4.18879020	$1/\sqrt{5}$ = 0.447	360° = 2π radians
$1/2\pi$ = 0.15915494	$1/\sqrt{6}$ = 0.408	1° = $\pi/180°$ = 0.017453 radian
$\sqrt{1}$ = 1.000	$1/\sqrt{7}$ = 0.377	base of natural logs ϵ = 2.718
	$1/\sqrt{8}$ = 0.354	
	$1/\sqrt{9}$ = 0.333	
	$1/\sqrt{10}$ = 0.316	

Greek Alphabet

Greek Capital Letter	Greek Lowercase Letter	Greek Name
A	α	Alpha
B	β	Beta
Γ	γ	Gamma
Δ	δ	Delta
E	ϵ	Epsilon
Z	ζ	Zeta
H	η	Eta
Θ	θ	Theta
I	ι	Iota
K	κ	Kappa
Λ	λ	Lambda
M	μ	Mu
N	ν	Nu
Ξ	ξ	Xi
O	o	Omicron
Π	π	Pi
P	ρ	Rho
Σ	σ	Sigma
T	τ	Tau
Υ	υ	Upsilon
Φ	ϕ	Phi
X	χ	Chi
Ψ	ψ	Psi
Ω	ω	Omega

Comparison of electric and magnetic circuits.

	Electric circuit	Magnetic circuit
Force......................	Volt, E, or e.m.f.	Gilberts, F, or m.m.f.
Flow.......................	Ampere, I	Flux, Φ, in maxwells
Opposition...............	Ohms, R	Reluctance, R, or rels
Law........................	Ohm's law, $I = \dfrac{E}{R}$	Rowland's law, $\Phi = \dfrac{F}{R}$
Intensity of force......	Volts per cm. of length	$H = \dfrac{1.257 IN}{l}$, gilberts per centimeter of length.
Density..................	Current density — for example, amperes per cm.²	Flux density — for example, lines per cm.², or gausses.

n	2^n	n	2^n
1	2	41	21990 23255 552
2	4	42	43980 46511 104
3	8	43	87960 93022 208
4	16	44	17592 18604 4416
5	32	45	35184 37208 8832
6	64	46	70368 74417 7664
7	128	47	14073 74883 55328
8	256	48	28147 49767 10656
9	512	49	56294 99534 21312
10	1024	50	11258 99906 84262 4
11	2048	51	22517 99813 68524 8
12	4096	52	45035 99627 37049 6
13	8192	53	90071 99254 74099 2
14	16384	54	18014 39850 94819 84
15	32768	55	36028 79701 89639 68
16	65536	56	72057 59403 79279 36
17	13107 2	57	14411 51880 75855 872
18	26214 4	58	28823 03761 51711 744
19	52428 8	59	57646 07523 03423 488
20	10485 76	60	11529 21504 60684 6976
21	20971 52	61	23058 43009 21369 3952
22	41943 04	62	46116 86018 42738 7904
23	83886 08	63	92233 72036 85477 5808
24	16777 216	64	18446 74407 37095 51616
25	33554 432	65	36893 48814 74191 03232
26	67108 864	66	73786 97629 48382 06464
27	13421 7728	67	14757 39525 89676 41292 8
28	26843 5456	68	29514 79051 79352 82585 6
29	53687 0912	69	59029 58103 58705 65171 2
30	10737 41824	70	11805 91620 71741 13034 24
31	21474 83648	71	23611 83241 43482 26068 48
32	42949 67296	72	47223 66482 86964 52136 96
33	85899 34592	73	94447 32965 73929 04273 92
34	17179 86918 4	74	18889 46593 14785 80854 784
35	34359 73836 8	75	37778 93186 29571 61709 568
36	68719 47673 6	76	75557 86372 59143 23419 136
37	13743 89534 72	77	15111 57274 51828 64683 8272
38	27487 79069 44	78	30223 14549 03657 29367 6544
39	54975 58138 88	79	60446 29098 07314 58735 3088
40	10995 11627 776	80	12089 25819 61462 91747 06176

n	2^n
81	24178 51639 22925 83494 12352
82	48357 03278 45851 66988 24704
83	96714 06556 91703 33976 49408
84	19342 81311 38340 66795 29881 6
85	38685 62622 76681 33590 59763 2
86	77371 25245 53362 67181 19526 4
87	15474 25049 10672 53436 23905 28
88	30948 50098 21345 06872 47810 56
89	61897 00196 42690 13744 95621 12
90	12379 40039 28538 02748 99124 224
91	24758 80078 57076 05497 98248 448

n	2^n
92	49517 60157 14152 10995 96496 896
93	99035 20314 28304 21991 92993 792
94	19807 04062 85660 84398 38598 7584
95	39614 08125 71321 68796 77197 5168
96	79228 16251 42643 37593 54395 0336
97	15845 63250 28528 67518 70879 00672
98	31691 26500 57057 35037 41758 01344
99	63382 53001 14114 70074 83516 02688
100	12676 50600 22822 94014 96703 20537 6

FUNDAMENTALS OF BOOLEAN ALGEBRA

Definitions

a, b, c, etc.......................Symbols used in symbolic logic

a • b or ab....................................Read as: a and b

a + b..Read as: a or b

a′ or $\bar{a}$...Read as: not a

1.."True" or "On"

0.."False" or "Off"

Relations and Rules of Operation

1. $a + b = (a'b')'$; $ab = (a' + b')'$
   DeMorgan's Theorem

2. $1 = 0'$; $0 = 1'$

3. $a + a = a$; $a \cdot a = a$

4. $a + 1 = 1$; $a \cdot 1 = a$

5. $a + b = b + a$; $ab = ba$
   Commutative Laws

6. $(a + b) + c = a + (b + c)$
   $(ab)c = a(bc)$
   Associative Laws

7. $a(b + c) = ab + ac$

8. $(a + b)(a + c) = a + bc$
   Special Distributive Law

9. $a + a' = 1$; $a \cdot a' = 0$

10. $(a')' = a$

225

SQUARES, CUBES AND ROOTS

n	n^2	$\sqrt{n}$	$\sqrt{10n}$	n^3
1	1	1.000000	3.162278	1
2	4	1.414214	4.472136	8
3	9	1.732051	5.477226	27
4	16	2.000000	6.324555	64
5	25	2.236068	7.071068	125
6	36	2.449490	7.745967	216
7	49	2.645751	8.366600	343
8	64	2.828427	8.944272	512
9	81	3.000000	9.486833	729
10	100	3.162278	10.00000	1,000
11	121	3.316625	10.48809	1,331
12	144	3.464102	10.95445	1,728
13	169	3.605551	11.40175	2,197
14	196	3.741657	11.83216	2,744
15	225	3.872983	12.24745	3,375
16	256	4.000000	12.64911	4,096
17	289	4.123106	13.03840	4,913
18	324	4.242641	13.41641	5,832
19	361	4.358899	13.78405	6,859
20	400	4.472136	14.14214	8,000
21	441	4.582576	14.49138	9,261
22	484	4.690416	14.83240	10,648
23	529	4.795832	15.16575	12,167
24	576	4.898979	15.49193	13,824
25	625	5.000000	15.81139	15,625
26	676	5.099020	16.12452	17,576
27	729	5.196152	16.43168	19,683
28	784	5.291503	16.73320	21,952
29	841	5.385165	17.02939	24,389
30	900	5.477226	17.32051	27,000
31	961	5.567764	17.60682	29,791
32	1,024	5.656854	17.88854	32,768
33	1,089	5.744563	18.16590	35,937
34	1,156	5.830952	18.43909	39,304
35	1,225	5.916080	18.70829	42,875
36	1,296	6.000000	18.97367	46,656
37	1,369	6.082763	19.23538	50,653
38	1,444	6.164414	19.49359	54,872
39	1,521	6.244998	19.74842	59,319
40	1,600	6.324555	20.00000	64,000
41	1,681	6.403124	20.24846	68,921
42	1,764	6.480741	20.49390	74,088
43	1,849	6.557439	20.73644	79,507
44	1,936	6.633250	20.97618	85,184
45	2,025	6.708204	21.21320	91,125
46	2,116	6.782330	21.44761	97,336
47	2,209	6.855655	21.67948	103,823
48	2,304	6.928203	21.90890	110,592
49	2,401	7.000000	22.13594	117,649
50	2,500	7.071068	22.36068	125,000

SQUARES, CUBES AND ROOTS—Continued

n	n^2	$\sqrt{n}$	$\sqrt{10n}$	n^3
50	2,500	7.071068	22.36068	125,000
51	2,601	7.141428	22.58318	132,651
52	2,704	7.211103	22.80351	140,608
53	2,809	7.280110	23.02173	148,877
54	2,916	7.348469	23.23790	157,464
55	3,025	7.416198	23.45208	166,375
56	3,136	7.483315	23.66432	175,616
57	3,249	7.549834	23.87467	185,193
58	3,364	7.615773	24.06319	195,112
59	3,481	7.681146	24.28992	205,379
60	3,600	7.745967	24.49490	216,000
61	3,721	7.810250	24.69818	226,981
62	3,844	7.874008	24.89980	238,328
63	3,969	7.937254	25.09980	250,047
64	4,096	8.000000	25.29822	262,144
65	4,225	8.062258	25.49510	274,625
66	4,356	8.124038	25.69047	287,496
67	4,489	8.185353	25.88436	300,763
68	4,624	8.246211	26.07681	314,432
69	4,761	8.306624	26.26785	328,509
70	4,900	8.366600	26.45751	343,000
71	5,041	8.426150	26.64583	357,911
72	5,184	8.485281	26.83282	373,248
73	5,329	8.544004	27.01851	389,017
74	5,476	8.602325	27.20294	405,224
75	5,625	8.660254	27.38613	421,875
76	5,776	8.717798	27.56810	438,976
77	5,929	8.774964	27.74887	456,533
78	6,084	8.831761	27.92848	474,552
79	6,241	8.888194	28.10694	493,039
80	6,400	8.944272	28.28427	512,000
81	6,561	9.000000	28.46050	531,441
82	6,724	9.055385	28.63564	551,368
83	6,889	9.110434	28.80972	571,787
84	7,056	9.165151	28.98275	592,704
85	7,225	9.219544	29.15476	614,125
86	7,396	9.273618	29.32576	636,056
87	7,569	9.327379	29.49576	658,503
88	7,744	9.380832	29.66479	681,472
89	7,921	9.433981	29.83287	704,969
90	8,100	9.486833	30.00000	729,000
91	8,281	9.539392	30.16621	753,571
92	8,464	9.591663	30.33150	778,688
93	8,649	9.643651	30.49590	804,357
94	8,836	9.695360	30.65942	830,584
95	9,025	9.746794	30.82207	857,375
96	9,216	9.797959	30.98387	884,736
97	9,409	9.848858	31.14482	912,673
98	9,604	9.899495	31.30495	941,192
99	9,801	9.949874	31.46427	970,299
100	10,000	10.00000	31.62278	1,000,000

$\sqrt[3]{n}$	$\sqrt[3]{10n}$	$\sqrt[3]{100n}$	n
1.000000	2.154435	4.641589	1
1.259921	2.714418	5.848035	2
1.442250	3.107233	6.694330	3
1.587401	3.419952	7.368063	4
1.709976	3.684031	7.937005	5
1.817121	3.914868	8.434327	6
1.912931	4.121285	8.879040	7
2.000000	4.308869	9.283178	8
2.080084	4.481405	9.654894	9
2.154435	4.641589	10.00000	10
2.223980	4.791420	10.32280	11
2.289428	4.932424	10.62659	12
2.351335	5.065797	10.91393	13
2.410142	5.192494	11.18689	14
2.466212	5.313293	11.44714	15
2.519842	5.428835	11.69607	16
2.571282	5.539658	11.93483	17
2.620741	5.646216	12.16440	18
2.668402	5.748897	12.38562	19
2.714418	5.848035	12.59921	20
2.758924	5.943922	12.80579	21
2.802039	6.036811	13.00591	22
2.843867	6.126926	13.20006	23
2.884499	6.214465	13.38866	24
2.924018	6.299605	13.57209	25
2.962496	6.382504	13.75069	26
3.000000	6.463304	13.92477	27
3.036589	6.542133	14.09460	28
3.072317	6.619106	14.26043	29
3.107233	6.694330	14.42250	30
3.141381	6.767899	14.58100	31
3.174802	6.839904	14.73613	32
3.207534	6.910423	14.88806	33
3.239612	6.979532	15.03695	34
3.271066	7.047299	15.18294	35
3.301927	7.113787	15.32619	36
3.332222	7.179054	15.46680	37
3.361975	7.243156	15.60491	38
3.391211	7.306144	15.74061	39
3.419952	7.368063	15.87401	40
3.448217	7.428959	16.00521	41
3.476027	7.488872	16.13429	42
3.503398	7.547842	16.26133	43
3.530348	7.605905	16.38643	44
3.556893	7.663094	16.50964	45
3.583048	7.719443	16.63103	46
3.608826	7.774980	16.75069	47
3.634241	7.829735	16.86865	48
3.659306	7.883735	16.98499	49
3.684031	7.937005	17.09976	50

$\sqrt[3]{n}$	$\sqrt[3]{10n}$	$\sqrt[3]{100n}$	n
3.684031	7.937005	17.09976	50
3.708430	7.989570	17.21301	51
3.732511	8.041452	17.32478	52
3.756286	8.092672	17.43513	53
3.779763	8.143253	17.54411	54
3.802952	8.193213	17.65174	55
3.825862	8.242571	17.75808	56
3.848501	8.291344	17.86316	57
3.870877	8.339551	17.96702	58
3.892996	8.387207	18.06969	59
3.914868	8.434327	18.17121	60
3.936497	8.480926	18.27160	61
3.957892	8.527019	18.37091	62
3.979057	8.572619	18.46915	63
4.000000	8.617739	18.56636	64
4.020726	8.662391	18.66256	65
4.041240	8.706588	18.75777	66
4.061548	8.750340	18.85204	67
4.081655	8.793659	18.94536	68
4.101566	8.836556	19.03778	69
4.121285	8.879040	19.12931	70
4.140818	8.921121	19.21997	71
4.160168	8.962809	19.30979	72
4.179339	9.004113	19.39877	73
4.198336	9.045042	19.48695	74
4.217163	9.085603	19.57434	75
4.235824	9.125805	19.66095	76
4.254321	9.165656	19.74681	77
4.272659	9.205164	19.83192	78
4.290840	9.244335	19.91632	79
4.308869	9.283178	20.00000	80
4.326749	9.321698	20.08299	81
4.344481	9.359902	20.16530	82
4.362071	9.397796	20.24694	83
4.379519	9.435388	20.32793	84
4.396830	9.472682	20.40828	85
4.414005	9.509685	20.48800	86
4.431048	9.546403	20.56710	87
4.447960	9.582840	20.64560	88
4.464745	9.619002	20.72351	89
4.481405	9.654894	20.80084	90
4.497941	9.690521	20.87759	91
4.514357	9.725888	20.95379	92
4.530655	9.761000	21.02944	93
4.546836	9.795861	21.10454	94
4.562903	9.830476	21.17912	95
4.578857	9.864848	21.25317	96
4.594701	9.898983	21.32671	97
4.610436	9.932884	21.39975	98
4.626065	9.966555	21.47229	99
4.641589	10.00000	21.54435	100

n	n^4	n^5	n^6	n^7	n^8
1	1	1	1	1	1
2	16	32	64	128	256
3	81	243	729	2187	6561
4	256	1024	4096	16384	65536
5	625	3125	15625	78125	390625
6	1296	7776	46656	279936	1679616
7	2401	16807	117649	823543	5764801
8	4096	32768	262144	2097152	16777216
9	6561	59049	531441	4782969	43046721
					$\times 10^8$
10	10000	100000	1000000	10000000	1.000000
11	14641	161051	1771561	19487171	2.143589
12	20736	248832	2985984	35831808	4.299817
13	28561	371293	4826809	62748517	8.157307
14	38416	537824	7529536	105413504	14.757891
15	50625	759375	11390625	170859375	25.628906
16	65536	1048576	16777216	268435456	42.949673
17	83521	1419857	24137569	410338673	69.757574
18	104976	1889568	34012224	612220032	110.199606
19	130321	2476099	47045881	893871739	169.835630
				$\times 10^9$	$\times 10^{10}$
20	160000	3200000	64000000	1.280000	2.560000
21	194481	4084101	85766121	1.801089	3.782286
22	234256	5153632	113379904	2.494358	5.487587
23	279841	6436343	148035889	3.404825	7.831099
24	331776	7962624	191102976	4.586471	11.007531
25	390625	9765625	244140625	6.103516	15.258789
26	456976	11881376	308915776	8.031810	20.882706
27	531441	14348907	387420489	10.460353	28.242954
28	614656	17210368	481890304	13.492929	37.780200
29	707281	20511149	594823321	17.249876	50.024641
			$\times 10^8$	$\times 10^{10}$	$\times 10^{11}$
30	810000	24300000	7.290000	2.187000	6.561000
31	923521	28629151	8.875037	2.751261	8.528910
32	1048576	33554432	10.737418	3.435974	10.995116
33	1185921	39135393	12.914680	4.261844	14.064086
34	1336336	45435424	15.448044	5.252335	17.857939
35	1500625	52521875	18.382656	6.433930	22.518754
36	1679616	60466176	21.767823	7.836416	28.211099
37	1874161	69343957	25.657264	9.493188	35.124795
38	2085136	79235168	30.109364	11.441558	43.477921
39	2313441	90224199	35.187438	13.723101	53.520093
			$\times 10^9$	$\times 10^{10}$	$\times 10^{12}$
40	2560000	102400000	4.096000	16.384000	6.553600
41	2825761	115856201	4.750104	19.475427	7.984925
42	3111696	130691232	5.489032	23.053933	9.682652
43	3418801	147008443	6.321363	27.181861	11.688200
44	3748096	164916224	7.256314	31.927781	14.048224
45	4100625	184528125	8.303766	37.366945	16.815125
46	4477456	205962976	9.474297	43.581766	20.047612
47	4879681	229345007	10.779215	50.662312	23.811287
48	5308416	254803968	12.230590	58.706834	28.179280
49	5764801	282475249	13.841287	67.822307	33.232931
50	6250000	312500000	15.625000	78.125000	39.062500

POWERS OF NUMBERS—Continued

n	n^4	n^5	n^6	n^7	n^8
			$\times 10^9$	$\times 10^{11}$	$\times 10^{13}$
50	6250000	312500000	15.625000	7.812500	3.906250
51	6765201	345025251	17.596288	8.974107	4.576794
52	7311616	380204032	19.770610	10.280717	5.345973
53	7890481	418195493	22.164361	11.747111	6.225969
54	8503056	459165024	24.794911	13.389252	7.230196
55	9150625	503284375	27.680641	15.224352	8.373394
56	9834496	550731776	30.840979	17.270948	9.671731
57	10556001	601692057	34.296447	19.548975	11.142916
58	11316496	656356768	38.068693	22.079842	12.806308
59	12117361	714924299	42.180534	24.886515	14.683044
		$\times 10^8$	$\times 10^{10}$	$\times 10^{11}$	$\times 10^{13}$
60	12960000	7.776000	4.665600	27.993600	16.796160
61	13845841	8.445963	5.152037	31.427428	19.170731
62	14776336	9.161328	5.680024	35.216146	21.834011
63	15752961	9.924365	6.252350	39.389806	24.815578
64	16777216	10.737418	6.871948	43.980465	28.147498
65	17850625	11.602906	7.541889	49.022279	31.864481
66	18974736	12.523326	8.265395	54.551607	36.004061
67	20151121	13.501251	9.045838	60.607116	40.606768
68	21381376	14.539336	9.886748	67.229888	45.716324
69	22667121	15.640313	10.791816	74.463533	51.379837
		$\times 10^8$	$\times 10^{10}$	$\times 10^{12}$	$\times 10^{14}$
70	24010000	16.807000	11.764900	8.235430	5.764801
71	25411681	18.042294	12.810028	9.095120	6.457535
72	26873856	19.349176	13.931407	10.030613	7.222041
73	28398241	20.730716	15.133423	11.047399	8.064601
74	29986576	22.190066	16.420649	12.151280	8.991947
75	31640625	23.730469	17.797852	13.348389	10.011292
76	33362176	25.355254	19.269993	14.645195	11.130348
77	35153041	27.067842	20.842238	16.048523	12.357363
78	37015056	28.871744	22.519960	17.565569	13.701144
79	38950081	30.770564	24.308746	19.203909	15.171088
		$\times 10^8$	$\times 10^{10}$	$\times 10^{12}$	$\times 10^{14}$
80	40960000	32.768000	26.214400	20.971520	16.777216
81	43046721	34.867844	28.242954	22.876792	18.530202
82	45212176	37.073984	30.400667	24.928547	20.441409
83	47458321	39.390406	32.694037	27.136051	22.522922
84	49787136	41.821194	35.129803	29.509035	24.787589
85	52200625	44.370531	37.714952	32.057709	27.249053
86	54700816	47.042702	40.456724	34.792782	29.921793
87	57289761	49.842092	43.362620	37.725479	32.821167
88	59969536	52.773192	46.440409	40.867560	35.963452
89	62742241	55.840594	49.698129	44.231335	39.365888
		$\times 10^9$	$\times 10^{11}$	$\times 10^{13}$	$\times 10^{15}$
90	65610000	5.904900	5.314410	4.782969	4.304672
91	68574961	6.240321	5.678693	5.167610	4.702525
92	71639296	6.590815	6.063550	5.578466	5.132189
93	74805201	6.956884	6.469902	6.017009	5.595818
94	78074896	7.339040	6.898698	6.484776	6.095689
95	81450625	7.737809	7.350919	6.983373	6.634204
96	84934656	8.153727	7.827578	7.514475	7.213896
97	88529281	8.587340	8.329720	8.079828	7.837434
98	92236816	9.039208	8.858424	8.681255	8.507630
99	96059601	9.509900	9.414801	9.320653	9.227447
100	100000000	10.000000	10.000000	10.000000	10.000000

TRIGONOMETRIC FUNCTIONS

Degrees	Sine	Tangent	Cotangent	Cosine	
0	.0000	.0000	......	1.0000	90
1	.0175	.0175	57.29	.9998	89
2	.0349	.0349	28.636	.9994	88
3	.0523	.0524	19.081	.9986	87
4	.0698	.0699	14.301	.9976	86
5	.0872	.0875	11.430	.9962	85
6	.1045	.1051	9.5144	.9945	84
7	.1219	.1228	8.1443	.9925	83
8	.1392	.1405	7.1154	.9903	82
9	.1564	.1584	6.3138	.9877	81
10	.1736	.1763	5.6713	.9848	80
11	.1908	.1944	5.1446	.9816	79
12	.2079	.2126	4.7046	.9781	78
13	.2250	.2309	4.3315	.9744	77
14	.2419	.2493	4.0108	.9703	76
15	.2588	.2679	3.7321	.9659	75
16	.2756	.2867	3.4874	.9613	74
17	.2924	.3057	3.2709	.9563	73
18	.3090	.3249	3.0777	.9511	72
19	.3256	.3443	2.9042	.9455	71
20	.3420	.3640	2.7475	.9397	70
21	.3584	.3839	2.6051	.9336	69
22	.3746	.4040	2.4751	.9272	68
23	.3907	.4245	2.3559	.9205	67
24	.4067	.4452	2.2460	.9135	66
25	.4226	.4663	2.1445	.9063	65
26	.4384	.4877	2.0503	.8988	64
27	.4540	.5095	1.9626	.8910	63
28	.4695	.5317	1.8807	.8829	62
29	.4848	.5543	1.8040	.8746	61
30	.5000	.5774	1.7321	.8660	60
31	.5150	.6009	1.6643	.8572	59
32	.5299	.6249	1.6003	.8480	58
33	.5446	.6494	1.5399	.8387	57
34	.5592	.6745	1.4826	.8290	56
35	.5736	.7002	1.4281	.8192	55
36	.5878	.7265	1.3764	.8090	54
37	.6018	.7536	1.3270	.7986	53
38	.6157	.7813	1.2799	.7880	52
39	.6293	.8098	1.2349	.7771	51
40	.6428	.8391	1.1918	.7660	50
41	.6561	.8693	1.1504	.7547	49
42	.6691	.9004	1.1106	.7431	48
43	.6820	.9325	1.0724	.7314	47
44	.6947	.9657	1.0355	.7193	46
45	.7071	1.0000	1.0000	.7071	45
	Cosine	Cotangent	Tangent	Sine	Degrees

CONVERSION OF INCHES TO MILLIMETERS

Inches	Milli-meters	Inches	Milli-meters	Inches	Milli-meters
0.001	0.025	0.290	7.37	0.660	16.76
0.002	0.051	0.300	7.62	0.670	17.02
0.003	0.076	0.310	7.87	0.680	17.27
0.004	0.102	0.320	8.13	0.690	17.53
0.005	0.127	0.330	8.38	0.700	17.78
0.006	0.152	0.340	8.64	0.710	18.03
0.007	0.178	0.350	8.89	0.720	18.29
0.008	0.203	0.360	9.14	0.730	18.54
0.009	0.229	0.370	9.40	0.740	18.80
0.010	0.254	0.380	9.65	0.750	19.05
0.020	0.508	0.390	9.91	0.760	19.30
0.030	0.762	0.400	10.16	0.770	19.56
0.040	1.016	0.410	10.41	0.780	19.81
0.050	1.270	0.420	10.67	0.790	20.07
0.060	1.524	0.430	10.92	0.800	20.32
0.070	1.778	0.440	11.18	0.810	20.57
0.080	2.032	0.450	11.43	0.820	20.83
0.090	2.286	0.460	11.68	0.830	21.08
0.100	2.540	0.470	11.94	0.840	21.34
0.110	2.794	0.480	12.19	0.850	21.59
0.120	3.048	0.490	12.45	0.860	21.84
0.130	3.302	0.500	12.70	0.870	22.10
0.140	3.56	0.510	12.95	0.880	22.35
0.150	3.81	0.520	13.21	0.890	22.61
0.160	4.06	0.530	13.46	0.900	22.86
0.170	4.32	0.540	13.72	0.910	23.11
0.180	4.57	0.550	13.97	0.920	23.37
0.190	4.83	0.560	14.22	0.930	23.62
0.200	5.08	0.570	14.48	0.940	23.88
0.210	5.33	0.580	14.73	0.950	24.13
0.220	5.59	0.590	14.99	0.960	24.38
0.230	5.84	0.600	15.24	0.970	24.64
0.240	6.10	0.610	15.49	0.980	24.89
0.250	6.35	0.620	15.75	0.990	25.15
0.260	6.60	0.630	16.00	1.000	25.40
0.270	6.86	0.640	16.26	......	......
0.280	7.11	0.650	16.51	......	......

CONVERSION OF MILLIMETERS TO INCHES

Milli-meters	Inches	Milli-meters	Inches	Milli-meters	Inches
0.01	0.0004	0.35	0.0138	C.68	0.0268
0.02	0.0008	0.36	0.0142	0.69	0.0272
0.03	0.0012	0.37	0.0146	0.70	0.0276
0.04	0.0016	0.38	0.0150	0.71	0.0280
0.05	0.0020	0.39	0.0154	0.72	0.0283
0.06	0.0024	0.40	0.0157	0.73	0.0287
0.07	0.0028	0.41	0.0161	0.74	0.0291
0.08	0.0031	0.42	0.0165	0.75	0.0295
0.09	0.0035	0.43	0.0169	0.76	0.0299
0.10	0.0039	0.44	0.0173	0.77	0.0303
0.11	0.0043	0.45	0.0177	0.78	0.0307
0.12	0.0047	0.46	0.0181	0.79	0.0311
0.13	0.0051	0.47	0.0185	0.80	0.0315
0.14	0.0055	0.48	0.0189	0.81	0.0319
0.15	0.0059	0.49	0.0193	0.82	0.0323
0.16	0.0063	0.50	0.0197	0.83	0.0327
0.17	0.0067	0.51	0.0201	0.84	0.0331
0.18	0.0071	0.52	0.0205	0.85	0.0335
0.19	0.0075	0.53	0.0209	0.86	0.0339
0.20	0.0079	0.54	0.0213	0.87	0.0343
0.21	0.0083	0.55	0.0217	0.88	0.0346
0.22	0.0087	0.56	0.0220	0.89	0.0350
0.23	0.0091	0.57	0.0224	0.90	0.0354
0.24	0.0094	0.58	0.0228	0.91	0.0358
0.25	0.0098	0.59	0.0232	0.92	0.0362
0.26	0.0102	0.60	0.0236	0.93	0.0366
0.27	0.0106	0.61	0.0240	0.94	0.0370
0.28	0.0110	0.62	0.0244	0.95	0.0374
0.29	0.0114	0.63	0.0248	0.96	0.0378
0.30	0.0118	0.64	0.0252	0.97	0.0382
0.31	0.0122	0.65	0.0256	0.98	0.0386
0.32	0.0126	0.66	0.0260	0.99	0.0390
0.33	0.0130	0.67	0.0264	1.00	0.0394
0.34	0.0134	....	.?...	....	.....

COMMON LOGARITHMS OF NUMBERS

N	0	1	2	3	4	5	6	7	8	9
10	0000	0043	0086	0128	0170	0212	0253	0294	0334	0374
11	0414	0453	0492	0531	0569	0607	0645	0682	0719	0755
12	0792	0828	0864	0899	0934	0969	1004	1038	1072	1106
13	1139	1173	1206	1239	1271	1303	1335	1367	1399	1430
14	1461	1492	1523	1553	1584	1614	1644	1673	1703	1732
15	1761	1790	1818	1847	1875	1903	1931	1959	1987	2014
16	2041	2068	2095	2122	2148	2175	2201	2227	2253	2279
17	2304	2330	2355	2380	2405	2430	2455	2480	2504	2529
18	2553	2577	2601	2625	2648	2672	2695	2718	2742	2765
19	2788	2810	2833	2856	2878	2900	2923	2945	2967	2989
20	3010	3032	3054	3075	3096	3118	3139	3160	3181	3201
21	3222	3243	3263	3284	3304	3324	3345	3365	3385	3404
22	3424	3444	3464	3483	3502	3522	3541	3560	3579	3598
23	3617	3636	3655	3674	3692	3711	3729	3747	3766	3784
24	3802	3820	3838	3856	3874	3892	3909	3927	3945	3962
25	3979	3997	4014	4031	4048	4065	4082	4099	4116	4133
26	4150	4166	4183	4200	4216	4232	4249	4265	4281	4298
27	4314	4330	4346	4362	4378	4393	4409	4425	4440	4456
28	4472	4487	4502	4518	4533	4548	4564	4579	4594	4609
29	4624	4639	4654	4669	4683	4698	4713	4728	4742	4757
30	4771	4786	4800	4814	4829	4843	4857	4871	4886	4900
31	4914	4928	4942	4955	4969	4983	4997	5011	5024	5038
32	5051	5065	5079	5092	5105	5119	5132	5145	5159	5172
33	5185	5198	5211	5224	5237	5250	5263	5276	5289	5302
34	5315	5328	5340	5353	5366	5378	5391	5403	5416	5428
35	5441	5453	5465	5478	5490	5502	5514	5527	5539	5551
36	5563	5575	5587	5599	5611	5623	5635	5647	5658	5670
37	5682	5694	5705	5717	5729	5740	5752	5763	5775	5786
38	5798	5809	5821	5832	5843	5855	5866	5877	5888	5899
39	5911	5922	5933	5944	5955	5966	5977	5988	5999	6010
40	6021	6031	6042	6053	6064	6075	6085	6096	6107	6117
41	6128	6138	6149	6160	6170	6180	6191	6201	6212	6222
42	6232	6243	6253	6263	6274	6284	6294	6304	6314	6325
43	6335	6345	6355	6365	6375	6385	6395	6405	6415	6425
44	6435	6444	6454	6464	6474	6484	6493	6503	6513	6522
45	6532	6542	6551	6561	6571	6580	6590	6599	6609	6618
46	6628	6637	6646	6656	6665	6675	6684	6693	6702	6712
47	6721	6730	6739	6749	6758	6767	6776	6785	6794	6803
48	6812	6821	6830	6839	6848	6857	6866	6875	6884	6893
49	6902	6911	6920	6928	6937	6946	6955	6964	6972	6981
50	6990	6998	7007	7016	7024	7033	7042	7050	7059	7067
51	7076	7084	7093	7101	7110	7118	7126	7135	7143	7152
52	7160	7168	7177	7185	7193	7202	7210	7218	7226	7235
53	7243	7251	7259	7267	7275	7284	7292	7300	7308	7316
54	7324	7332	7340	7348	7356	7364	7372	7380	7388	7396

COMMON LOGARITHMS OF NUMBERS — Continued

N	0	1	2	3	4	5	6	7	8	9
55	7404	7412	7419	7427	7435	7443	7451	7459	7466	7474
56	7482	7490	7497	7505	7513	7520	7528	7536	7543	7551
57	7559	7566	7574	7582	7589	7597	7604	7612	7619	7627
58	7634	7642	7649	7657	7664	7672	7679	7686	7694	7701
59	7709	7716	7723	7731	7738	7745	7752	7760	7767	7774
60	7782	7789	7796	7803	7810	7818	7825	7832	7839	7846
61	7853	7860	7868	7875	7882	7889	7896	7903	7910	7917
62	7924	7931	7938	7945	7952	7959	7966	7973	7980	7987
63	7993	8000	8007	8014	8021	8028	8035	8041	8048	8055
64	8062	8069	8075	8082	8089	8096	8102	8109	8116	8122
65	8129	8136	8142	8149	8156	8162	8169	8176	8182	8189
66	8195	8202	8209	8215	8222	8228	8235	8241	8248	8254
67	8261	8267	8274	8280	8287	8293	8299	8306	8312	8319
68	8325	8331	8338	8344	8351	8357	8363	8370	8376	8382
69	8388	8395	8401	8407	8414	8420	8426	8432	8439	8445
70	8451	8457	8463	8470	8476	8482	8488	8494	8500	8506
71	8513	8519	8525	8531	8537	8543	8549	8555	8561	8567
72	8573	8579	8585	8591	8597	8603	8609	8615	8621	8627
73	8633	8639	8645	8651	8657	8663	8669	8675	8681	8686
74	8692	8698	8704	8710	8716	8722	8727	8733	8739	8745
75	8751	8456	8762	8768	8774	8779	8785	8791	8797	8802
76	8808	8814	8820	8825	8831	8837	8842	8848	8854	8859
77	8865	8871	8876	8882	8887	8893	8899	8904	8910	8915
78	8921	8927	8932	8938	8943	8949	8954	8960	8965	8971
79	8976	8982	8987	8993	8998	9004	9009	9015	9020	9025
80	9031	9036	9042	9047	9053	9058	9063	9069	9074	9079
81	9085	9090	9096	9101	9106	9112	9117	9122	9128	9133
82	9138	9143	9149	9154	9159	9165	9170	9175	9180	9186
83	9191	9196	9201	9206	9212	9217	9222	9227	9232	9238
84	9243	9248	9253	9258	9263	9269	9274	9279	9284	9289
85	9294	9299	9304	9309	9315	9320	9325	9330	9335	9340
86	9345	9350	9355	9360	9365	9370	9375	9380	9385	9390
87	9395	9400	9405	9410	9415	9420	9425	9430	9435	9440
88	9445	9450	9455	9460	9465	9469	9474	9479	9484	9489
89	9494	9499	9504	9509	9513	9518	9523	9528	9533	9538
90	9542	9547	9552	9557	9562	9566	9571	9576	9581	9586
91	9590	9595	9600	9605	9609	9614	9619	9624	9628	9633
92	9638	9643	9647	9652	9657	9661	9666	9671	9675	9680
93	9685	9689	9694	9699	9703	9708	9713	9717	9722	9727
94	9731	9736	9741	9745	9750	9754	9759	9763	9768	9773
95	9777	9782	9786	9791	9795	9800	9805	9809	9814	9818
96	9823	9827	9832	9836	9841	9845	9850	9854	9859	9863
97	9868	9872	9877	9881	9886	9890	9894	9899	9903	9908
98	9912	9917	9921	9926	9930	9934	9939	9943	9948	9952
99	9956	9961	9965	9969	9974	9978	9983	9987	9991	9996

BINARY NUMBERS

	16	8	4	2	1
0					0
1					1
2				1	0
3				1	1
4			1	0	0
5			1	0	1
6			1	1	0
7			1	1	1
8		1	0	0	0
9		1	0	0	1
10		1	0	1	0

	16	8	4	2	1
11		1	0	1	1
12		1	1	0	0
13		1	1	0	1
14		1	1	1	0
15		1	1	1	1
16	1	0	0	0	0
17	1	0	0	0	1
18	1	0	0	1	0
19	1	0	0	1	1
20	1	0	1	0	0
21	1	0	1	0	1

	16	8	4	2	1
22	1	0	1	1	0
23	1	0	1	1	1
24	1	1	0	0	0
25	1	1	0	0	1
26	1	1	0	1	0
27	1	1	0	1	1
28	1	1	1	0	0
29	1	1	1	0	1
30	1	1	1	1	0
31	1	1	1	1	1

DECIMAL TO BINARY CONVERSION RULES

(a) Write number $n + 0$ if even or $(n-1) + 1$ if odd.

(b) Divide even number obtained in (a) by 2.
Write answer (m) below in same form:
$m + 0$ if even, $(m - 1) + 1$ if odd.

(c) Continue until m or $(m - 1)$ becomes zero.

(d) Column of ones and zeros so obtained is binary equivalent of n with least significant digit at the top.

EXAMPLE: $n = 327$

$$326 + 1$$
$$162 + 1$$
$$80 + 1$$
$$40 + 0$$
$$20 + 0$$
$$10 + 0$$
$$4 + 1$$
$$2 + 0$$
$$0 + 1$$

Therefore the binary equivalent of 327 is 101000111

BINARY TO DECIMAL CONVERSION RULES

(a) Start at left with first significant digit—double it if the next digit is a zero or "dibble" it (double and add one) if the next digit is a one.

(b) If the 3rd digit is a zero, double value obtained in (a), if it is a one "dibble" value obtained in (a).

(c) Continue until operation indicated by least significant digit has been performed.

FUSING CURRENTS OF WIRES

This table gives the fusing currents in amperes for 5 commonly used types of wires. The current I in amperes at which a wire will melt can be calculated from $I = Kd^{3/2}$ where d is the wire diameter in inches and K is a constant that depends on the metal concerned. A wide variety of factors influence the rate of heat loss and these figures must be considered as approximations.

AWG B&S gauge	d in inches	copper $K =$ 10,244	aluminum $K =$ 7585	german silver $K =$ 5230	iron $K =$ 3148	tin $K =$ 1642
40	0.0031	1.77	1.31	0.90	0.54	0.28
38	0.0039	2.50	1.85	1.27	0.77	0.40
36	0.0050	3.62	2.68	1.85	1.11	0.58
34	0.0063	5.12	3.79	2.61	1.57	0.82
32	0.0079	7.19	5.32	3.67	2.21	1.15
30	0.0100	10.2	7.58	5.23	3.15	1.64
28	0.0126	14.4	10.7	7.39	4.45	2.32
26	0.0159	20.5	15.2	10.5	6.31	3.29
24	0.0201	29.2	21.6	14.9	8.97	4.68
22	0.0253	41.2	30.5	21.0	12.7	6.61
20	0.0319	58.4	43.2	29.8	17.9	9.36
19	0.0359	69.7	51.6	35.5	21.4	11.2
18	0.0403	82.9	61.4	42.3	25.5	13.3
17	0.0452	98.4	72.9	50.2	30.2	15.8
16	0.0508	117	86.8	59.9	36.0	18.8
15	0.0571	140	103	71.4	43.0	22.4
14	0.0641	166	123	84.9	51.1	26.6
13	0.0719	197	146	101	60.7	31.7
12	0.0808	235	174	120	72.3	37.7
11	0.0907	280	207	143	86.0	44.9
10	0.1019	333	247	170	102	53.4
9	0.1144	396	293	202	122	63.5
8	0.1285	472	349	241	145	75.6
7	0.1443	561	416	287	173	90.0
6	0.1620	668	495	341	205	107

ROMAN NUMERALS*

1	I	8	VIII
2	II	9	IX
3	III	10	X
4	IV	50	L
5	V	100	C
6	VI	500	D
7	VII	1000	M

The chief symbols are $I = 1$; $V = 5$; $X = 10$; $L = 50$; $C = 100$; $D = 500$; and $M = 1000$. Note that $IV = 4$, means 1 short of 5; $IX = 9$, means 1 short of 10; $XL = 40$, means 10 short of 50; and $XC = 90$, means 10 short of 100. Any symbol following one of equal or greater value adds its value—$II = 2$. Any symbol preceding one of greater value subtracts its value—$IV = 4$. When a symbol stands between two of greater value its value is subtracted from the second and the remainder is added to the first—$XIV = 14$; $LIX = 59$. Of two equivalent ways of representing a number, that in which the symbol of larger denomination preceded is preferred—XIV instead of VIX for 14.

Used currently to determine dates of cornerstones and vintage of T.V. films.

NUMERICAL DATA

1 cubic foot of water at 4° C (weight)................62.43 lb

1 foot of water at 4° C (pressure)...............0.4335 lb/in^2

Velocity of light in
vacuum, c...........186,280 mi/sec = 2.998×10^{10} cm/sec

Velocity of sound in dry air at 20° C, 76 cm Hg....1127 ft/sec

Degree of longitude at equator.................69.173 miles

Acceleration due to gravity at sea-level,
40° Latitude, g..............................32.1578 ft/sec^2

$\sqrt{2g}$..8.020

1 inch of mercury at 4° C........1.132 ft water = 0.4908 lb/in^2

Base of natural logs ϵ...................................2.718

1 radian....................................180° $\div$ π = 57.3°

360 degrees......................................2π radians

π..3.1416

Sine 1′...0.00029089

Arc 1°...0.01745 radian

Side of square..................0.707 $\times$ (diagonal of square)

COMMON INTEGRALS

1. $\int a\, dx = ax.$

2. $\int a \cdot f(x)dx = a \int f(x)dx.$

3. $\int \phi(y)dx = \int \dfrac{\phi(y)}{y'}dy,$ where $y' = dy/dx.$

4. $\int (u + v)\, dx = \int u\, dx + \int v\, dx,$ where u and v are any functions of $x.$

5. $\int u\, dv = uv - \int v\, du.$

6. $\int u\,\dfrac{dv}{dx}\, dx = uv - \int v\,\dfrac{du}{dx}\, dx.$

7. $\int x^n\, dx = \dfrac{x^{n+1}}{n + 1},$ except $n = -1.$

8. $\int \dfrac{f'(x)\, dx}{f(x)} = \log f(x),$ $[d\, f(x) = f'(x)\, dx].$

9. $\int \dfrac{dx}{x} = \log x,$ or $\log (-x).$

10. $\int \dfrac{f'(x)\, dx}{2\,\sqrt{f(x)}} = \sqrt{f(x)},$ $[d\, f(x) = f'(x)\, dx].$

11. $\int e^x\, dx = e^x.$

12. $\int e^{ax}\, dx = e^{ax}/a.$

13. $\int b^{ax}dx = \dfrac{b^{ax}}{a \log b}.$

14. $\int \log x\, dx = x \log x - x.$

15. $\int a^x \log a\, dx = a^x.$

16. $\int \dfrac{dx}{a^2 + x^2} = \dfrac{1}{a}\tan^{-1}\left(\dfrac{x}{a}\right),$ or $-\dfrac{1}{a}\cot^{-1}\left(\dfrac{x}{a}\right).$

17. $\int \dfrac{dx}{a^2 - x^2} = \dfrac{1}{a}\tanh^{-1}\left(\dfrac{x}{a}\right),$ or $\dfrac{1}{2a}\log\dfrac{a + x}{a - x}$

18. $\int \dfrac{dx}{x^2 - a^2} = -\dfrac{1}{a} \coth^{-1}\left(\dfrac{x}{a}\right)$, or $\dfrac{1}{2a} \log \dfrac{x - a}{x + a}$.

19. $\int \dfrac{dx}{\sqrt{a^2 - x^2}} = \sin^{-1}\left(\dfrac{x}{a}\right)$, or $-\cos^{-1}\left(\dfrac{x}{a}\right)$.

20. $\int \dfrac{dx}{\sqrt{x^2 \pm a^2}} = \log(x + \sqrt{x^2 \pm a^2})$.

21. $\int \dfrac{dx}{x \sqrt{x^2 - a^2}} = \dfrac{1}{a} \cos^{-1}\left(\dfrac{a}{x}\right)$.

22. $\int \dfrac{dx}{x \sqrt{a^2 \pm x^2}} = -\dfrac{1}{a} \log\left(\dfrac{a + \sqrt{a^2 \pm x^2}}{x}\right)$.

23. $\int \dfrac{dx}{x \sqrt{a + bx}} = \dfrac{2}{\sqrt{-a}} \tan^{-1} \sqrt{\dfrac{a + bx}{-a}}$, or

$$\dfrac{-2}{\sqrt{a}} \tanh^{-1} \sqrt{\dfrac{a + bx}{a}}.$$

LINEAR MEASURE

12 inches = 1 foot
3 feet = 1 yard = 36 inches
5½ yards = 1 rod or pole = 16½ feet
40 rods = 1 furlong = 220 yards = 660 feet = ⅛ mile
8 furlongs = 1 statute mile = 1760 yards = 5280 feet
3 miles = 1 league = 5280 yards = 15,840 feet

SQUARE MEASURE

144 square inches = 1 square foot
9 square feet = 1 square yard = 1296 square inches
30¼ square yards = 1 square rod = 272¼ square feet
160 square rods = 1 acre = 4840 square yards
640 acres = 1 square mile = 3,097,600 square yards

CUBIC MEASURE

1728 cubic inches = 1 cubic foot
27 cubic feet = 1 cubic yard
144 cubic inches = 1 board foot
128 cubic feet = 1 cord

LIQUID MEASURE

4 gills = 1 pint
2 pints = 1 quart = 8 gills
4 quarts = 1 gallon = 8 pints = 32 gills
31½ gallons = 1 barrel = 126 quarts
2 barrels = 1 hogshead = 63 gallons = 252 quarts

DRY MEASURE

2 pints = 1 quart
8 quarts = 1 peck = 16 pints
4 pecks = 1 bushel = 32 quarts = 64 pints
105 quarts = 1 barrel (for fruits, vegetables, and other dry
commodities) = 7056 cubic inches

CIRCULAR MEASURE

60 seconds (") = 1 minute (')
60 minutes = 1 degree (°)
90 degrees = 1 quadrant
4 quadrants = 1 circle of circumference

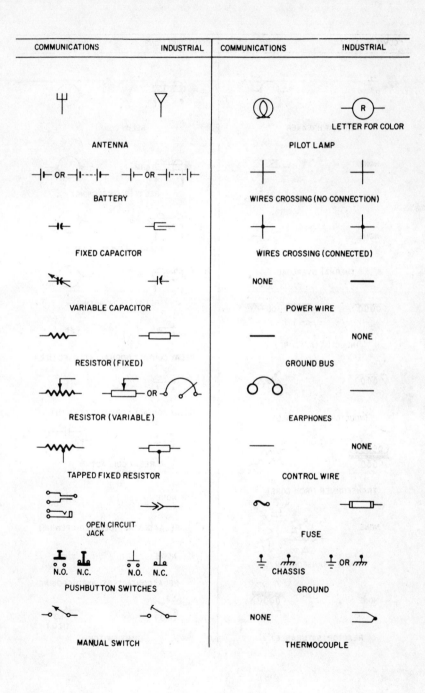

COMMUNICATIONS	INDUSTRIAL	COMMUNICATIONS	INDUSTRIAL

ANTENNA

BATTERY

FIXED CAPACITOR

VARIABLE CAPACITOR

RESISTOR (FIXED)

RESISTOR (VARIABLE)

TAPPED FIXED RESISTOR

OPEN CIRCUIT JACK

N.O.   N.C.   N.O.   N.C.

PUSHBUTTON SWITCHES

MANUAL SWITCH

LETTER FOR COLOR

PILOT LAMP

WIRES CROSSING (NO CONNECTION)

WIRES CROSSING (CONNECTED)

NONE

POWER WIRE

NONE

GROUND BUS

EARPHONES

NONE

CONTROL WIRE

FUSE

CHASSIS   OR

GROUND

NONE

THERMOCOUPLE

COMMUNICATIONS	INDUSTRIAL	COMMUNICATIONS	INDUSTRIAL

CIRCUIT BREAKER

RELAY COIL

NONE — MAGNETIC OVERLOAD

RELAY (SLOW CLOSING)

ARM — SO

NONE — THERMAL OVERLOAD

RELAY (SLOW-RELEASE)

ARM — SR

INDUCTOR (AIR CORE)

OR

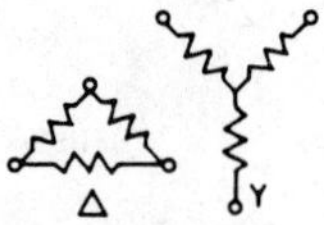

RELAY (SLOW-ACTING)

ARM — SA

INDUCTOR (SLUG TUNED)

RELAY CONTACT NORMALLY CLOSED (N.C.)

TRANSFORMER (IRON-CORE)

RELAY CONTACT NORMALLY OPEN (N.O.)

NONE — 3-PHASE TRANSFORMER

Δ   Y

RELAY CONTACT
SPDT

NONE — RELAY CONTACT (DELAYED-OPENING)

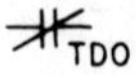

TDO

NONE — RELAY CONTACT (DELAYED-CLOSING)

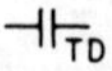

TD

NONE — REACTOR (SATURABLE)

LIMIT SWITCH

LS
(N.O.)

LS
(N.O.)

COMMUNICATIONS	INDUSTRIAL	COMMUNICATIONS	INDUSTRIAL

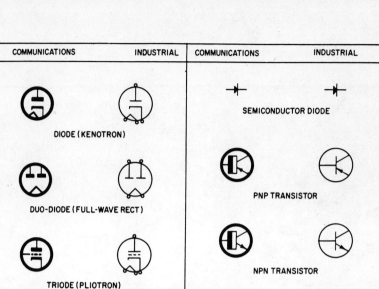

DIODE (KENOTRON)

DUO-DIODE (FULL-WAVE RECT)

TRIODE (PLIOTRON)

PENTODE

NEON LAMP

PHOTOCELL

THYRATRON

NONE

IGNITRON

SEMICONDUCTOR DIODE

PNP TRANSISTOR

NPN TRANSISTOR

PNP TETRODE TRANSISTOR

CONTROLLED RECTIFIER

PNP FIELD-EFFECT TRANSISTOR

UNIJUNCTION TRANSISTOR

THERMISTOR

Index

A

Abbreviations, electronic 219
AC circuits 51
  capacitive divider 51
  charging 51
AC:
  bridge 213
  circuits, power in DC 59
  Ohm's law for 142, 201
Adcock antenna 201
Admittance of a series circuit 117
Alpha, values of 159
Alpha, cutoff frequency 166
Alphabet, Greek 51
Alternation, negative 51
Alternation, positive 51
Ambient temperature 25
Ammeter range extended
  by shunting formula 208
Amplification:
  at high frequencies (pentodes) 151
  at high frequencies (triodes) 148
  at intermediate or medium
    frequencies (triodes) 148
  at low frequencies (pentodes) 150
  at low frequencies (triodes) 148
  at medium frequencies
    (pentodes) 150
  current 159
  factor 141
  factor, current 161
  voltage 144
Amplifiers:
  base current factor 165
  power 152
  resistance-coupled audio 146
  voltage 144

Amplifier, second harmonic
  distortion of 155
Angle, phase 95
Angle, wave 188
Angles 57
Antenna:
  Adcock 201
  Beverage 203
  center-fed Hertz 194
  coaxial 199
  corner reflector 194
  cosecant-square reflector 193
  crow-foot 199
  elevation 188
  end-fed Hertz 194
  folded dipole 203
  Fuchs 194
  full wave 185
  gain related to height 188
  ground-plane 199
  half rhombic 203
  horn 193
  Ilas 200
  impedances 185
  inverted V 203
  length 183, 189
  length, modified 184
  length, physical, in inches 184
  loop 201
  Marconi 195
  omni-range 201
  parabolic reflector 193
  parasitic array 198
  radiation resistance 186
  resonance frequency 183
  rhombic 198
  skin 200

sleeve	199
standard	186
stub mast	201
tilted wire	203
transmission lines	183
tuned doublet	194
turnstile	200
vertical J	198
vor	201
without feedback, formulas	152
Zepp	194
Antennas	183
Apparent power formula	120
Area of wire	22
Aspect ratio	177
Attenuation	190
Attenuators and pads	137
Audio amplifiers:	
resistance-coupled (pentodes)	418
resistance-coupled (triodes)	146
Audio power output, single	
pentode	155
Audio transformer color code	94
Average value	54

B

Band-elimination filter	132
Band-pass filter (constant K)	131
Basic transistor circuits	162
Basic units	29
Beat interference	180
Beta	166
Beverage antenna	203
Binary numbers	237
Binary to decimal conversion	
rules	237
Bridge:	
AC	213
slide wire	214
Wheatstone	213

C

Capacitance increase formula	26
Capacitive	73
circuit, Ohm's law for a	73
circuits, phase angle in	97
inductive voltage divider	83
reactance	70
as voltage dividers	70
Capacitor:	
charge of	67
coupling	146
energy stored in a	69
in parallel formula	65
in series	67
in series parallel	68
Q of a	89
working voltage	69
Capacitive effect of temperature	
coefficient	25
Cathode current	144
Cathode followers	164
Cathode ray oscilloscope	123
Cells in parallel	40
Cells in series aiding	174
Celsius, Fahrenheit conversion	25
Channel monochrome or color	173
Channel numbers, TV finding	174
Channels TV broadcast	173
Characteristic impedance	192
Charge of a capacitor	41
Circuits, vacuum tube	141
Circular measure	242
Coaxial antenna	199
Coaxial transmission line,	
resistance of	191
Coefficient of coupling	78
Coefficient of resistance	25
Coil:	
Q of a	89
single layer air coil	77
moving meter	207
subcarrier	179
Color code:	
audio transformer	94
IF transformer	93
output transformer	94
power transformer	92
push pull transformer	94
resistor	20
subcarrier	179

Common:
  base circuit 163
  collector circuit 164
  emitter circuit 162
  integrals 240
  logarithms of numbers 235
Comparison of electric and
  magnetic circuits 223
Complex series diagram and
  formula 109
Components, operated 157
Concentric transmission line (air
  insulated) 190
Conductance:
  AC current 51
  formulas 118
  mutual 143
  plate 141
  time 45
Conversion factors for
  electronic multiples 64, 66
Conversion, inches to
  millimeters 233
Conversion of millimeters to
  inches 234
Corner reflector 194
Cosecant-square reflector 193
Coupling and mutual inductance 78
Coupling capacitor 146
Crowfoot antennas 199
Cube root of numbers 226
Cubic measure 242
Current:
  amplification 159
  amplification factor 161
  and voltage measurements 54, 55
  average value 55
  cathode 141
  flow direction 158
  gain 159
  efficiency formulas 169
  electrode 159
  effective values 158
  law Kirchhoff's 41, 42
  measurement methods 54
  peak-to-peak 54

  rms 57
  sine wave 51
  transformers 91
  value, measurements 55
Cutoff frequency, alpha 166
Cycles per second / Hertz 52

D
Data and tables 217
Db 126
DC current 211
DC plate resistance 142
Decibels and Nepers 126, 127
Decimal equivalents 220
Decimal to binary conversion
  rules 237
Deflection frequencies 179
Degenerative feedback 151
Diagrams, capacitors in service 67
Diameter of wire 22
Dielectric constant listing 191
Distortion of a power amplifier 156
Distortion of voltage and current
  along half-wave antenna 186
Distortion, second-harmonic 94
Dividing AC circuits by
  capacitors and formula 71
Dry measure 242
Dynamic plate circuit 153
Dynamic plate resistance 141

E
Effective 57
  current 57
  resistance 88
  voltage 57
Efficiency, plate 143
EHF 146
Electronic:
  abbreviations 219
  prefixes 65
  symbols 65
Emitter transistor collector
  leakage circuit 168
Energy stored in a capacitor 64
Energy vs power 34

End-fed Hertz 194
Extremely high frequency 146

F

Factor
   amplification 141
   power 120
   velocity factor formula 205
Fahrenheit, Celsuis conversion 24
Feedback, negative 151
Filter:
   band elimination 132
   (constant K) band-pass 131
   pi-type high-pass 134
   pi-type, low-pass 134
   T-type, low-pass 133
Filters 129
Filters:
   (constant K) high-pass 129
   (constant K), low-pass 129
   m-derived 135
   types of m-derived 136
Folded dipole 203
Frequency:
   alpha circuit 166
   and wavelength 51
   measurements 207
   ratio calculations 216
   calculations, unknown 215
Fuchs antenna 185
Full wave antennas 185
Fundamental and harmonic
   relationships 139
Fusing currents of wires 238

G

Gain:
   power 160, 186
   resistance 160
   voltage 160
Gauge of wire 20
Gigacycle 221
Greek alphabet 223
Grid effectivity control 141
Ground plane antenna 199
Grounded cathode circuit 162
Grounded grid circuit 163

H

Half rhombic 203
Harmonic fundamental
   relationships 139
Height of antenna 183
Hertz, Lissajous patterns 215
High frequency 221
High frequency range 151
High-pass filter (constant K)
   formulas and diagram 129
High-pass filter, pi-type 134
High-pass filters (constant K) 129
Horn antennas 193

I

IF transformer color code 93
Ilas antennas 200
Impedance:
   characteristic 192
   impedance and phase angle
   of series R-L shunted by C 114
   impedance and phase angle
   of series R-L shunted by R 113
   in an R-L circuit 86, 114
   of a parallel L-C circuit 112
   of a parallel R-C circuit 111
   of a parallel R-L circuit 115
   of a parallel R-L-C circuit 107
   of a series L-C circuit 106
   of series R-L-C circuit 107
   of transmission line 189
   of an R-C circuit 73
   surge 189
   transformers 92
Impedance, antenna 185
Impedance matching 192
Inches to millimeters 233
Inductance, mutual 80
Inductive:
   circuit, Ohm's law for an 81
   circuits, phase angle in 97
   resistance 80
Inductance Q 69
Inductor, reactance of 80
Inductors 79
   in parallel 77

in parallel aiding 80
in parallel opposing 80
in series 79
in series aiding 79
in series opposing 79
Input resistance 167
Instantaneous value 56
Integrals, common 240
Inverse feedback 151
Inverted V antenna 203

K
Kirchhoff's current law 44
Kirchhoff's voltage law 41

L
L-C circuit:
  impedance of a parallel 112, 113
  impedance of a series 111
  phase angle of a parallel 112, 113
  phase angle of a series 111
Length of transmission line 192
Levels, reference 127
LF 221
Linear measure 242
Lines, transmission 188, 189
Liquid measure 242
Load, maximum transfer of
  power to the 154
Load, power in the plate 155
Logarithms of numbers,
  common 235
Logs, common 235
Loop antenna 201
Low-frequency 221
Low-frequency range 150
Low-pass filter, pi type 134
Low-pass filter, T-type 133
Low-pass filters, (constant K) 130

M
Marconi antenna 195
Matching impedance 192
Mathematical symbols 222

Maximum transfer of power 154
Maximum voltage 55
M-derived filters 135
M-derived filters, types of 136
Measurements 207
Measurements:
  resistance 210
  voltage and current 54
Medium frequency 221
Medium frequency range 510
MF 221
Millimeters to inches 234
Multiples and submultiples 64
Multiplier resistance 209
Mutual conductance 143
Mutual inductance 78

N
Negative feedback 151
Nepers and decibels 126
Nonsinusoidal waves 60, 138
Numbers:
  binary 237
  common logarithms of 235
Numerals, Roman 239
Numerical data 239

O
Ohm's law 142
Ohm's law for:
  a capacitive circuit 73
  AC 119
  an inductive circuit 81
  basic units by exponents 29
  basic units by numbers 28
  capacitive circuit 74
  summary of 29
Omni-range antenna 201
Operated components 157
Oscilloscope 207
Output:
  power 153
  resistance 167
  transformer color code 91
  undistorted power 155

P

Parabolic reflector antenna   201
Parallel:
  aiding inductors in   29
  capacitors   65
  inductors   80
  L-C circuit, impedance of   112, 113
  L-C circuit, phase angle of   112, 113
  opposing inductors in   81
  R-C circuits, impedance of   112, 113
  resistors in   12
  R-L circuit, impedance of   112, 113
  R-L circuit, phase angle of   112, 113
  R-L-C circuit,
    impedance of   107, 108
  R-L-C circuit, phase
    angle of   107, 108
Parallel-series capacitors   68
Parallel-series, resistors in   18
Parasitic array   198
Peak-to-peak current   57
Peak-to-peak voltage   57
Peak voltage   54
Period   53
Phase   35
Phase angle   95
Phase angle:
  and impedance of series
    R-L shunted by C   117
  and impedance of series
    R-L shunted by R   113
  in capacitive circuits   97
  in inductive circuits   97
  in resistive circuits   96
  of a parallel L-C circuit   112, 113
  of a parallel R-L circuit   112, 113
  of a parallel R-L-C circuit   113
  of a series L-C circuit   98
  of a series R-L circuit   115
  of a series R-L-C circuit   113
Pi-type high-pass filter   135
Pi-type low-pass filter   135
Plate efficiency   143
Plate load, power in the   155
Plate resistance   142

Potentiometer voltage divider   37
Power   29
Power:
  amplifiers   152
  amplifier, second harmonic
    distortion of   155
  apparent   120
  basic formula   30
  factor   120, 121
  gain   186
  gain, transistor   160
  in AC circuit   65
  in DC circuit   29
  in the plate load   155
  laws, summary of   29
  maximum transfer of   155
  output   153
  output, single pentode audio   155
  output, undistorted   155
  radiated   186
  sensitivity   153
  transformer color code   91
  units   29
  vs energy   35
Power of numbers   230
Preferred value of resistors   20
Pulse, horizontal blanking   179
Pulse, time delay   171
Pulse, vertical blanking   179
Pushpull transformer color code   91

Q

Q of a:
  capacitor   89
  coil   89
  series resonant circuit   125

R

Radiated power   186
Radiation resistance   185
Ratio:
  standing wave   192
  turns   89
R-C:
  audio amplifiers, (pentode)   148
  audio amplifiers, (triodes)   146

circuit, impedance of a
  parallel   112, 113
circuit, impedance of   115
circuit, phase angle of a series   113
circuit, voltages in a series   98
series   58

Reading meter to measure
  resistance   211

Reference levels   127

Resistance:
  base   167
  capacitive   83
  coefficient of   25
  collector   168
  computing unknown values   214
  coupled audio amplifiers
    (pentodes)   149
  coupled audio amplifiers
    (triodes)   146
  effective   88
  gain   159
  input and output   167
  measurements   210
  multiplier   191
  of a coaxial transmission line   191
  of an inductor   81
  of open two-wire copper line   191
  of wire   23
  plate   142
  radiation   185
  shunt   208

Resistive circuits, phase angle in   97
Resistor color code   20
Resistors   11
Resistors:
  in parallel   12, 13
  in series   11
  in series-parallel   18
  preferred values of   20

Resonance in a series circuit   123
Resonant circuit, Q of a series   125
Rhombic antenna   198
R-L:
  circuit, impedance in an   185

circuit, impedance of a
  parallel   112, 113
circuit, phase angle of a
  parallel   112
circuit, phase angle of a series   115
circuit, voltages in a series   69
series   58
shunted by C, impedance
  and phase angle of   117
shunted by R, impedance
  and phase angle of   107, 108
R-L-C:
  circuit, impedance of a
    parallel   107, 108
  circuit, impedance of a series   113
  circuit, phase angle of   107, 108
RMS:
  current   57
  voltage   57
Roman numerals   239

S
Scope   214
Second harmonic distortion   155
Sensitivity, power   152
Series:
  aiding, inductors in   80
  aiding, voltages in   39
  capacitors   65
  circuit, admittance of   117
  circuit, resonance in   123
  inductors   80
  L-C circuit, impedance of   113
  L-C circuit, phase angle of a   113
  opposing, inductors in   80
  parallel capacitors   68
  parallel, resistors in   18
  R-C   58
  R-C circuit, phase angle of   113
  R-C circuit, voltages in a   98
  resistors in   11
  resonant circuit, Q of a   125
  R-L   45
  R-L circuit, phase angle of   115
  R-L circuit, voltages in   69

R-L shunted by C, impedance
and phase angle of 117
R-L shunted by R, impedance
and phase angle of 107, 108
R-L-C circuit, impedance of 113
R-L-C circuit, phase angle of 113
SHF 221
Shunt:
 law 35
 resistance 207, 208
Sine values 58
Single pentode audio power
 output 155
Skin antennas 200
Sleeve antenna 199
Slide-wire bridge 213
Square:
 measure 242
 root of numbers 226
Square of numbers 226
Standard antenna 185
Standing wave ratio 192
Static leakage 169
Step down transformers 89
Step up transformers 89
Stub mast antenna 201
Super-high frequency 201
Surge impedance 188, 189
Susceptance 117
SWR 191, 192
Symbols:
 electronic 244
 mathematical 222

T

Tables and data 217
Temperature 22
Time constants 45
Transformer color code:
 audio 91
 IF 93
 output 91
 power 91
 pushpull 91
 turns ratio 89

Transformers:
 current 91
 impedance 91, 92
 step down 91
 step up 91
 voltage 91
Transistor:
 circuits, basic 162
 common base transistor circuit 163
 grounded base circuit 167
 power gain 186
 voltage gain 186
Transistors 155
Transmission line:
 concentric 190
 line, length of 205
 two wire open 189
Transmission lines 183
Trigonometric functions 232
Triode, base 157
Triode , collector 157
Triode resistance-coupled
 audio amplifiers 146
T-type low-pass filter 133
Tube characteristics 141
Tube circuits, vacuum 141
Tubes, vacuum 141
Tuned doublet 194
Turns ratio 89
Turnstile antenna 200
Two wire:
 copper line, resistance
  of open 191, 192
 open transmission line 191

U

UHF 221
Ultra-high frequency 221
Undistorted power output 155
Unidirectional formula 55
Units, volume (VU) 128

V

Vacuum tube circuits 141
Vacuum tubes 141
Velocity factor 204

Velocity of a wave 53
Vertical J antenna 198
Very-high frequency 221
Very-low frequency 221
VHF 221
VLF 221
Voltage:
  amplification 144
  amplifiers 144
  and current measurements 29
  average value 55
  base 159
  bias 141
  collector 158
  divider (potentiometer) 37
  dividers, capacitors as 70
  effective 57
  gain of transistor 160
  law, Kirchhoff's 41
  of a capacitor, working 70
  peak 54
  peak-to-peak 57
  rms 57
  transformers 89
Voltages:
  in a series R-C circuit 75

in a series R-L circuit 88
in series, aiding 39
Volume units 128
VU 128

W

Wave angle, determination of antenna 188
Wave length and frequency 511
Wave length, duration time 178
Wavelength of frequency bands 221
Wave, nonsinusoidal 138
Wave, sine, effective values of voltage on current 58
Wave, velocity of 53
Wheatstone bridge 214
Wire, copper, dia. in mils 22
Wire, resistance of 20
Wire table 22
Wires, fusing currents of 238
Working voltage of a capacitor 70

Z

Zepp antenna 194